All In One
Barcelona
Guide
&
Spanish
Phrasebook

Above: *blue skies over the fountain of Parc de la Ciutadella*

AA Publishing

Above: *Barcelona has a strong musical tradition*

All In One guide first published 2003
Barcelona Guide written by Teresa Fisher
© Automobile Association Developments Limited 2002
Maps © Automobile Association Developments Limited 2002

Automobile Association Developments Limited retains the copyright in the orginal edition © 1998 and in all subsequent editions, reprints and amendments.

Spanish Phrasebook: English edition prepared by First Edition Translations Ltd, Great Britain
Designed and produced by AA Publishing.

First published in 1995 as Wat & Hoe Spaans, © Uitgeverij Kosmos bv - Utrecht/Antwerpen.

Van Dale Lexicografie bv - Utrecht/Antwerpen

Published by AA Publishing, a trading name of Automobile Association Developments Limited, whose registered office is Millstream, Maidenhead Road, Windsor, Berkshire SL4 5GD. Registered number 1878835.
A CIP catalogue record for this book is available from the British Library.

ISBN 0 7495 3982 8

A01882

Colour separation: Pace Colour, Southampton

Printed and bound in Italy by Printer Trento Srl

Find out more about AA Publishing and the wide range of services the AA provides by visiting our website at www.theAA.com

Contents

About this Book

KEY TO SYMBOLS

➕ map reference to the maps in the What to See section

✉ address

☎ telephone number

🕐 opening times

🍴 restaurant or café on premises or near by

🚇 nearest underground train station

🚌 nearest bus/tram route

🚆 nearest overground train station

⛴ nearest ferry stop

♿ facilities for visitors with disabilities

✋ admission charge

↔ other places of interest near by

❓ other practical information

➤ indicates the page where you will find a fuller description

The **Barcelona Guide** is divided into five sections to cover the most important aspects of your visit to Barcelona.

Viewing Barcelona pages 5–14
An introduction to Barcelona by the author.
Barcelona's Features
Essence of Barcelona
The Shaping of Barcelona
Peace and Quiet
Barcelona's Famous

Top Ten pages 15–26
The author's choice of the Top Ten places to see in Barcelona, listed in alphabetical order, each with practical information.

What to See pages 27–90
An extensive guide to Barcelona, with a brief introduction and an alphabetical listing of the main attractions, followed by a shorter guide to Catalonia.
Practical information
Snippets of 'Did you know…' information
6 suggested walks and 2 suggested drives
2 features

Where To… pages 91–116
Detailed listings of the best places to eat, stay, shop, take the children and be entertained.

Practical Matters pages 117–24
A highly visual section containing essential travel information.

Maps
All map references are to the individual maps found in the What to See section of this guide.

For example, Tibidabo has the reference ➕ 47D5 – indicating the page on which the map is located and the grid square in which the hill is to be found. A list of the maps that have been used in this travel guide can be found in the index.

Prices
Where appropriate, an indication of the cost of an establishment is given by **£** signs:

£££ denotes higher prices, **££** denotes average prices, while **£** denotes lower charges.

Star Ratings
Most of the places described in this book have been given a separate rating:

✪✪✪   Do not miss
✪✪   Highly recommended
✪   Worth seeing

Viewing
Barcelona

Above: *Gaudí chimney faces – the 'witch-scarers' – at Casa Milà*
Right: *a proud Catalan*

5

Teresa Fisher's Barcelona

Orientating Yourself
Downtown Barcelona is divided into distinctive districts including *La Ribera*, today a popular museum quarter; *El Raval* (or *Barri Xinès*, China Town), a run-down area with a high crime rate (and perhaps best avoided); the bohemian 'village' of *Grácia*; *Barceloneta*, the former fishermen's quarter; and smart seafront developments – *Port Vell*, the **Olympic village** and **port**.

Below: *Christopher Columbus surveys the port*
Below right: *aerial view of Passeig de Grácia – one of Barcelona's main thoroughfares*

Inventive and innovative, radical and racy, Barcelona is one of Europe's most dynamic cities. Strolling through its streets is like wandering through a living museum, a legacy of its remarkable two thousand years of history. From the ancient maze-like Gothic quarter, built within the Roman city walls, to the astonishing regimental grid plan of the turn-of-the-19th-century Eixample district, studded with eye-catching jewels of *Modernista* architecture, and the space-age constructions for the 1992 Olympiad, the city contains some of the finest and most eccentric art and architecture in the world. Outstanding even by Barcelonan standards is Gaudí's extraordinary Sagrada Família – for many, reason enough to visit the city.

Just as *Modernisme* – the movement that has made Barcelona unique – emerged at the end of the 19th century as a desire for change and renovation, so today the city is celebrating its past. Rather than suffer a post-Olympic slump, it is restoring its old buildings, introducing new art and architecture and eradicating some severe urban problems, while staying at the forefront of contemporary culture.

As a result, Barcelona today is very much alive – a city bursting with new pride and self-confidence, which cannot fail to excite and delight. So before you leave, consider the city's motto – *Barcelona Es Teva* ('Barcelona Belongs to You') – and drink from the famous Canaletes fountain on La Rambla. It is said that after just one sip, you will fall under the city's spell and are sure to return again, and again…and again.

Barcelona's Features

Geography

• Barcelona is in northeastern Spain, 160km from the French border. The city occupies 99sq km, with 13km of Mediterranean coastline, including 4.2km of sandy beaches. It is bounded by the mountains of Montjuïc (to the south) and Tibidabo (to the northwest), and framed by the rivers Llobregat (to the south) and Besós (to the north).

Climate

• Barcelona enjoys a Mediterranean climate. Summers are hot and humid with an average temperature of 24°C. Winters are mild and sunny with an average temperature of 11°C. December can be very wet.

People and Economy

• Barcelona's population is 1,503,451 (or 4,264,039 within the *area metropolitana* of greater Barcelona). Many inhabitants originated from southern Spain, drawn to Catalonia in the 1950s and '60s by the prospect of work in the capital of Spain's most progressive and prosperous region.

Leisure Facilities

• Barcelona boasts 53 museums and galleries, 143 cinemas, 41 theatres, an amusement park, 2 luxury marinas, a zoo, 6 beaches, 61 parks and gardens, and over 2,300 restaurants. A special tourist bus (*bus turístic*) connects 18 of the most popular attractions. Thanks to the 1992 Olympics, the city has top facilities for every kind of sport.

Catalunya (Catalonia)

The autonomous region of Catalunya (Catalonia) covers an area of 31,930sq km (6.3 per cent of Spain) and has a population of over 6 million (15 per cent of the Spanish population), 70 per cent of whom live in greater Barcelona. It is Spain's leading economic region, producing 8 per cent of the country's gross national product. Nearly 40 per cent of all visitors to Spain come to Catalonia.

Above: *children play in the famous Canaletes fountain on La Rambla*

Barcelona for Wheelchair Users

Barcelona is a popular destination for wheelchair users as it is a compact city, and the modern attractions are wheelchair-friendly. However, many of the streets are cobbled, which can be uncomfortable unless appropriate tyres are fitted. The Bus Turístic has low-entry doors and wheelchair points, and some of the other main routes have wheelchair-accessible buses. The metro system is easy enough to get into and out of, but changing lines within it is difficult as there are generally no lifts.

Essence of Barcelona

Barcelona is unique. It has something for everyone and is one of Europe's top destinations. The only problem you will encounter is that there will never be enough time to explore its many museums and monuments, churches and galleries, its fascinating seaboard and, above all, its delectable cuisine.

Below: *the fountain in the Plaça d'Espanya*
Bottom: *aerial view of the city from the Columbus monument*

To enjoy your stay to the full, you will need to adopt the Barcelonan lifestyle – a striking blend of businesslike efficiency combined with long alfresco lunches, lazy siestas, ritual evening *passeixus* (promenades) and an intoxicating nightlife. You will long remember its proud yet generous people, who will welcome you back with open arms when you return, as you surely will.

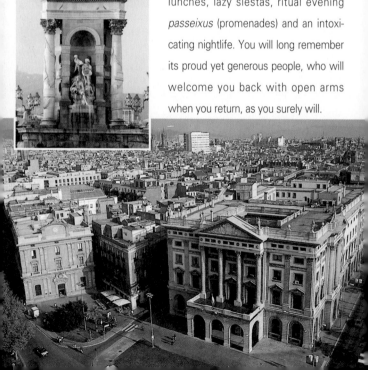

THE **10** ESSENTIALS

If you have only a short time to visit Barcelona and would like to get a really complete picture of the city, here are the essentials:

• **Stroll along La Rambla** (➤ 23), pause for a coffee and listen to the street performers.

• **Get into Gaudí**, especially Casa Milà (➤ 37), Parc Güell (➤ 21) and the famous Sagrada Família (➤ 24–25).

• **Follow in the footsteps** of Picasso and Dalí and wander at length through the maze of narrow streets in the Barri Gòtic (➤ 40–41).

• **Enjoy the wide variety** of *tapas* (➤ 97–100) available in the local bars.

• **Join locals to dance** the *sardana*, the national dance of Catalonia (➤ 69).

• **Experience the tastes**, fragrances and colours of the Mediterranean at Mercat de la Boqueria (➤ 49).

• **Visit Museu Picasso** (➤ 20).

• **Shop for Spanish fashion** and designer gifts in the smart Eixample district (➤ 42–43).

• **Watch FC Barça play** a home match (➤ 54, 55).

• **Walk the waterfront** (➤ 70–71) and sample the freshest of seafood.

Below: *the main entrance to Parc Güell* Bottom: *human tower building in the city's Castellets festival*

The Shaping of Barcelona

c15 BC
Roman colony of Barcino founded. Roman stone city walls built in AD 4.

531
Barcelona becomes a Visigothic capital.

711
Arabs gain control of Barcelona and call it Barjelunah.

801
Barcelona seized by Franks, making it part of Charlemagne's empire.

878
Guifré el Pilós (Wilfred 'The Hairy') founds the independent county of Catalonia.

1131–62
Reign of Count Ramon Berenguer IV of Barcelona and union of Catalonia and Aragon. Barcelona becomes a major trading city.

1213–76
Reign of Jaume I.

1229
Jaume I conquers Mallorca, then Ibiza (1235), then Valencia (1238) from the Moors.

1249
Council of One Hundred (*Consell de Cent*) set up as the municipal government of Barcelona.

1298
Gothic Cathedral begun.

1323–24
Conquest of Corsica and Sardinia shows Barcelona's maritime supremacy.

1354
The *Corts Catalans*, legislative council of Catalonia, establishes the *Generalitat* to control city finances.

1355
Thousands of Jews massacred in Barcelona's *Call*.

1356
Martí I, last ruler of the House of Barcelona, dies heirless. Ineffective rule from Madrid.

1462–73
Catalan civil war. Economy deteriorates.

1492
Final expulsion of Jews. Discovery of America.

1516
Charles of Habsburg (Charles V), becomes King of Spain.

1640
Catalan *Guerra dels*

Le Petit Journal

Bloody history – leaders of the Setmana Tràgica rising are executed

Segadors (Revolt of the Reapers) against Castilian rule.

1714
City falls to Franco-Spanish army during the War of the Spanish Succession. The *Nova Planta* (1715) decree abolishes Catalan institutions and Catalonia becomes a mere province of Spain.

1808–13
Departure of Napoleonic troops following five years of French occupation.

1832
Spain's first steam-driven factory opens in Barcelona.

1844
Liceu opera house opens.

1859
Cerdà's plan for the Eixample is approved.

1882
Work begins on the Sagrada Família.

1888
Universal Exhibition attracts 2 million visitors.

Late 19th to early 20th century
The Eixample district is created, containing many *Modernista* buildings.

1899
FC Barcelona founded. First electric trams.

1909
Churches and convents looted and burned by anti-establishment rioters during *Setmana Tràgica* (Tragic Week).

1914–18
Spanish neutrality in World War I helps boost Barcelona's economy.

1921
First metro line opened.

1929
International Exhibition on Montjuïc.

1931
Second Spanish Republic. Francesc Macià declares Catalan independence.

1936
Franco comes to power. His army uprising is defeated by armed city workers. Civil War starts.

1939
City falls to Nationalists. Franco's troops occupy Catalonia. Catalan language banned and Catalan culture crushed during dictatorship. Economic decline.

1975
Following Franco's death, Juan Carlos I is declared king, and acknowledges the re-establishment of the *Generalitat* as the Parliament of an autonomous regional government of Catalonia.

1992
Barcelona Olympic Games on Montjuïc.

1994
Liceu opera house gutted by fire. It reopens in 1999.

1995–96
Opening of three new museums – the Museu Nacional d'Art de Catalunya, the Museu d'Història de Catalunya and the Museu d'Art Contemporani de Barcelona – reflects continuing pride in the Catalan nation.

2002
Gaudí International Year: a variety of events, exhibitions and festivals celebrating 150 years since the birth of architect Antoni Gaudí (► 14)

2004
Barcelona will host the Universal Forum of Cultures, sponsored by UNESCO.

The 1992 Olympics helped put Barcelona back on the world map

Peace & Quiet

Barcelona is not a quiet city, yet it is always possible to find small pockets of peace – a quiet alley, a hidden square, a fountain-filled park – and the expansive greenery of Barcelona's twin mountains, Montjuïc (➤ 18) and Tibidabo (➤ 73), provides a joyful respite from frenetic city life. Alternatively, leave behind the hustle and bustle of Barcelona, and head instead for the Catalan countryside, where you will find a naturalist's paradise, blessed with more than its fair share of magnificent scenery, flora and fauna.

The Coast
Although many of the beaches in Barcelona's immediate vicinity have been spoilt, further afield lies some of the Mediterranean's most attractive coastal scenery. To the north, the charming maritime towns and villages, the warm turquoise sea, craggy cliffs and spacious sandy beaches have made the Costa Brava (wild coast) one of the most famous coastlines in Spain. Despite mass tourism, it is still possible to find small, welcoming and surprisingly unspoilt coves, their steep banks cloaked in wild flowers and cactus plants.

Take a rest from sightseeing and visit one of the city's many beautiful parks

To the south of Barcelona, beyond the long, wide, sandy beaches of the Costa Daurada (golden coast, ➤ 87), running from Alcanar and Vilanova i la Geltrú, is the vast Ebro Delta – the second largest wetland habitat on the Mediterranean and home to over 300 species of bird. The area has been made a protected nature reserve, due to the importance of its wildlife and its diversity of habitats – ranging from rice paddies to sand dunes maintained by marram grass, and from riverside woods of white poplar and water-willow to freshwater lagoons framed by reeds and rushes. Look out for otters, white-toothed shrews and water voles, flamingos, purple herons, spade-foot toads, stripeless tree frogs and spiny-footed lizards.

Parc de la Ciutadella in the centre of Barcelona

The Hinterland
Catalonia's hinterland offers a variety of landscapes. Just inland from the coast, the hills are clad in Aleppo pines, stone pines and cork oaks, and splashed with the yellows and mauves of broom, gorse, heathers and orchids. Further inland, one of Catalonia's

special delights is to ramble through the region's extensive, sun-baked scrubland habitats of olives, kermes oaks and strawberry trees. The air is fragrant with lavender and wild herbs, their sweet, heady perfume attracting a busy insect life of butterflies, bugs and beetles – an endless feast for the local hoopoes, bee-eaters and warblers. Southwest of Barcelona in the Alt Penedès wine region (► 84–85), where the land is striped with a patchwork of tidy vines, the dramatic gorges of the Serra d'Ancosa, beyond, shelter wild boar and genets, salamanders, badgers, goshawks, tawny owls and other birds of prey.

The Mountains

If you have a couple of days to spare, a trip to the craggy, snow-topped Pyrenees provides a complete contrast to the Mediterranean coast surrounding Barcelona. The Aigüestortes, Estany de Sant Maurici and Ordesa National Parks provide sanctuary for chamois, wild boar and other mountain species. Glacial lagoons, jagged granite formations and verdant valleys with myriad alpine flowers and forests of sober black pine represent the quintessence of this great mountain range. One of the most important preserves of upland wildlife in Europe, the Pyrenean range is every walker's dream.

Above: a complete change of scene – the impressive mountains of Ordesa National Park
Below: getting away from it all: Cardona in the foothills of the Pyrenees

Barcelona's Famous

Arantxa Sanchez Vicario
One of Spain's greatest tennis players, Arantxa was born in Barcelona in 1971. She has won over 75 major titles, including four Grand Slam singles titles and nine Grand Slam doubles titles. Between tournaments she returns home and joins the rest of Barcelona, shopping on the Diagonal, walking her dogs in the Collserola mountains and socialising at Port Vell or Port Olímpic.

Wilfred 'The Hairy'

Few people have heard of Count Guifré 'el Pilós' (c860–98), yet not only was he the first to unite several northeastern counties, creating the basis for a future Catalan state, but he also declared Barcelona capital of the region and founded the dynasty of the Counts of Barcelona. Sadly he met an early death, in battle against the Saracens. It is said that, in recognition of his heroism, the Emperor dipped his fingers into Wilfred's bloody wounds then ran them down his golden shield, thereby creating the four red stripes of today's Catalan flag – the *Quatre Barres* (Four Bars), the oldest flag in Europe.

Antoni Gaudí

Gaudí (1852–1926), Barcelona's most famous son, occupies a unique position in the history of modern architecture. He was a true genius of the *Modernista* movement, without predecessor or successor. To this day his flamboyant art is unique. For many people, Gaudí alone is sufficient reason to visit Barcelona, to see his remarkable organic structures, his trademark pinnacles, towers and rooftop terraces and, above all, the church of the Sagrada Família (► 24–25). Tragically, Gaudí was run over by a tram on the Gran Via and died unrecognised in hospital. When his identity was discovered, Barcelona gave him what was almost a state funeral.

Pablo Ruiz Picasso

Málaga-born Picasso (1881–1973) spent many of his formative years (from the age of 14 to 23) in Barcelona, and is said to have considered himself more Catalan than Andalucian. He was particularly fond of the Catalan capital and, even after his move to Paris in 1904, continued to visit Barcelona regularly, until the Civil War (the subject of his famous painting, *Guernica*) put an end to his visits. Museu Picasso (► 20), the city's most visited museum, is particularly rich in paintings from his Barcelona period.

Left: *Picasso never forgot his early adulthood spent in Barcelona*
Above left: *Arantxa Sanchez Vicario*

Top Ten

Above: *Casa Bruno Quadras on La Rambla*
Right: *Gaudí ironwork*

15

1
Catedral

🕇 62C3

✉ Plaça de la Seu

☎ 93 315 15 54

🕐 Daily 9–1, 4–7

🚇 Jaume I

🚌 17, 19, 40, 45

♿ Few

✋ Free

↔ Ciutat Vella (➤ 38–39);
Museu Frederic Marès
(➤ 55)

Museum

☎ 93 310 25 80

🕐 Daily 10:30–1

✋ Cheap

❓ Small gift shop

Barcelona's great cathedral is not only one of the most celebrated examples of Catalan Gothic style, but also one of the finest cathedrals in Spain.

The cathedral is located at the heart of the Barri Gòtic (➤ 40), on the remains of an early Christian basilica and a Romanesque church. Most of the building was erected between the late 13th century and the middle of the 15th century, although the heavily ornate main façade and octagonal dome were constructed at the beginning of the 20th century.

The impressive interior represents a harmonious blend of Medieval and Renaissance styles, with a lofty triple nave, graceful arches, 29 side chapels and an intricately carved choir. Beneath the main altar is the crypt of Santa Eulàlia (the patron saint of Barcelona), which contains her tomb.

Near the main entrance is the Chapel of Christ of Lepanto (formerly the Chapter House), which is widely considered to be the finest example of Gothic art in the cathedral. It contains the crucifix carried on board *La Real*, the flagship of Don Juan of Austria (➤ 41), during the famous Battle of Lepanto. The 14th-century cloister is the

most beautiful part of the cathedral, its garden of magnolias, palms and fountains making a cool retreat from the heat of Barcelona. There is even a small pond, with a flock of white geese, supposedly symbolising Santa Eulàlia's virginal purity. A small **museum** just off the cloister shelters many of the cathedral's most precious treasures.

Despite its grandeur, the cathedral remains very much a people's church. Worshippers outnumber tourists and on Sundays Barcelonans gather in Plaça de la Seu at noon to perform the *sardana*, a stately Catalan folk dance which symbolises unity (➤ 69).

Soaring arches in the great cathedral

2
Fundació Joan Miró

This dazzling gallery pays homage to Joan Miró, one of Catalonia's greatest artists, famous for his childlike style and use of vibrant colours.

Vibrant colours typify Miró's work

The Miró Foundation was set up by Joan Miró in 1971, and is devoted to the study of his works and to the promotion of all contemporary art. The gallery – a modern building of white spaces, massive windows and skylights designed by Josep Lluís Sert – is itself a masterpiece and a perfect place in which to pursue the Foundation's aims. It contains some 200 Mironian paintings, 153 sculptures, nine tapestries, his complete graphic works and over 5,000 drawings, making it one of the world's most complete collections of this great master.

Fragment of the Tapis de la Fundació Joan Miró, Joan Miró © ADAGP, Paris and DACS, London 1998

Miró was born in Barcelona in 1893 and, apart from a brief spell in Paris, spent most of his life in the city developing his bold style of vigorous lines and intense primary colours. In 1956 he moved to Mallorca, and remained on the island until his death in 1983.

Highlights of the gallery include some of Miró's earliest sketches, the tapestry *Tapis de la Fundació* and a set of black-and-white lithographs entitled *Barcelona Series* (1939–44) – an artistic appraisal of the war years. The roof terrace and gardens contain several striking sculptures.

The Foundation also presents temporary exhibitions of modern art, contemporary music recitals (► 114) and a special permanent collection called 'To Joan Miró', with works by Ernst, Tàpies, Calder and Matisse among others, a touching tribute to the person and his work.

✚ 28C2

✉ Avinguda de Miramar, Parc de Montjuïc

☎ 93 443 94 79

🕐 Oct–Jun Tue–Sat 10–7, Thu till 9:30; Jul–Sep Tue–Sat 10–8, Thu till 9:30; Sun 10–2:30

🍴 Café-restaurant (££)

🚇 Espanya   🚌 50

♿ Good   Expensive

3
Montjuïc

28C1

Cafés and restaurants
(£–££)

Espanya

50

Montjuïc funicular from
Paral.lel Metro

Free

Anella Olímpica (➤ 32)

*Few can resist the charms of the city's local hill,
with its museums, galleries, gardens and other
attractions set in an oasis of natural calm.*

The history of Montjuïc, a 213m-high hill south of the city
and the dominant feature of its coast and skyline, has been
linked to the city's history since prehistoric times. The
Romans later called it 'Jove's Mountain' but today it is
called 'Mountain of the Jews', after an early Jewish
necropolis here. The castle, standing on the bluff, dates
from the 16th to 18th centuries and houses the **Museu
Militar**, exhibiting collections of military weaponry and
uniforms from different countries and periods.

Museums

Museu Militar: 93 329
86 13; Museu
Arqueològic: 93 424 65
77; Museu Etnològic: 93
424 64 02;

Tue–Sun, times vary

Cheap; Museo Etnològic
free first Sun of month

Above: *view of Montjuïc
from the Columbus
monument*

In 1929 Montjuic was the venue for the International
Expo. Today many of its buildings are filled with museums.
The **Museu Arqueològic** and the **Museu Etnològic** typify
the Expo's architecture, as does the Palau Nacional, home
of the Museu Nacional d'Art de Catalunya (➤ 19).

Beneath the Palau Nacional, Plaça d'Espanya marks the
main entrance to the Expo with Venetian towers, and an
avenue leading to Plaça de la Font Màgica – 'Magic
Fountain' – a spectacular sight that always draws the
crowds. The road continues up past the Pavello Barcelona
(➤ 66) and the Poble Espanyol (➤ 22) to Fundació Joan
Miró (➤ 17) and the Anella Olímpica (➤ 32), venue for
much of the 1992 Olympic Games.

4

Museu Nacional d'Art de Catalunya (MNAC)

Dominating the northern flank of Montjuïc, this imposing neoclassical palace contains a treasure trove of Catalan art spanning several centuries.

The National Museum of Catalan Art is one of the best museums of medieval art in the world. Housed in an extravagant National Exhibition building, built as the symbol of the 1929 World Exhibition (➤ 22), the museum is currently undergoing renovation by architect Gae Aulenti, who also converted the Gare d'Orsay into one of Paris's foremost museums.

The MNAC boasts the world's most eminent Romanesque art collection, with stone sculptures, wood carvings, gold and silverwork, altar cloths, enamels and coins and a beautifully presented series of 11th- and 12th-century murals, carefully stripped from church walls throughout Catalonia and precisely reconstructed in apses, as if they were still in their original locations.

The idea for this collection originated in the early 20th century when the theft of national architectural treasures in Catalonia was at its height, necessitating a church-led crusade to move some of the region's most precious treasures to a safe location.

The museum's Gothic collection forms a striking contrast with over 400 highly ornate retables and sculptures, including an extraordinary 15th-century Virgin in full flamenco dress. A somewhat fragmented collection of Renaissance and baroque paintings embraces works by Tintoretto, El Greco and Zurbarán.

The museum also contains the Museum of Drawings and Prints, the Numismatic Museum of Catalonia, and will eventually house the General Library of Art History and the Museu d'Art Modern (➤ 54), which is currently located in the Ciutadella Park.

✚ 28C2

✉ Palau Nacional, Parc de Montjuïc

☎ 93 622 03 75

🕐 Tue–Sat 10–7; Sun and hols 10–2:30. Closed Mon

🍴 Café-bar (£)

Ⓜ Espanya

🚌 9, 13, 30, 50, 55

♿ Excellent

💰 Expensive

↔ Anella Olímpica (➤ 32)

The MNAC – a treasure house of Barcelonan history

5
Museu Picasso

Below and bottom: *the Museu Picasso draws thousands of vistors*

This fascinating museum traces the career of the most acclaimed artist of modern times, from early childhood sketches to the major works of later years.

,The Picasso Museum is the city's biggest tourist attraction. It contains one of the world's most important collections of Picasso's work and the only one of any significance in his native country.

Pablo Ruiz Picasso was born in Andalucia, but moved to the Catalan capital in 1895, aged 14. He was already an exceptionally gifted artist, and, by the time of his first exhibition here in 1900, was well known. In 1904 he moved to Paris, but nevertheless remained in close contact with Barcelona.

The museum contains work from his early years, notably a series of impressionistic landscapes and seascapes, a portrait of his aunt, Tía Pepa (1896), notebook sketches and paintings of street scenes, including *Sortida del Teatre* (1896) and *La Barceloneta* (1897), and the menu for *Els Quatre Gats* (Four Cats) café (➤ 94). Other selected works are from the Blue Period (1901–1904), the Pink Period (1904–1906), the Cubist (1907–20) and Neo-classical (1920–25) periods, through to the mature works of later years. There are also 41 ceramic pieces donated by his wife, Jacqueline in 1982, which graphically demonstrate the astonishing artistic development of this great master.

✝ 29E4

✉ Carrer Montcada 15–23

☎ 93 319 63 10

🕐 Tue–Sat and hols 10–8, Sun 10–3. Closed Mon

🍴 Café-restaurant (££)

Ⓜ Jaume I

🚌 14, 17, 19, 36, 39, 40 45, 51, 57, 59, 64, 157

♿ Very good

💵 Expensive (free first Sun of month)

↔ Museu Tèxtil i d'Indumentària (➤ 57)

6
Parc Güell

Deemed a failure in its day, Gaudí's eccentric hilltop park is now considered one of the city's treasures and a unique piece of landscape design.

The architectural work of Gaudí is inseparable from Barcelona, largely thanks to his relationship with the Güells, a family of industrialists who commissioned from him a number of works. For Parc Güell, Don Eusebi Güell, Gaudí's main patron, had grand ideas for a residential English-style garden city, with 60 houses set in formal gardens. Gaudí worked on the project from 1900 to 1914, but it proved an economic disaster: only three houses were completed, and the park became city property in 1923.

The park's main entrance is marked by two eccentric pavilions. A grand stairway, ornamented by a dragon fountain, leads to a massive cavernous space, originally intended as the marketplace. Its forest of pillars supports a rooftop plaza bordered by a row of curved benches, covered in multicoloured *trencadís* (broken ceramics).

Throughout the 20 hectares of Mediterranean-style parkland, there are sculptures, steps and paths raised on columns of 'dripping' stonework. Gaudí himself lived in one of the houses from 1906 to 1926. Built by his pupil Berenguer, it is now the Casa-Museu Gaudí (☎ 93 219 38 11) and contains models, furniture, drawings and other memorabilia of the architect and his colleagues.

☩ 47D4

✉ Main entrance: Carrer Olot

☎ 93 213 04 88

🕐 Oct–Jun daily 10–6:30; Jul–Sep daily 10–7

🍴 Self-service bar

Ⓜ Lesseps or Vallcarca (and uphill walk)

🚌 24, 25, 28, 87

✋ Free

↔ Hospital de la Santa Creu i Sant Pau (➤ 45); Parc de la Creueta del Coll (➤ 65)

Sit on one of Europe's most unusual park benches

7
Poble Espanyol

This charming Andalucian square is the centrepiece of the Poble Espanyol

You can tour the whole of Spain in an afternoon here at Barcelona's 'Spanish Village', a remarkable showcase of regional architectural styles.

✚ 28B2

✉ Avinguda de Marqués de Comillas s/n

☎ 93 325 78 66

🕐 Mon 9AM–8PM; Tue–Thu 9AM–2AM; Fri & Sat 9AM–4AM; Sun 9AM–midnight

🍴 Plenty (£–££)

Ⓜ Espanya

🚌 13, 50

♿ Only partially accessible to wheelchair users, who have free entry

💷 Expensive

↔ Anella Olímpica (➤ 32); Fundació Joan Miró (➤ 17); Montjuïc (➤ 18); Museu Nacional d'Art de Catalunya (➤ 19)

Built for the 1929 World Exhibition, the Poble Espanyol (Spanish Village) was intended as a re-creation of the diversity of Spanish regional architecture through the ages. It could easily have resembled a stage set or a theme park, but instead, the 115 life-sized reproductions of buildings, clustered around 6 squares and 3km of streets, form an authentic village, where visitors can identify famous or characteristic buildings ranging from the patios of Andalucia to Mallorcan mansions and the granite façades of Galicia.

Within the village are bars and restaurants serving regional specialities, and over 60 shops selling folk crafts and regional artefacts. Some are undeniably over-priced, but there are also some real finds (➤ 107).

The Museum of Popular Arts, Industries and Traditions and the Museum of Graphic Arts are also located here and every Sunday at midday, a *festa* enlivens the main square.

The Poble Espanyol was smartened up for the 1992 Olympics, with the introduction of 'The Barcelona Experience' (a half-hour audio-visual history of the city) and several restaurants and bars, including the extraordinary Torres de Ávila (➤ 113), a trendy 'designer bar'-cum-nightclub, one of Barcelona's hottest night spots. Excellent flamenco shows can also be seen at El Tablao de Carmen (➤ 114).

8
La Rambla

Sooner or later, every visitor joins the locals swarming day and night down La Rambla, the most famous walkway in Spain.

Life on Barcelona's most famous street is never dull

The name La Rambla, derived from *ramla* (Arabic for 'torrent'), serves as a reminder that in earlier times, the street was a sandy gully that ran parallel to the medieval wall, and carried rainwater down to the sea. Today's magnificent 18th-century tree-lined walkway, running through the heart of the old city down to the port, is the pride of Barcelona. The central promenade is split into various distinctive sections strung head-to-tail, each with their own history and characteristics, from the flower stalls along Rambla de les Flors to the birdcages of Rambla dels Ocells (Walk, ➤ 51). And it is said if you drink from the famous fountain (➤ 51) in La Rambla de Canaletes you are sure to return to the city.

Promenading La Rambla is never the same twice, changing with the seasons, by the day and by the hour. It's an experience eagerly shared by people from every walk of life – tourists, locals, bankers, Barça fans, artists, beggars, street-performers, newspaper-sellers, pickpockets, night-clubbers, students, lovers and theatre crowds – all blending together with the noise of the traffic, the birdsong, the buskers, and the scent of the flowers. Such is the significance to the city of this promenade *par excellence*, that two words – *ramblejar* (a verb meaning 'to walk down the Rambla') and *ramblista* (an adjective describing someone addicted to the act of *ramblejar*) – have been adopted in its honour.

✚ 29D3

🍽 Plenty (£–£££)

🚇 Catalunya, Drassanes, Liceu

🚌 14, 38, 59, 91

📷 Boat excursions from Moll de les Drassanes (➤ 110)

↔ Ciutat Vella (➤ 38–39); Drassanes and Museu Marítim (➤ 41); Mercat de la Boqueria (➤ 49); Palau Güell (➤ 57); Plaça de Catalunya (➤ 67); Plaça Reial (➤ 69)

❓ Sant Jordi (St George's Day) celebrations on 23 April (➤ 116. panel). Beware of pickpockets

9
La Sagrada Família

Opposite and below: *the Sagrada Família must be seen to be believed*

Big Ben, the Eiffel Tower...most cities have a distinctive monument. Barcelona has Gaudí's Sagrada Família, his, as yet unfinished, cathedral.

🔢 29E6

✉️ Plaça Sagrada Família

☎️ 93 207 30 31

🕐 Daily Nov–Feb 9–6; Mar, Sep and Oct 9–7; Apr–Aug 9–8

Ⓜ️ Sagrada Família

🚌 19, 33, 34, 43, 44, 50, 51

♿ Few

✋ Expensive (additional charge for lift)

↔️ L'Eixample (► 42–43); Hospital de la Santa Creu i Sant Pau (► 45)

❓ Crypt museum, gift shop, lift and stairway to the towers

Antoni Gaudí, the internationally prestigious figure of Catalan architecture, started work on La Sagrada Família (Temple of the Holy Family) in 1882, and for the latter part of his life dedicated himself entirely to his great vision for Europe's biggest cathedral. His dream was to include three façades representing the birth, death and resurrection of Christ, and eighteen mosaic-clad towers symbolising the Twelve Apostles, the four Evangelists, the Virgin Mary, and Christ. On his untimely death in 1926 (► 14), only the crypt, one of the towers, the majority of the east (Nativity) façade, and the apse were completed. Ever since, the fate of the building has been the subject of often bitter debate.

With a further estimated 80 years of work (which would include the destruction of several buildings in Carrer Mallorca and Carrer Valencia), it seems that the Sagrada Família will probably never be more than a shell. Even as it stands today, it has become a world-wide symbol of Barcelona, one of the great architectural wonders of the world, and a must on every visitor's itinerary.

10
Santa Maria del Mar

🔲 29E4

✉ Plaça de Santa Maria

☎ 93 310 23 90

🕐 Daily 9–1:30, 4:30–8

🚊 Barceloneta, Jaume I

🚌 14, 17, 36, 39, 40, 45, 51, 57, 59, 64, 157

♿ Good

🖐 Free

↔ Museu Picasso (➤ 20); Palau de Mar (➤ 58)

Right and below: *Santa Maria epitomises Catalan Gothic architecture*

Barcelona's seaside cathedral is a Gothic triumph, built to demonstrate Catalan supremacy in Mediterranean commerce.

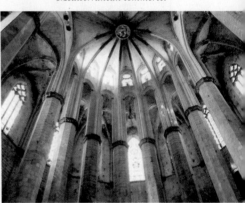

The 14th-century church of Santa Maria del Mar (St Mary of the Sea) is located at the heart of La Ribera (The Waterfront), the medieval city's maritime and trading district. This neighbourhood's link with the sea dates back to the 10th century, when a settlement grew up along the seashore outside the city walls, around a chapel called Santa Maria de les Arenes (St Mary of the Sands). During the 13th century, the settlement grew and became known as Vilanova de Mar. Its identity was eventually firmly established with the transformation of the tiny chapel into the magnificent church of Santa Maria del Mar, built on what was then the seashore, as a show of maritime wealth and power. Indeed, the foundation stone commemorated the Catalan conquest of Sardinia.

The church was built between 1329 and 1384 and has a purity of style that makes it one of the finest examples of Barcelona's Gothic heritage. The plain exterior is characterised by predominantly horizontal lines and two octagonal, flat-roofed towers. Inside, the wide, soaring nave and high, narrow aisles, all supported by slim, octagonal columns, provide a great sense of spaciousness. Sadly, the ornaments of the side chapels were lost when the city was besieged, once by Bourbon troops in 1714 and again during the Spanish Civil War. The resulting bareness of the interior, apart from the sculpture of a 15th-century ship that sits atop the altar, enables you to admire the church's striking simplicity without distraction.

What to See

Above: *chimney detail on Gaudí's Casa Mila*
Right: *street entertainer on La Rambla*

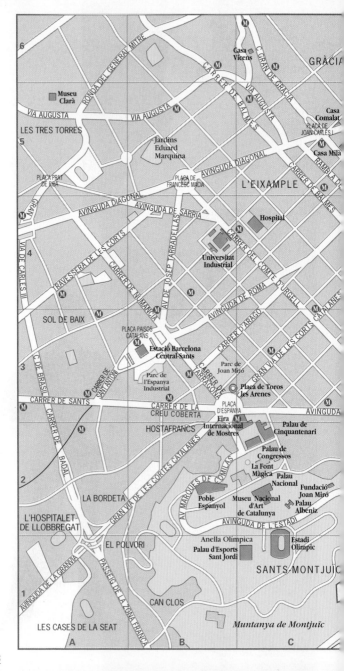

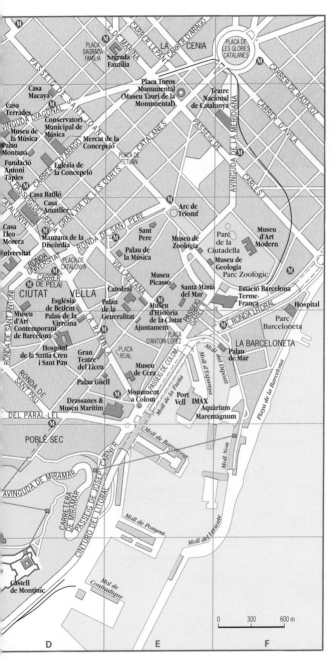

Barcelona

 Ever since it was founded over 2,000 years ago, Barcelona has been striving to become a great metropolis. To its inhabitants, it is not Spain's second city but the capital of Catalonia; not a Spanish metropolis but a European one, and the Spanish leader in both *haute couture* and *haute cuisine*. The best time to see Barcelona in its true colours is after FC Barça wins an important match, and the streets erupt with excitement to the sound of car horns and popping champagne corks.

Visitors to Barcelona, on the other hand, are entranced by the Mediterranean atmosphere of the city, the richness of its art and architectural treasures both ancient and modern, the proud but not narrowly nationalistic character of the people, the strong tradition of theatre and music and the exuberant nightlife. In this dynamic and passionate city, it is easy to live life to the full, both day and night.

> *'I would rather be Count of Barcelona than King of the Romans.'*
>
> CHARLES V
> *Holy Roman Emperor (1519)*

The City of Barcelona

Barcelona is easy to get to know. It is a compact city, small enough to explore on foot but great enough to be enormously varied. Most of the main sights are in three main areas: the Ciutat Vella (Old City), the Eixample and the Waterfront.

It is easy to lose yourself in the hidden corners of the Old City, to stumble upon a colourful market in a fountain-splashed square, to explore the city's boutiques, or to write some postcards in the geese-filled cloisters of the cathedral. The Eixample is particularly remarkable for the way the great turn-of-the-19th-century Modernists (*Modernistas*) created some of the most imaginative and bizarre buildings in the world within the confines of a rigid grid system of streets.

The city has often been accused of ignoring the sea on which so much of its fame and prosperity depended. The extension of the seafront began with the naming of Barcelona as host city for the 1992 Olympics. Today, with its smart coastal promenades, sandy beaches, and a plethora of open-air bars and restaurants, Barcelona's image is 'Cara al Mar' ('Face to the Sea'). Leading from the seafront, La Rambla is a must-see, a bustling avenue of cafés, bookstalls and flower kiosks, the best place to people-watch and to feel the city's true pulse. By contrast, twin hills Montjuïc and Tibidabo provide a welcome refuge from downtown Barcelona, with their panoramic views over the rooftops to the Pyrenean mountains beyond and the sparkling Mediterranean sea.

Below: *buskers on La Rambla*
Bottom: *Avinguda Portal de l'Angel, a popular shopping precinct*

What to See in Barcelona

L'ANELLA OLÍMPICA ✪✪

In 1992, Montjuïc mountain (➤ 18) was temporarily renamed 'Mount Olympus' and became Barcelona's main venue for the Olympic Games. Atop its western crest lies the Anella Olímpica (Olympic Ring), a monumental complex of concrete and marble that contains some of the city's most celebrated new buildings: Ricardo Bofills' neoclassical sports university; the Institut Nacional de Educació Física de Catalunya (INEFC); the Complex Esportiu Bernat Picornell swimming-pool complex; Santiago Calatrava's space-age communications tower, which dominates the skyline; and the remarkable black steel and glass domed Palau de Sant Jordi, designed by Japanese architect Arata Isozaki, which looks more like a UFO than a covered sports stadium.

Barcelona had bid for the games three times previously and had built Europe's biggest stadium for the 1929 World Exhibition with the clear intention of using it for the 1936 'People's Olympics' (organised as an alternative to the Nazi's infamous Berlin Games). These never took place due to the outbreak of Spanish Civil War the day before the official opening. For the 1992 games, local architects managed to preserve the stadium's original façade, while increasing the seating capacity from 25,000 to 70,000 by excavating deep into the interior. Today, highlights of the 1992 games can be relived through video clippings and souvenir showcases in the Galería Olímpica, located beneath the stadium.

✚ 34C3
✉ Avinguda de l'Estadi/Passeig Olímpic, Montjuïc
☎ Estadi Olimpic: 93 426 20 89; Palau Sant Jordi: 93 426 20 89
Ⓔ Espanya, or Paral.lel, then Funicular de Montjuïc
🚌 61
♿ Very good
🎟 Free

Galeria Olímpica
☎ 93 426 06 60
🕐 Apr–Sep Mon–Sat 10–2, 4–6 (7 in Jun, 8 Jul–Sep), Sun and hols 10–2; Oct–Mar Mon–Fri 10–1, 4–6
🚌 61
♿ Good
🎟 Cheap

Above: *the stadium that hosted the XXVth Olympic and the IXth Paralympic Games*

LA BARCELONETA AND PORT OLÍMPIC ✪✪

Following the siege and conquest of Barcelona by Felipe V in 1714, a large area of the Ribera district was destroyed to make way for a new citadel (➤ 64, Did You Know?). The displaced residents lived for years in makeshift shelters on the beach, until in 1755 a new district was developed on a triangular wedge of reclaimed land between the harbour and the sea, named La Barceloneta (Little Barcelona).

In the 19th century, La Barceloneta became home to seamen and dockers and it is still very much a working district, retaining its distinctive shanty-town atmosphere, fishy smells, and a quayside lined with the boats and nets of the local fleet. Today most visitors come here to eat in the many fine seafood eateries (*chiringuitos*), in particular those along the main harbourside thoroughfare, Passeig Joan de Borbó, and the restaurants of the converted Palau de Mar warehouse (➤ 58).

By contrast, Port Olímpic, with its smart promenades and glittering new marina, has given new impetus to Barcelona's nautical activities. Its chic restaurants, cafés and bars have become a lively night spot for both locals and tourists. Spain's two tallest buildings preside over the port – the office-filled Torre Mapfre and the five-star hotel Arts Barcelona, Barcelona's top hotel (➤ 101). Near by, a striking bronze fish sculpture (➤ 71, 74) by Frank Gehry (architect of the Guggenheim Museum in Bilbao) heralds the start of the Passeig Marítim, which links the port with La Barceloneta.

🔒 47D1

✉ Barceloneta/Port Olímpic

🍴 Plenty (£–£££)

🚇 Barceloneta, Ciutadella/Vila Olímpica

🚌 Barceloneta: 17, 36, 39, 40, 45, 57, 59, 64, 157. Port Olímpic: 10, 45, 57, 59, 71, 92, 157

↔ Parc de la Ciutadella (➤ 64); Port Vell (➤ 72); Vila Olímpica (➤ 73)

Hotel Arts and Gehry's Fish – symbols of a new and progressive city

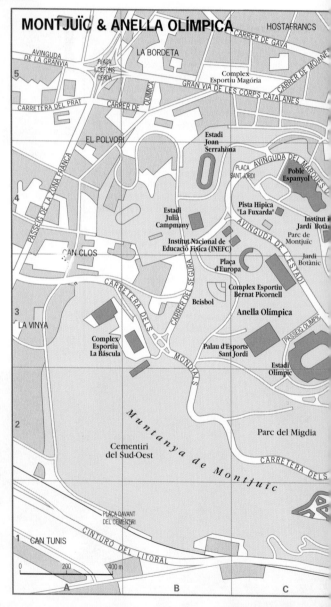

MONTJUÏC & ANELLA OLÍMPICA

HOSTAFRANCS

CARRER DE GAVA

AVINGUDA
DE LA GRANVIA

LA BORDETA

CARRER DE MOIANE

PLAÇA
ILDEFONS
CERDA

Complex
Esportiu Magória

GRAN VIA DE LES CORPS CATALANES

CARRETERA DEL PRAT

CARRER DE

EL POLVORI

Estadi
Joan
Serrahima

PLAÇA
SANT JORDI

AVINGUDA DEL MARQUES

Poble
Espanyol

Pista Hipica
"La Fuxarda"

Institut
Jardí Botà

Estadi
Julià
Campmany

AVINGUDA DE L'ESTADI

Parc de
Montjuic

Institut Nacional de
Educació Física (INEFC)

Jardi
Botànic

PASSEIG DE LA ZONA FRANCA

CAN CLOS

Plaça
d'Europa

Complex Esportiu
Bernat Picornell

Anella Olímpica

LA VINYA

CARRETERA DELS

Beisbol

CARRER DEL SEGURA

PASSEIG OLÍMPIC

Complex
Esportiu
La Báscula

MONDIALS

Palau d'Esports
Sant Jordi

Estadi
Olímpic

Muntanya de Montjuïc

Parc del Migdia

Cementiri
del Sud-Oest

CARRETERA DELS

PLAÇA DAVANT
DEL CEMENTIRI

CAN TUNIS

CINTURÓ DEL LITORAL

0   200   400 m

A   B   C

1   2   3   4   5

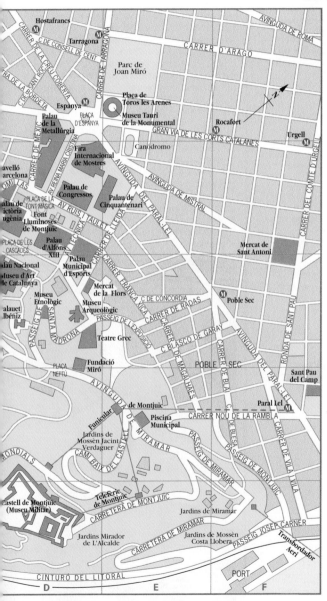

Hostafrancs
CARRER DE LA CREU COBERTA
C. DE CONSELL DE CENT
Tarragona
CARRER DE TARRAGONA
AVINGUDA DE ROMA
CARRER D'ARAGO
TRA DE LA BORDETA
DE LA BORDETA
Espànya
Parc de
Joan Miró
Plaça de
Toros les Arenes
Museu Tauri
de la Monumental
Rocafort
Urgell
CARRER DEL COMTE D'URGELL
Palau
de la
Metallúrgia
CARRER DE MÉXIC
VERNA MARIA CRISTINA
PLAÇA
D'ESPANYA
GRAN VIA DE LES CORTS CATALANES
Canòdromo
avelló
arcelona
OMILLAS
Fira
Internacional
de Mostres
alau de
ictòria
ugènia
PLAÇA DE LA
FONT MAGICA
Font
Lluminoses
de Montjuïc
Palau de
Congressos
AV RUIS I TAULET
Palau de
Cinquantenari
AVINGUDA DEL PARAL·LEL
AVINGUDA DE MISTRAL
Mercat de
Sant Antoni
PLAÇA DE LES
CASCADES
Palau
d'Alfons
XIII
TÉCNICA
Palau
Municipal
d'Esports
CARRER DE LLEIDA
CARRER FRANÇA VICA
lau Nacional
Museu d'Art
de Catalunya
Museu
Etnològic
alauet
lbéniz
PASSEIG DE SANTA MADRONA
Mercat
de la Flors
Museu
Arqueològic
C. DE CONCORDIA
CARRER DE RADAS
Poble Sec
PASSEIG DE L'EXPOSICIO
Teatre Grec
C. BLASCO DE GARAY
CARRER DE MAGALHAES
POBLE SEC
RONDA DE SANT PAU
AVINGUDA DEL PARAL·LEL
Sant Pau
del Camp
PLAÇA
NEPTU
Fundació
Miró
AVINGUDA DE MONTJUIC
de Montjuïc
Piscina
Municipal
CARRER NOU DE LA RAMBLA
Paral Lel
Funicular
Jardins de
Mossen Jacint
Verdaguer
CAMI BAIX DEL CASTELL
MIRAMAR
PASSEIG DE MIRAMAR
PASSEIG DE MONTJUIC
CARRER DE VILA VILA
MONDIALS
Castell de Montjuïc
(Museu Militar)
Teleféric
de Montjuïc
CARRETERA DE MONTJUIC
Jardins de Miramar
PASSEIG JOSEP CARNER
Transbordador
Aeri
Jardins Mirador
de L'Alcalde
CARRETERA DE MIRAMAR
Jardins de Mossèn
Costa Llobera
CINTURÓ DEL LITORAL
PORT
D
E
F

🔲 29D4
✉ Passeig de Gràcia 41
☎ 93 488 01 39
🕐 Mon–Sat 10–7, Sun 10–2
🚇 Passeig de Gràcia
♿ Good
🎫 Free
↔ Eixample (➤ 42–43);
  Fundació Antoni Tàpies
  (➤ 44)
❓ The entrance hall, open
  to the public, contains the
  information centre for *La
  Ruta del Modernisme*

🔲 29D4
✉ Passeig de Gràcia 43
🕐 Interior not open to the
  public
🚇 Passeig de Gràcia
♿ Good
↔ Eixample (➤ 42–43);
  Fundació Antoni Tàpies
  (➤ 44)

CASA AMATLLER

Chocolate manufacturer Antonio Amatller i Costa commissioned Josep Puig i Cadafalch to remodel Casa Amatller into an extravagant home with a neo-Gothic façade decorated with sculptures, coats of arms and floral reliefs, and crowned by a stepped gable. Inside the broad entranceway, the beautiful wooden lift was one of Barcelona's earliest elevators. Note also the amazing carvings on one interior doorway depicting animals making chocolate. A combined ticket is available for a guided tour, *La Ruta del Modernisme*, which includes the three façades of Casa Amatller, Casa Batlló and Casa Lleó-Morera and discounted entry to attractions.

CASA BATLLÓ

Casa Batlló is one of the most famous buildings of the *Modernista* school, designed by Gaudí for Josep Batlló i Casanovas and completed in 1907. It is said to illustrate the triumph of Sant Jordi (St George) over the dragon, with its mosaic façade, covered in glazed blue, green and ochre ceramics, representing the scaly skin of the dragon, its knobbly roof the dragon's back, the tower the saint's cross, and the wave-like balconies the skulls and bones of victims.

Casa Batlló – Gaudí's famous 'dragon' building

36

CASA LLEÓ-MORERA ✪✪

This striking *Modernista* building is considered Lluís Domènech i Montaner's most exuberant decorative work. Its flamboyant façade cleverly minimises the corner by placing visual emphasis on ornate circular balconies, columned galleries and oriel windows. Inside, a florid pink mosaic vestibule and open staircase lead to first-floor living quarters, lavishly decorated with stencilled stuccowork, stained glass, marquetry and mosaics, portraying roses (the nationalist symbol of Catalonia), lions (*lleó*) and mulberry bushes (*morera*). It is closed to the public.

CASA MILÀ ✪✪

Known locally as La Pedrera (the quarry), Spain's most controversial apartment block and Antoni Gaudí's last and most famous secular building was built between 1906 and 1912 and shows this great Catalan architect at his most inventive. It also shows Gaudí's genius as a structural engineer, with seven storeys built entirely on columns and arches, supposedly without a single straight line or right-angled corner. Its most distinctive features are the rippling limestone façade, with its intricate ironwork, and the strangely shaped chimneys of the roof terrace.

After years of neglect, Casa Milà was declared a World Heritage Site by UNESCO in 1984, and purchased by the Caixa Catalunya Foundation, which invested over 8,000 million ptas to restore it to its original glory.

CATEDRAL (➤ 16, TOP TEN)

✚ 29D4
✉ Passeig de Gràcia 35
☎ No phone
🕐 Interior currently not open to the public
🚇 Passeig de Gràcia
♿ Good
↔ Eixample (➤ 42–43); Fundació Antoni Tàpies (➤ 44)
❓ Guided tours of the *Manzana de la Discòrdia* and *La Rute del Modernisme* (a tour connecting all the *Modernista* sights in the city) ➤ 36, Casa Amatller. Includes discounts to many attractions.

Although Casa Milà is now a World Heritage Site, it so shocked Barcelonans when built that they nicknamed it 'La Pedrera' (the Quarry)

✚ 28C5
✉ Carrer Provença 261–265
☎ 93 484 59 00
🕐 Daily 10–8. Guided tours: Mon–Fri at 5:30 in English and Catalan and at 6:30 in Spanish
🚇 Diagonal
♿ Good (but not on roof); excellent toilet
💵 Expensive
↔ Eixample (➤ 42–43); Gracià (➤ 44–45); Manzana de la Discòrdia (➤ 36–37); Sagrada Família (➤ 24–25)
❓ Audio guide available

Did you know?
The Passeig de Gràcia between Carrer d'Aragó and Consell de Cent, containing Casa Amatller, Batlló and Lleó-Morera, is known as the Manzana de la Discòrdia *(Block of Discord), because of the clashing architectural styles.*

✚ 29D4

🍴 Plenty (£–£££)

Ⓜ Jaume I, Liceu, Plaça de
   Catalunya, Urquinaona

↔ Plaça de Catalunya
   (➤ 67); Port Vell (➤ 72);
   La Rambla (➤ 23)

*Explore the atmospheric
lanes of the Ciutat Vella, a
world away from the
modern city*

CIUTAT VELLA ★★★

The tightly packed maze of narrow streets and alleyways of Barcelona's Ciutat Vella (Old City), bordered by the Ramblas, the Ciutadella Park, Plaça Catalunya and the sea, was once enclosed by medieval city walls and, until the massive building boom of the Eixample (➤ 42–43), 150 years ago, comprised the entire city.

At its heart is the Barri Gòtic (Gothic Quarter), one of several clearly identifiable *barris* or districts which make up the Old City. Its roots can be traced back to 15BC, when Roman soldiers established a small settlement called Barcino on a slight hill here called Mons Taber. This remarkable cluster of dark, twisting streets, quiet patios, sun-splashed squares and grand Gothic buildings was built

inside the Roman fortifications, at a time when Barcelona, along with Genoa and Venice, was one of the three most important merchant cities in the Mediterranean and possessed untold riches. Its crowning glory, the Catedral (➤ 16), is surrounded by former residences of the counts of Barcelona and the Kings of Catalonia and Aragón. To the northwest lies Carrer Portaferrissa, the Old City's principal shopping street, with trendy boutiques and shopping arcades. To the south lies the spacious Plaça Sant Jaume (➤ 69) and a cobweb of narrow streets and interconnecting squares, including Plaça Sant Felip Neri, with its fine baroque church, Plaça del Pi, with its market of local produce (➤ 75), and leafy Plaça Sant Josep Oriol, the 'Montmartre of Barcelona', where local artists display their works at weekends and buskers entertain the café crowds. Just off the square, the narrow streets bounded by Carrer Banys Nous, Call and Bisbe once housed a rich Jewish ghetto called *El Call*, but now the area is known for its antique shops.

As the city grew more prosperous in the early Middle Ages, new *barris* developed around the Roman perimeter, including La Mercè to the south and La Ribera to the east. The area south of Carrer de Ferran – La Mercè – is focused around the elegant, arcaded Plaça Reial (➤ 69) and the Church of La Mercè, Barcelona's patron Virgin. Though once very prosperous, this *barri* has become shabby and run-down, but is still worth exploring if only to seek out the excellent locals' *tapas* bars along Carrer de la Mercè.

The *barri* of La Ribera, east of Via Laietana, holds much to interest the visitor. Its name (The Waterfront) recalls the time when the shoreline reached considerably further inland during Barcelona's Golden Age, when it was the city's main centre of commerce and trade and the favourite residential area of the merchant élite. Their handsome Gothic palaces still line its main street, Carrer Montcada. Several have since been converted into museums and galleries including Museu Picasso (➤ 20) and Galeria Maeght (➤ 107). The street leads to Santa Maria del Mar, the 'seaside cathedral' (➤ 26) and the Passeig del Born, with its popular restaurants, bars and craft shops.

Above: *tiled detail on a drinking fountain in the Barri Gòtic*
Below: *look for the ornate balconies and other hidden details above the shop fronts*

Barri Gòtic

Distance
2km

Time
1 hour (excluding visits)

Start/end point
Plaça Nova
➕ 41B3
Ⓜ Catalunya, Urquinaona

Coffee break
Mesón del Café (£)
✉ Carrer Llibreteria 16, just off Plaça Sant Jaume I
☎ 93 315 07 54

Leave Plaça Nova via the Portal del Bisbe (part of the Roman wall) into Carrer del Bisbe. Turn first left into Carrer de Santa Llúcia.

Note the tiny chapel of Santa Llúcia to your right, and the Gothic Archdeacon's House (Casa de l'Ardiaca) to your left. Just beyond is the main entrance to the Catedral (➤ 16).

From Plaça de la Seu, follow Carrer dels Comtes beside the cathedral, past Museu Frederic Marès (➤ 55). A left turn into Baixada de Santa Clara leads to Plaça del Rei (➤ 68). Return to the cathedral and skirt round its buttresses past the 14th-century Canon's House (Casa del Cánonges).

Stone plaques on the façade portray twin towers supported by winged goats with lions' feet, the heraldic symbols of medieval Barcelona.

Intricate stone lacework makes this bridge on Carrer del Bisbe unique

Turn sharp left, then left again onto Carrer del Bisbe, under a bridge and into Plaça Sant Jaume (➤ 69). Take Carrer de la Ciutat, then the first left until you reach Plaça Sant Just.

Here, the Església dels Sants Just i Pastor is reputedly the oldest church in Barcelona. Opposite, note the faded frescos on an elegant townhouse.

Leave the square along Carrer del Lledó. Turn first left then left again at the House of the Blue Tiles. Following the line of the Roman wall, cross Carrer Jaume I and continue up Carrer de la Tapineria, once the main street of medieval shoemakers.

Constructed between 270 and 310 AD, Barcelona's Roman walls were outgrown by the 11th century.

Continue along Carrer de la Tapineria past more Roman remains and return to Plaça Nova.

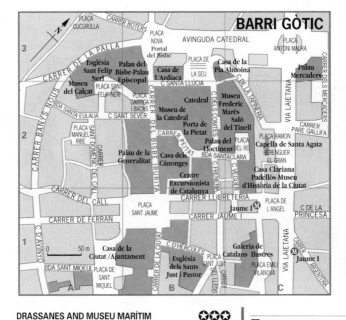

BARRI GÒTIC

DRASSANES AND MUSEU MARÍTIM ✪✪✪

Barcelona's Museu Marítim (Maritime Museum) is located in the magnificent Drassanes Reials (Royal Shipyards), a splendid example of Gothic civil architecture. Since the 13th century, these impressive yards have been dedicated to the construction of ships for the Crowns of Catalonia and Aragon.

Today, their vast, cathedral-like, stone-vaulted halls contain maps, charts, paintings, pleasure craft and a huge range of other seafaring memorabilia chronicling the remarkable maritime history of Barcelona. The most impressive exhibit is a 60m replica of *La Real*, flagship of Don Juan of Austria, which forms part of an exciting 45-minute spectacle – 'The Great Sea Adventure'.

Through headphones, visual and acoustic effects, visitors can experience life as a galley slave, encounter a Caribbean storm, join emigrants bound for the New World, and explore the seabed on board *Ictineo*, claimed to be the world's first submarine and built by Catalan inventor Narcís Monturiol.

➕ 29E3
✉ Avinguda de les Drassanes s/n
☎ 93 342 99 20
🕐 Daily 10–7
🍴 Café-restaurant (£)
Ⓜ Drassanes
🚌 14, 18, 36, 38, 57, 59, 64, 91
♿ Few
💰 Expensive
🔁 Ciutat Vella (➤ 38–39); Monument a Colom (➤ 50); Port Vell (➤ 72); La Rambla (➤ 23)
❓ Library, bookshop, gift shop

Life on the ocean wave is explored in the Museu Marítim

L'EIXAMPLE ✪✪

L'Eixample means 'The Extension' in Catalan, and this district was laid out between 1860 and 1920 to expand the city beyond the confines of its medieval walls and to link it with the outlying municipalities of Sants, Sarrià-Sant Gervasi and Gràcia.

The innovative plan, drawn up by liberal-minded civil engineer Ildefons Cerdà, broke completely with the tradition of Spanish urban planning, with its geometric grid of streets running parallel to the seafront, neatly dividing an area of 9sq km into 550 symmetrical blocks. The aptly named Avinguda Diagonal cuts through the rectilinear blocks at 45° to add a touch of originality. The utopian features of Cerdà's plan – such as gardens in the middle of each block and buildings on only two sides – have been largely forgotten, and today many people scorn the district for its monotony while others praise it as a visionary example of urban planning.

The Eixample is divided into two *barris*, either side of Carrer Balmes. *L'Esquerra* (The Left) is largely residential and of less interest to visitors, whereas *La Dreta* (The Right) contains many of Barcelona's greatest *Modernistame* landmarks, including Casa Milà, the three properties of La Manzana de la Discòrdia, the Fundació Antoni Tàpies, the Hospital de la Santa Creu i Sant Pau, and the Sagrada Família. It is also a district of offices, banks and hotels. Chic boutiques and shops line its streets and, at night, Barcelona's smart set frequents its many restaurants, designer bars and discos.

Above: Passeig de Gràcia, with its many shops, bars and restaurants, is one of the city's liveliest streets

The Eixample District

This walk explores some of Barcelona's lesser-known examples of *Modernista* architecture.

Start in Plaça de Catalunya, and walk up Passeig de Gràcia.

This elegant avenue has its original wrought-iron street lamps with ceramic mosaic seats dating from 1906. Note Nos 6–14 (one of the last *Modernista* constructions), No 18 (the only surviving example of rationalist commercial architecture in Barcelona) and No 21.

Turn left at Casa Lleó–Morera (➤ 37), along Carrer Consell de Cent then first left into Rambla de Catalunya, past several contrasting Modernista buildings (Nos 47, 54 and 77) until Diagonal. Turn right past Gaudí-influenced Casa Comalat at No 442 by Salvador Valery and continue until Puigi Cadafalch's Palau Quadras at No 373.

This striking neo-Gothic building contains the Museu de la Música. Near by, UNESCO-listed Casa Terrades (Nos 416–20) is sometimes known as Casa de les Punxes ('House of Spikes') because of its steep gables and red-tiled turrets.

Turn right into Carrer Roger de Lluria, past Palau Montaner (Carrer Mallorca 278), an early work by Domènech i Montaner, and turn left into Carrer València, past Nos 285, 293, and 312, striking Modernista buildings, and a large enclosed market. At Avinguda Diagonal, turn right.

Don't miss the extraordinary undulating wooden façade of Casa Planells (No 332), by one of Gaudí's early collaborators, Josep Maria Jujol.

Turn left into Carrer Sicilia and continue on to the Sagrada Família (➤ 24–25).

Distance
4km

Time
2–2½ hours (excluding visits)

Start point
Plaça de Catalunya
🚇 29D4
Ⓜ Catalunya

End point
Sagrada Família
🚇 29E6
Ⓜ Sagrada Família

Lunch break
Buy a picnic in the large, covered market (Mercat de la Concepció) to eat in Plaça Sagrada Família.
✉ Mercat de la Concepció, Carrer València

Above: *Casa Josefa Villanueva in Carrer València – one of the many Modernista buildings in the Eixample*

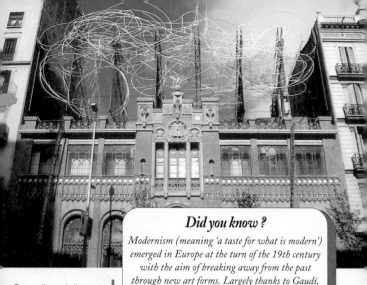

Extraordinary skyline – Fundació Tàpies' Cloud and Chair sculpture

FUNDACIÓ ANTONI TÀPIES ✪

The Tàpies Foundation was founded by Catalan artist Antoni Tàpies in 1984 to promote the study and understanding of modern art. It is housed in the former Montaner i Simon publishing house, built by Lluis Domènech i Montaner between 1880 and 1889, an unusual building that is considered the initiator of the Modernist movement. The striking *Mudejar*-style façade is crowned by an eye-catching tangle of wire and tubing by Tàpies, entitled *Cloud and Chair* (1990). Inside, there is an exhaustive library documenting art and artists of the 20th century, and one of the most complete collections of Tàpies' own works.

FUNDACIÓ JOAN MIRÓ (➤ 17, TOP TEN)

GRÀCIA ✪

In 1820, Gràcia was a mere village of about 2,500 inhabitants. By 1897, the population had swollen to 61,000, making it the ninth-largest city in Spain, known as a radical centre of Catalanism and anarchism, still reflected in some street names – Mercat de la Llibertat and Plaça de la Revolució. Since then, Gràcia has been engulfed by the expanding metropolis, yet even now it maintains a village-like, no-frills, bohemian atmosphere and the *Graciencs* still call the cityfolk *Barcelonins*.

+ 29D5
✉ Carrer d'Aragó 255
☎ 93 487 03 15
⏱ Tue–Sun 10–8. Closed Mon
🚌 7, 16, 17, 20, 22, 24, 28, 43, 44
Ⓜ Passeig de Gràcia
♿ Good
💷 Moderate
↔ Manzana de la Discòrdia (➤ 36–37, and panel)
❓ Library and small bookshop

+ 28C6
🍴 Plenty (£–£££)
Ⓜ Fontana, Gràcia, Joanic, Plaça Molina
❓ Festa Major every August (➤ 116)

There are no real 'tourist' attractions here, except Gaudí's first major commission, Casa Vicens (✉ Carrer de les Carolines 24). Gràcia's real appeal is its muddle of narrow atmospheric streets and squares, and a concentration of reasonably priced bars, restaurants and popular night venues.

HOSPITAL DE LA SANTA CREU I SANT PAU ✪✪

This remarkable hospital complex is a masterpiece of *Modernisme* by innovative architect Lluís Domènech i Montaner. Not only did he deliberately defy the orderliness of the Eixample by aligning the buildings at 45 degrees to the street grid, but he also built the complex in contradiction to established hospital concepts by creating a 'hospital-village' of 48 small pavilions connected by underground passages and surrounded by gardens, rather than one single massive building.

Construction began in 1902, as a long-overdue replacement for the old hospital in the Raval, following a bequest from a Catalan banker called Pau Gil. The new hospital was inaugurated in 1930. The main pavilion, with its graceful tower and ornate mosaic façade, serves as a majestic entrance to the whole ensemble. Inside, the various pavilions are grouped around gardens that occupy an area equivalent to nine blocks of the Eixample, where both doctors and patients alike can enjoy a peaceful natural environment. The pavilions are decorated in ornate *Modernista* style using brick, colourful ceramics and natural stone. Over the years, the hospital complex has been restored several times and in 1984 it was declared a World Cultural Heritage site by UNESCO.

✚ 62A4
✉ Carrer de Sant Antoni Maria Claret 167–71
☎ 93 291 90 00
🍴 Small coffee shop in one of the pavilions (£)
🚇 Hospital de Sant Pau
↔ Gràcia (► 44); Parc Güell (► 21); Sagrada Família (► 24–25)
❓ Please remember that this is a hospital and not a tourist attraction

The main hospital of the Eixample – more palatial than most!

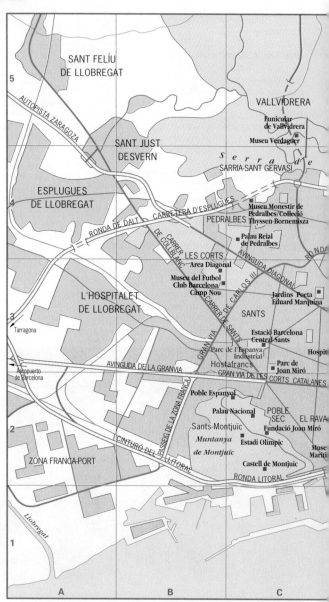

BARCELONA ENVIRONS

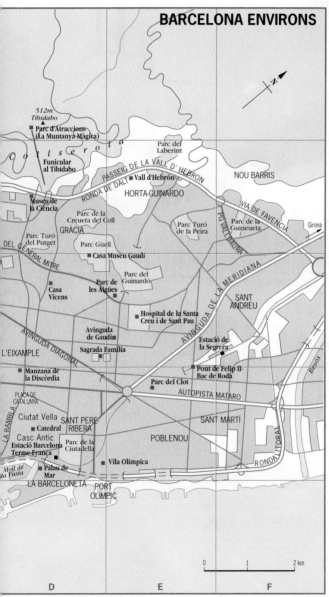

512m
Tibidabo
■ Parc d'Atraccions
(La Muntanya Màgica)

C o l l s e r o l a

Funicular
al Tibidabo

Parc del
Laberint

PASSEIG DE LA VALL D' HEBRON

RONDA DE DALT ■ Vall d'Hebron

NOU BARRIS

■ Museu de
la Ciència

HORTA-GUINARDÓ

VIA DE FAVENCIA

Girona

Parc de la
Creueta del Coll

GRÀCIA

Parc Turó
de la Peira

Parc de la
Guineueta

PG VALL D'AURA

Parc Turó
del Putget

DEL GENERAL MITRE

Parc Güell

■ Casa Museu Gaudí

Casa
Vicens

Parc de
les Aigües

Parc del
Guinardó

AVINGUDA DE LA MERIDIANA

■ Hospital de la Santa
Creu i de Sant Pau

SANT
ANDREU

Besòs

AVINGUDA DIAGONAL

Avinguda
de Gaudí ■

Sagrada Família

Estació de
la Segrera

L'EIXAMPLE

■ Manzana de
la Discòrdia

■ Pont de Felip II-
Bac de Roda

Parc del Clot

PLAÇA DE
CATALUNYA

AUTOPISTA MATARO

LA RAMBLA

Ciutat Vella

SANT PERE-
RIBERA

SANT MARTÍ

■ Catedral

Casc Antic

Estació Barcelona
Terme-França

Parc de la
Ciutadella

POBLENOU

RONDA LITORAL

Moll de
la Fusta

■ Palau de
Mar

■ Vila Olímpica

LA BARCELONETA

PORT
OLÍMPIC

0   1   2 km

D   E   F

47

MERCAT DE LA BOQUERIA ✪✪

Of more than 40 food markets in Barcelona, La Boqueria is the best and the busiest – always bustling with local shoppers, restaurateurs, gourmands and tourists. Its cavernous market hall (best entered through an imposing wrought-iron entranceway halfway up La Rambla) was built in the 1830s to house the food stalls that cluttered La Rambla and surrounding streets.

Inside is a riot of noise, perfumes and colours, with a myriad stalls offering all the specialities of the Mediterranean and the Catalonian hinterland – mouth-watering displays of fruit and vegetables, a glistening array of exotic fish, endless strings of sausages and haunches of ham, and sweetly scented bunches of herbs.

🚩 62A3
✉ Rambla 91
☎ 93 318 25 84
🕑 Mon–Sat 7AM–8PM. Closed Sun
🍴 Snack bars (£)
Ⓜ Liceu
♿ Few
👍 Free
🔁 Ciutat Vella (➤ 38–39); Drassanes and Museu Marítim (➤ 41); Plaça Reial (➤ 69); La Rambla (➤ 23); Gran Teatre del Liceu (➤ 114)

MONESTIR DE PEDRALBES AND COLLECCIÓ THYSSEN-BORNEMISZA ✪✪

The monastery of Pedralbes was founded by King Jaume II and Queen Elisenda de Montcada in 1326 to accommodate nuns of the St Clare of Assisi order. Following the king's death in 1327, Elisenda spent the last 37 years of her life here.

The spacious, three-storey cloisters – one of the architectural jewels of Barcelona – are still used by the Clarista nuns. Step inside and it is hard to believe you are just a short bus ride from frenetic downtown Barcelona. From here, there is access to the refectory, the chapter house, the Queen's grave and St Michael's cell, with its remarkable wall murals.

Recently, Baron von Thyssen-Bornemisza donated part of his priceless art collection to the monastery, with 79 works housed in two former dormitories – mostly 13th- to 18th-century Italian and German paintings, including works by Fra Angélico, Lucas Cranach, Velázquez and Rubens .

🚩 46C4
✉ Baixada de Monestir 9
☎ Monastery: 93 203 92 82. Thyssen-Bornemisza Collection: 93 280 14 34
🕑 Monastery and museums: Tue–Sun 10–2. Closed Mon and hols. Church: Tue–Sun 11–1
🚌 22, 63, 64, 75
♿ Excellent
👍 Monastery: moderate. Thyssen-Bornemisza: moderate
🔁 Palau Reial de Pedralbes (➤ 61)
❓ Bookshop, gift shop

MONTJUÏC (➤ 18, TOP TEN)

Left: *the lively, colourful Mercat de la Boqueria* Opposite: *enjoy a peaceful stroll through the Monestir de Pedralbes*

49

🔲 62A1
✉ Plaça Portal de la Pau
☎ 93 302 52 24
🕐 10–1:30, 3:30–6:30,
longer in summer and
weekends.
Ⓜ Drassanes
💷 Cheap
↔ Port Vell (► 72)

MONUMENT A COLOM ✪

This vast monument, commemorating the return of Christopher Columbus to Barcelona in 1493 from his first trip to the Americas, stands outside the naval headquarters of Catalonia, at the seaward end of the Ramblas. It was designed by Gaietà Buigas for the Universal Exposition of 1888, with Columbus standing at the top of a 50m column, pointing out to sea – towards Italy! Take the lift to the top for breathtaking bird's-eye views of the harbourfront.

🔲 62A5
✉ Plaça dels Àngels 1
☎ 93 412 08 10
🕐 Mon, Wed–Fri 11–7:30,
Sat 10–8, Sun and hols
10–3. Closed Tue. Longer
opening hours in summer
🍴 Café (£)
Ⓜ Catalunya, Universitat
♿ Excellent
💷 Expensive
↔ Ciutat Vella (► 38–39);
La Rambla (► 23)

MUSEU D'ART CONTEMPORANI DE BARCELONA (MACBA) ✪✪

The new Barcelona Museum of Contemporary Art (MACBA), inaugurated in 1995, focuses on the art movements of the second half of the 20th century.

The museum building, itself a work of art designed by the American architect Richard Meier, has been the subject of much controversy but is increasingly being included as one of Barcelona's must-see landmarks. The vast white edifice with swooping ramps and glass-walled galleries almost upstages the works on display. Its location – surrounded by shabby old houses in the rundown district of Raval – is intended to spearhead investment in the neighbourhood.

MACBA's extensive collection (exhibited in rotation) covers the 1940s to the 1990s, with special emphasis on Catalan and Spanish artists. It contains works by Klee, Miró and Tàpies, along with many others, including Joan Brossa, Maurizio Cattelan and Damien Hirst.

Above: *the Monument a Colom makes an impressive sight*

La Rambla

Start at Plaça Portal de la Pau, with your back to the sea and La Colom Monument (➤ 50), and head up the Ramblas, beginning at La Rambla de Santa Mònica. The convent here is the only 17th-century building still standing on La Rambla.

This first section of Barcelona's famous street can be dangerous, especially at night, as it borders the Barri Xinès (China Town) district, renowned as a centre of drugs and crime. If you visit El Ravel after dark, take a taxi.

Continue up to Plaça del Teatre and the Rambla dels Caputxins, on the site of an ancient Capuchin convent.

This was once the heart of the old theatre district, marked by a statue of Serafí Pitarra, 'father' of contemporary theatre in Catalonia. Today, only the shabby Teatro Principal remains.

Continue north past the Gran Teatre del Liceu (➤ 114) to Rambla de Sant Josep, which begins where the street widens, at Mercat de la Boqueria (➤ 49).

A meat market used to be held in the Plaça de la Boqueria. Indeed, 'boqueria' means 'butcher'. Today the square is decorated with a mosaic by Joan Miró. Flower-stands line this section, commonly called the Rambla de les Flors, whereas birds and other small creatures are sold in the Rambla dels Estudis, named after a university which once stood here, although now dubbed the Rambla dels Ocells (Boulevard of the Birds).

The final Rambla – La Rambla de Canaletes, named after its famous fountain (➤ 23) – leads to Plaça de Catalunya, the square where the city's heart beats fastest (➤ 67).

Distance
1km

Time
1 hour

Start point
Plaça Portal de la Pau
➕ 62A1
Ⓜ Drassanes

End point
Plaça de Catalunya
➕ 62B5
Ⓜ Catalunya

Coffee break
Café de l'Òpera (➤ 98)
✉ Rambla dels Caputxins 74
☎ 93 302 41 80

You can frequently find street artists in the Rambla dels Caputxins

Food & Drink

No one visiting Barcelona should leave without trying *la cuina Catalana*, its cuisine, described by the American food critic Colman Andrews as 'the last great culinary secret in Europe'. Rooted in the fresh local ingredients of the mountains, the plains and sea, the food is delicious and suprisingly subtle in flavour.

Mediterranean Flavours

The main ingredients of traditional Catalan dishes are typically Mediterranean: tomatoes, garlic, olive oil, aubergines, courgettes, peppers and herbs, which, when blended, form *samfaina*, a delicious sauce served with many dishes. Other principal sauces include *picada* (nuts, bread, parsley, garlic and saffron), *sofregit* (a simple sauce of onion, tomato and garlic lightly fried in olive oil) and *allioli* (a strong, garlicky mayonnaise).

For centuries pork (*llom*) has been the cornerstone of the Catalan diet. Little is wasted – even the *peus de porc* (pigs' trotters) are considered a delicacy. No bar would be complete without its haunch of *pernil* (cured ham), a popular *tapas* dish (► 95 panel), and you often see a variety of sausages hanging from the rafters of restaurants and delicatessens. Lamb, chicken, duck, beef and game also feature strongly, often prepared *a la brasa* (on an open charcoal grill) and served with lashings of *allioli.*

Fresh fish is one of the gourmet delights of la Cuina Catalana

Mar i Muntanya

In Catalan cuisine, meat is commonly combined with fruit, creating such mouth-watering dishes as *pollastre amb pera* (chicken with pears) and *conill amb prunes* (rabbit with prunes). However, it is the unique 'surf'n'turf' combinations that sea and mountain (*Mar i Muntanya*) produce which differentiate *la cuina Catalana* from the cookery of other Spanish regions. *Sípia amb mandonguilles* (cuttlefish with meatballs) and *mar i cel* ('sea and heaven' – made with sausages, rabbit, shrimp and fish) are especially tasty.

Near the coast, fish dishes reign supreme, ranging from simple grilled *sardinas* (sardines) and hearty *sarsuela* (seafood stew) to eye-catching shellfish displays. Try *suquet de peix* (fish and potato soup) or the more unusual *broudegos* ('dog soup') made with fresh fish, onions and orange juice, followed by speciality dishes *arròs negre* (rice cooked in black squid ink), *fideuà* (a local variant of paella, using pasta and not rice) or *bacallà* (salt cod), which comes *a la llauna* (with garlic, parsley, tomato and white wine), *esqueixada* (in an onion, olive and tomato salad), *amb samfaina* or *amb romesco* (a piquant sauce, made from a mixture of crushed nuts, tomatoes and spicy red pepper).

Fine Wines

A short distance south of Barcelona, the Penedès is the main Catalan wine region, producing red (*negre*), white (*blanc*) and rosé (*rosat*) wines. Look for the reliable Torres, Masia Bach and René Barbier labels. Catalan *cava* (sparkling wine) also comes from the Penedès wineries, made by the *méthode champenoise* (➤ 113 panel). Famous names include Freixenet and Codorníu, which can be sampled in the champagne bars of Barcelona. To the north, the Alella and Empordà regions produce white wines, while Priorat produces excellent, heavy reds.

Visitors with a sweet tooth also find sustenance in Barcelona (➤ 96 panel)

Tasty tapas; *tucking into portions of prawns and snails*

Above: *entrance to the Museu d'Art Modern*

MUSEU D'ART MODERN – MNAC ⭐⭐

The Museum of Modern Art shares a wing of the imposing Palau de la Ciutadella with the Parliament of Catalonia, on the far side of the Parc de la Ciutadella (➤ 64). Its collections follow on from those of the National Museum of Catalan Art (➤ 19), completing a period spanning the 11th to 20th centuries, and are devoted to Catalan art from the mid-19th century to around 1930.

The collection starts with works by Maria Fortuny, the earliest of the *Modernistas* and the first Catalan artist to be known widely abroad, and friends Ramon Casas, whose work once hung on the walls of Els Quatre Gats (➤ 94), and Santiago Rusinyol. However, the highlight of the museum is, without doubt, its decorative arts collection: jewellery, textiles, stained glass, ironwork, sculptures, ceramics and painted screens by Homar, Puig I Cadafalch and Gaudí, among others.

The extravagance of *Modernisme* was succeeded by the less adventurous *Noucentisme* movement, which attempted to reintroduce the more harmonious values of Classical and Mediterranean art, epitomised by the works of Casanovas and Sunyer. The fascinating exhibition draws to a close with a series of striking avant-garde sculptures by Gargallo and Juli González, dating from the 1920s and 30s.

Did you know?

FC Barcelona, or Barça for short, is more than Spain's top football club, the fifth most successful business in Spain, and the richest sports club in the world. During the Franco era, it stood as a Catalan symbol around which people could rally, and this emotional identification still remains today. It also explains why this legendary club has the world's largest soccer club membership (over 100,000 members) and why the streets still erupt with ecstatic revellers following a win over arch-rivals, Real Madrid.

MUSEU FREDERIC MARÈS ✪

Entrance to this museum, founded by local sculptor Frederic Marès in 1946, is via a beautiful medieval courtyard, which was once part of the Royal Palace of the Kings and Queens of Catalonia and Aragon. The museum itself is divided into two main sections: the sculpture collection, featuring works from the pre-Roman period to the 20th century, and the 'Sentimental Museum', which portrays daily life from the 15th to 20th centuries through an astonishing assortment of household items. Highlights include the women's section (with collections of fans, parasols, hat pins and jewellery), the smoker's room, and the charming entertainments room, with its puppet theatres, wind-up toys and dolls.

➕ 62C3
✉ Plaça de Sant Iu 5–6
☎ 93 310 58 00
🕐 Tue and Thu 10–5, Wed, Fri and Sat 10–7, Sun and hols 10–3. Closed Mon
🍴 Summer café (£)
Ⓜ Jaume I
♿ Few
💰 Moderate. Free 1st Sun of month and every Wed PM
🔄 Catedral (➤ 16); Ciutat Vella (➤ 38–39); Museu d'Història de la Ciutat (➤ 56); Plaça del Rei (➤ 68); Plaça Sant Jaume (➤ 69)
❓ Library, shop, guided visits

Religious imagery in the Museu Frederic Marès

MUSEU DEL FUTBOL CLUB BARCELONA ✪✪

If you can't get a ticket to see Europe's top football team in action, then at least visit the Barcelona Football Club Museum, the city's most visited museum after the revered Picasso Museum (➤ 20). Even those who loathe football can't help marvelling at the vast Nou Camp stadium, which seats 120,000 spectators. The museum, under the terraces, presents a triumphant array of trophies, photographs and replays of highlights in the club's history before leading you to the shop, where everyone can buy a club shirt, pen, scarf, badge, mug...

➕ 46B3
✉ Nou Camp – Entrance 7 or 9, Carrer Arístides Maillol
☎ 93 496 36 00
🕐 Mon–Sat 10–6:30, Sun and hols 10–2
🍴 Café (£)
Ⓜ Collblanc, Maria Cristina
💰 Moderate ♿ Good
❓ Gift shop

+ 62C3
✉ Plaça del Rei s/n
☎ 93 315 11 11
🕐 Tue–Sat 10–2, 4–8,
(Jul–Sep 10–8), Sun and
hols 10–2.
Ⓜ Jaume I, Liceu
♿ Few
🎟 Moderate (free 1st Sat
afternoon of the month)
↔ Catedral (➤ 16); Ciutat
Vella (➤ 38–39); Museu
Frederic Marès (➤ 55);
Plaça Sant Jaume (➤ 69)
❓ Information service, shop
and guided tours

Above: *the entrance of
the Museu d'Història de
la Ciutat*

+ 35E5
✉ Gran Via de les Corts
Catalanes 749
☎ 93 245 58 03
🕐 Mon–Sat 10:30–2, 4–7;
Sun 10–1
Ⓜ Monumental
🎟 Moderate

MUSEU D'HISTÒRIA DE LA CIUTAT ✪✪✪

The Museu d'Història de la Ciutat (City History Museum) is responsible for researching, conserving and publicising Barcelona's heritage. It is split into several sections in various locations around the Plaça del Rei (➤ 68). To start, visitors can familiarise themselves with the earliest origins of the city by wandering around the underground walkways beneath the square, which explore a vast area of excavations that have exposed the ancient Roman settlement of Barcino.

The main entrance to the museum complex is at the opposite end of the square, in Casa Padellàs, a medieval mansion which was moved here stone by stone when the Via Laietana was created in 1930. Inside, carefully chosen, thoroughly documented exhibits trace Barcelona's remarkable evolution through two thousand years of history from a Roman trading-post to a wealthy 18th-century metropolis. Climb to the lookout point high above the galleries for memorable views of the square and the old city.

Back in the square, a visit to the medieval buildings of the Palau Reial Major (the Great Royal Palace ➤ 68), completes the tour of the museum.

MUSEU NACIONAL D'ART DE CATALUNYA
(➤ 19, TOP TEN)

MUSEU PICASSO (➤ 20, TOP TEN)

MUSEU TAURI DE LA MONUMENTAL ✪

Even though bullfighting has never had a particularly passionate following in Catalonia, the Museu Tauri De La Monumental (Bullfighting Museum), located inside the Monumental Bullring, is undoubtedly one of Barcelona's more unusual museums, with its dazzling array of fancy capes and costumes, photographs, old bullfighting posters and the mounted heads of bulls.

MUSEU TÈXTIL I D'INDUMENTÀRIA ⭐

The Museu Tèxtil i d'Indumentària (Textile and Clothing Museum) acts as a reminder of how, thanks to its thriving textile industry, Barcelona rose to prosperity in the 1800s. It occupies a beautiful 14th-century palace, in what would then have been the aristocratic heart of Barcelona.

The museum collections include textiles, tapestries, lace and clothes from medieval to modern times, with displays of textile machinery, dolls, shoes, and other fashion accessories.

- 🕇 63D2
- ✉ Carrer Montcada 12–14
- ☎ 93 310 45 16
- 🕐 Tue–Sat 10–6, Sun and hols 10–3. Closed Mon
- 🍴 Café–restaurant (£)
- Ⓜ Jaume I
- ♿ Good
- ✋ Moderate
- ↔ Museu Picasso (➤ 20)

PALAU GÜELL ⭐⭐⭐

This extraordinary building, constructed in 1886–88 and declared a World Cultural Heritage site by UNESCO, was Antoni Gaudí's first major architectural project, commissioned by the Güell family.

The façade is particularly striking, with its twin arches leading into the central vestibule. Off the latter are various rooms decorated with *Modernista* fittings. A ramp leads down to the basement stables, constructed with bare-brick columns and arches. The rooftop terrace is a mixture of random spires, battlements and chimneys of differing shapes and sizes, decorated with coloured ceramic mosaics. Look closely and on one you will find a reproduction of Cobi, the 1992 Barcelona Olympics mascot.

Unfortunately, the Güell family did not live here long. In 1936, the palace was confiscated by Spanish Civil War anarchists, who used it as their military headquarters and prison.

- 🕇 29D3
- ✉ Carrer Nou de la Rambla 3–5
- ☎ 93 317 39 74
- 🕐 Mon–Sat 10–6. Closed Sun & hols
- Ⓜ Liceu
- ♿ None
- ✋ Cheap. Guided tours only (45 mins each)
- ↔ Mercat de la Boqueria (➤ 49); Ciutat Vella (➤ 38–39); Plaça Reial (➤ 69); La Rambla (➤ 23)

Plaça de Toros Monumental – Barcelona's main bullring

*The newly renovated
Palau de Mar warehouse
is renowned for its
excellent seafood
restaurants*

PALAU DE MAR ✪✪✪

Thanks to the influence of the Olympic Games, and the opening up of the old port as a leisure area, the Palau de Mar (Palace of the Sea) – an impressive late 19th-century warehouse – has recently been converted into offices, harbourside restaurants and the spectacular Museu d'Història de Catalunya (Museum of Catalan History).

This is one of Barcelona's most sophisticated museums, opened in 1996. Some critics have dubbed it a 'theme park', because of its lack of original exhibits, but it is nevertheless a dynamic and stimulating museum, covering the history of Catalonia in an entertaining fashion, through state-of-the-art displays, films, special effects, interactive screens and hands-on exhibits – tread an Arab waterwheel, mount a cavalier's charger, drive an early tram, take cover in a Civil War air-raid shelter...

The museum is divided into eight sections, each presenting a thorough picture of the economy, politics, technology, culture and everyday life of Catalonia over the centuries: the region's prehistory, the consolidation of Catalonia in the Middle Ages, its maritime role, links with the Austrian Empire in the 16th and 17th centuries, its economic growth and industrialisation, the 1936 Civil War and the ensuing repression of Catalonia under Franco, through to the restoration of democracy in 1979. The insight this innovative museum provides makes it easier for the visitor to understand the complexities of this 'nation within a nation'.

PALAU DE LA MÚSICA CATALANA ✪✪✪

In a city bursting with architectural wonders, the Palau de la Música Catalana (Palace of Catalan Music) – commissioned by the Orfeó Català (Catalan Musical Society) in 1904 and created by local architect Lluís Domènech i Montaner between 1905 and 1908 – stands out as one of Barcelona's greatest Modernist masterpieces and a symbol of the renaissance of Catalan culture.

The bare brick façade is highlighted with colourful ceramic pillars, fancy windows and busts of Palestrina, Bach, Beethoven and Wagner. The sculptural group projecting from the corner of the building symbolises popular song. A balcony runs around the building and the main structure is supported by ornate columns that form huge dramatic archways over the entrance.

The interior continues the ornamental theme with a profusion of decoration in the entrance hall, foyer and staircase – almost overpowering in its attention to detail. The *pièce de résistance*, however, must be the concert hall, with its exquisite roof (an inverted cupola made of stained glass), its sculptures, ceramics and paintings dedicated to musical muses (including Josep Anselm Clavé, the great 19th-century reviver of Catalan music), and its beautiful balconies and columns, designed to enhance the perspective of the auditorium.

It's no surprise that this is one of the city's main venues for classical music, and, until the restoration of the Liceu Opera House and the opening of the Auditorium, was home to two orchestras, the Liceu and the Orquestra Simfònica de Barcelona i Nacional de Catalunya. It's a memorable experience to attend one of the weekly concerts; the acoustics are as fine as the surroundings.

✚ 63D4
✉ Carrer Sant Francesc de Paula 2
☎ 93 295 72 00
🕐 Daily 10–3:30 (6 in summer)
Ⓜ Jaume 1, Urquinaona
♿ Few
💲 Cheap
❓ Guided tours. Early booking for concerts essential

The Palau de la Música Catalana is a feast for the eyes as well as the ears

The Pedralbes District

Distance
3km

Time
1 hour (excluding visits)

Start point
Palau Reial de Pedralbes
⊞ 46C4
Ⓜ Palau Reial

End point
Monestir de Pedralbes
⊞ 46C4
🚌 22, 63, 64, 75, 78

The cool cloisters of Monestir de Pedralbes provide some welcome shade from the midday sun

Start at the Palau Reial de Pedralbes (➤ 61). Walk eastwards along the Avinguda de la Diagonal past the Law School and turn left up Avinguda de Pedralbes.

After a short distance on the left is the former Güell Estate (No 15). Note Gaudí's extraordinary wrought-iron entrance gate, which represents a dragon. Today the buildings house La Càtedra Gaudí, an institution specialising in subjects connected with this famous architect.

Continue up Avinguda de Pedralbes until the T-junction. Branch left into Carretera d'Esplugues.

At No 103, the Church of Montserrat was commissioned in 1920 as a gift for the Monastery of Montserrat (➤ 83) for use as a monastic foundation. The bequest was refused, so the property became part of the bishopric of Barcelona in the 1960s.

Turn right in front of the church, up Carrer Abadessa Olzet, left along Avinguda Pearson then right again up Carrer Miret i Sans as far as Carrer de Panama 21.

Here, near the corner (No 21), a charming medieval farmhouse underlines the former rural character of Pedralbes. By contrast, No 13, a magnificent *Modernista* mansion with a gleaming polychromatic tiled roof, reflects the wealth of this district.

The road turns into Carrer de Montevideo and passes behind the monastery of Pedralbes (➤ 49), hidden behind bougainvillaea-smothered walls and framed by the hills of Tibidabo beyond. A flight of steps leads down Baixada del Monestir, past a small, leafy square, to the main entrance.

PALAU REIAL DE PEDRALBES ✪

The Palau Reial de Pedralbes (Royal Palace of Pedralbes) is the result of the conversion in 1919 of the ancient villa of Can Feliu into a residence to accommodate the Spanish Royal family during the International Exhibition of 1929. After 1939, it became Franco's residence on visits to the city and, after various subsequent uses by royalty and heads of state, was opened to the public in 1960. The geometric gardens were landscaped by Nicolau Rubió i Turdurí, who integrated the existing trees into his design, and there is even a fountain by Gaudí.

Today the state rooms house two museums. The Museu de Ceràmica traces the development of Spanish ceramics from the 12th century onwards, and includes the 18th-century Catalan panels *La Cursa de Braus* (the Bullfight) and *La Xocolotada* (The Chocolate Party), together with works by Picasso and Miró. The Museu de les Arts Decoratives has an impressive collection of decorative arts that spans the early Middle Ages to the present day. Special emphasis is placed on 20th-century developments, from decorative *Modernisme* to such movements as Functionalism and Minimalism, which are both totally void of decoration. The exhibits include some unlikely objects such as coffee-grinders, ice trays and even a urinal!

Above: of all the luxury mansions in Pedralbes, the Palau Reial is the finest

✚ 46C4
✉ Avinguda de la Diagonal 686
☎ Museu de les Arts Decoratives: 93 280 50 24. Museu de Ceràmica: 93 280 16 21
🕐 Tue–Sat 10–6, Sun 10–3. Closed Mon
🚇 Palau Reial
♿ Museu d'Arts Decoratives: good. Museu de Ceràmica: few
💶 Museums: moderate (free 1st Sun of month). Gardens: free
🔁 Monestir de Pedralbes and Col·lecció Thyssen-Bornemisza (➤ 49)
❓ Shop, library, guided visits, educational services

Did you know?

The Zona Alta consists of old villages like Pedralbes, Sarriá, Bonanova and Sant Gervasi. In the 19th century, Barcelona's wealthy would spend their summer months here, in magnificent houses with lush gardens. Along with Horta ('market garden') to the east, with its gentrified farmhouses, this is still the home of many upper middle class Barcelonans.

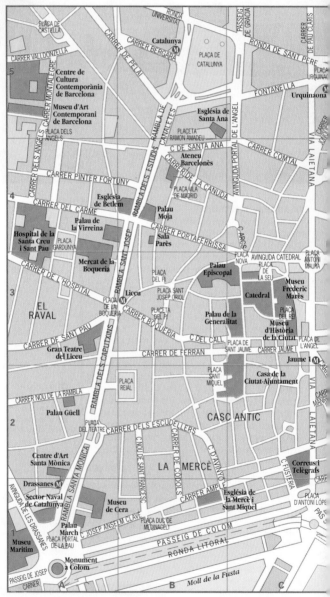

CENTRAL BARCELONA

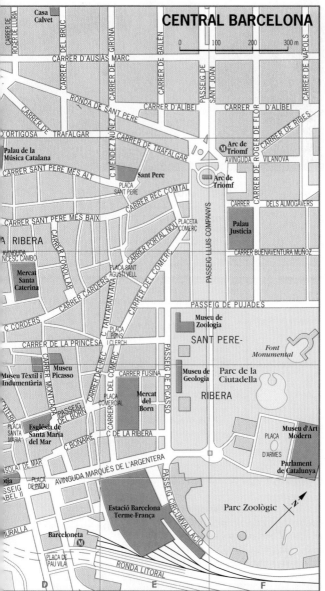

Casa Calvet

CARRER DE ROGER DE LLÚRIA

CARRER DEL BRUC

CARRER DE GIRONA

CARRER DE BAILEN

PASSEIG DE SANT JOAN

CARRER DE NÀPOLS

CARRER D'AUSIÀS MARC

RONDA DE SANT PERE

CARRER D'ALIBEI

CARRER D'ALIBEI

CARRER DE FLOR

PORTIGOSA DE TRAFALGAR

Palau de la Música Catalana

CARRER SANT PERE MÉS ALT

Sant Pere

CARRER DE TRAFALGAR

MENDEZ NUÑEZ

CARRER DE RIBES

CARRER DE ROGER DE FLOR

Arc de Triomf

AVINGUDA VILANOVA

PLAÇA SANT PERE

Arc de Triomf

CARRER REC COMTAL

CARRER SANT PERE MÉS BAIX

CARRER FONOLLAR

CARRER PORTAL NOU

PLACETA COMERÇ

PASSEIG LLUÍS COMPANYS

CARRER DELS ALMOGÀVERS

Palau Justícia

CARRER BUENAVENTURA MUÑOZ

RIBERA

AVINGUDA NCESC CAMBÓ

Mercat Santa Caterina

CARRER CARDERS

PLAÇA SANT AGUSTÍ VELL

CARRER DEL COMERÇ

CARRER DE TANTARANTANA

PASSEIG DE PUJADES

C. CORDERS

PLAÇA PONS I CLERCH

Museu de Zoologia

SANT PERE-

Font Monumental

CARRER DE LA PRINCESA

CARRER MONTCADA

Museu Picasso

CARRER FUSINA

PASSEIG DE PICASSO

Museu de Geologia

Parc de la Ciutadella

Museu Tèxtil i Indumentària

PLAÇA COMERCIAL

Mercat del Born

RIBERA

PASSEIG DEL BORN

CARRER DE LA RIBERA

PLAÇA SANTA MARIA

Església de Santa Maria del Mar

C. BONAIRE

Museu d'Art Modern

PLAÇA D'ARMES

NTERIA

CARRER DEL COMERÇ

Parlament de Catalunya

NSOLAT DE MAR

PLAÇA DE PALAU

AVINGUDA MARQUÈS DE L'ARGENTERA

PASSEIG CIRCUMVALACIÓ

otja

PASSEIG BEL II

MURALLA

Estació Barcelona Terme-França

Parc Zoològic

Barceloneta

PLAÇA DE PAU VILA

RONDA LITORAL

D   E   F

63

➕ 63F2
✉ Main entrance: Passeig
   Lluís Companys
🚇 Ciutadella, Arc de Triomf,
   Barceloneta, Jaume I
♿ Good 🎟 Free

Museu de Zoologia
➕ 63E3
✉ Passeig de Picasso
☎ 93 319 69 12
🕐 Tue–Sun 10–2 (Thu until
   6:30)
🎟 Moderate

Museu de Geologia
➕ 63E2
✉ Parc de la Ciutadella
☎ 93 319 68 95
🕐 Tue–Sun 10–2 (Thu until
   6:30)
🎟 Moderate

PARC DE LA CIUTADELLA ✪✪

This delightful walled park is a haven of shade and tranquillity just a stone's throw from the old city and waterfront. What's more, hidden among the trees, lawns, promenades and a boating lake, lies the Parc Zoológic (➤ 111) and a host of other attractions.

In 1888 the park was the site of the Universal Exposition and still contains some impressive relics of that great fair, including a striking *Modernista* café which now houses the **Museu de Zoologia**, with highlights that include a fascinating Whale Room and a Sound Library of recordings of animal sounds.

Near by, the neoclassical **Museu de Geologia**, with its rare and valuable minerals, fossils and rocks, opened in 1878 as Barcelona's first public museum. The impressive Hivernacle greenhouse, originally built for the display of exotic plants, is today a popular café (➤ 98), and the arsenal of Felip V's citadel houses the Museum of Modern Art (MNAC) (➤ 54). But the main showpiece of the park is the Font Monumental – a huge, neoclassical-style fountain, smothered in allegorical sculptures, which Gaudí contributed to as a student.

Outside the park on Passeig Lluís Companys, the monumental Arc de Triomf was constructed by Josep Vilaseca i Casanovas as the grand entrance to the Universal Exhibition.

Did you know?

Ciutadella Park takes its name from the mighty citadel constructed here by Felip V, following his victory in the 1714 Siege of Barcelona (➤ 33). The people's hatred of this fortress and their continual protests led to its eventual demolition, and the creation of this large, leafy park in its place, which first opened to the public in 1869.

Above: *the imposing Font Monumental – Niagara meets Brandenburg Gate!*

PARC DEL CLOT ✪

This park in the eastern suburbs has been built on the site of a disused railway yard and combines the walls and arches of the former rail buildings with a low-lying playing-field (the name 'Clot' in Catalan means 'hole') and a shady plaça, linked to a high grassy area of artificial hills and enigmatic sculptures by a lengthy overhead walkway.

🕂 47E2
✉ Carrer Escultors Claperós
🕐 Nov–Feb 10–6; Mar and Oct 10–7; Apr and Sep 10–8; May–Aug 10–9
🚇 Clot, Glories   🎫 Free
↔ Sagrada Familia (➤ 24–25)

PARC DE LA CREUETA DEL COLL ✪

This new park was built in a disused quarry by Olympic architects Martorell and Mackay in 1987. Surrounded by dramatic cliff-faces, scattered with modern sculptures and embracing wooded pathways and a small sand-fringed boating lake, it serves the densely inhabited suburb of Vallcarca and is always packed in summer.

🕂 47D4
✉ Passeig Mare de Déu del Coll
🕐 10–6, 7, 8 or 9 according to season
🚌 25, 28, 87
🎫 Free
↔ Gràcia (➤ 44)

PARC DE L'ESPANYA INDUSTRIAL ✪✪

With works by many Catalan artists, this is Barcelona's most controversial park – a *nou urbanisme* project, built between 1982 and 1985 on the site of an old textile factory. It is built on two levels, the lower part comprising a large lake and grassy area, with steep white steps up to the much-scorned upper esplanade, where there are ten lighthouses, a series of water spouts and an immense metal play-sculpture entitled the *Dragon of St George*.

🕂 28B3
✉ Carrer de Muntadas
🚇 Sants-Estació
🎫 Free
↔ Montjuïc (➤ 18); Parc de Joan Miró (➤ 66)

The Parc de l'Espanya Industrial defies all traditional concepts of park design

PARC GÜELL (➤ 21, TOP TEN)

35E5
- Carrer de Tarragona
- Snack bar
- Tarragona, Espanya
- Free
- Montjuïc (➤ 18); Parc de la Creueta del Coll (➤ 65)

PARC DE JOAN MIRÓ

This is one of Barcelona's most popular parks, occupying an entire city block on what was formerly the site of a massive abattoir, hence its nickname Parc de l'Escorxador (slaughter-house). It was created in the 1980s, and is always full of people reading, jogging, dog-walking or playing *petanca* (boules) amid the attractive pergolas and orderly rows of shady palm trees. The park's most famous feature, however, is a startling 22m-high sculpture by Joan Miró, covered in multicoloured ceramic fragments, named *Dona i Ocell* (Woman and Bird).

Woman and Bird –
centrepiece of Parc de Joan Miró

47E4
- Passeig dels Castanyers or Carrer Germans Desvalls, Vall d'Hebron
- Nov–Feb 10–6; Mar and Oct 10–7; Apr and Sep 10–8; May–Aug 10–9
- 10, 27, 60, 73, 76, 85
- Free

PARC DEL LABERINT

These romantic, Italian-style gardens, on the wooded outer rim of Barcelona near the Vall d'Hebrón, present a pleasing contrast to the stark modern *espais urbans* (urban spaces) of the city centre. They originally surrounded a grand 18th-century mansion, which has long since been demolished, but the park has maintained its formal flowerbeds, canals and fountains, its ornamental statuary and its centrepiece – the 'Labyrinth' – a beautiful topiary maze with a statue of Eros at its centre that has given the park its name.

35D4
- Avinguda del Marquès de Comillas s/n
- 93 423 40 16
- Daily 10–8
- Espanya
- 27, 50, 91, 157
- Good
- Cheap
- L'Anella Olímpica (➤ 32); Fundació Joan Miró (➤ 17); Montjuïc (➤ 18); Poble Espanyol (➤ 22)

PAVELLÓ BARCELONA

Bauhaus architect Ludwig Mies van der Rohe created this masterpiece of modern rationalist design for the 1929 Exhibition, a construction of astonishing simplicity and finesse in marble, onyx, glass and chrome, widely acknowledged as one of the classic buildings of the 20th century. Astonishingly, it was dismantled at the end of the fair and subsequently meticulously reconstructed and reopened (in its original location) in 1986, on the centenary of Mies van der Rohe's birth.

Inside, take time to enjoy the quality of the colours, textures and materials, as well as a striking bronze sculpture entitled *Der Morgen* (The Morning) and the famous 'Barcelona' chair, a design of timeless elegance created especially for the Expo, which has since been copied worldwide.

PLAÇA DE CATALUNYA ✪

The Plaça de Catalunya is the heart of Barcelona and the hub of the city's transport system. It was first landscaped at the end of the 19th century and soon became of major importance as the pivotal point between the old and new city, with the Barri Gòtic (► 40–41) to the east, the carefully planned new Eixample district (► 42–43) to the north and west, and, to the southeast, La Rambla (► 23) running down to the port.

In 1927 the square was further developed, with the construction of hotels, restaurants and other important buildings. Its main landmarks today are the overpowering head office of Banco Espanol de Crédito, former headquarters of the unified Socialist Party of Catalonia during the Civil War; the monstrous El Corte Inglés department store (► 104, panel); and a medley of fountains and statues, including work by important sculptors such as Gargallo, Marès and Subirachs. Today, its benches, trees and splashing fountains make it a popular place to meet friends and have a coffee or simply to sit and soak up the Mediterranean sun.

🞤 62B5
🍴 Several (£–££)
🚇 Catalunya
↔ Ciutat Vella (► 38–39);
  L'Eixample (► 42–43);
  Palau de la Música
  Catalana (► 59);
  La Rambla (► 23)

Bird's-eye view of Plaça de Catalunya, a popular meeting point at the heart of the city

62C3

Jaume I

Catedral (➤ 16); Ciutat
Vella (➤ 38–39); Museu
Frederic Marès (➤ 55);
Museu d'Història de la
Ciutat (➤ 56); Plaça Sant
Jaume (➤ 69)

Palau Reial Major

☎ 93 315 11 11

Palace: Tue–Sat 10–2,
4–8, Sun and hols 10–2
Tower: temporarily
closed for restoration

Moderate

Part of the Museu
d'Historia de la Ciutat
(➤ 56)

*The Palau Reial Major and
St Marti's tower dominate
the Plaça del Rei*

PLAÇA DEL REI ✪✪

The charming King's Square was once a bustling
medieval marketplace. Today, it forms a frequent
backdrop to summer open-air concerts and theatrical
events, especially during the Grec festival (➤ 116), and
is the location not only of the City History Museum
(➤ 56) but also of the **Palau Reial Major** (Great Royal
Palace), former residence of the Counts of Barcelona.

It was on the steps leading up to the Palau Reial Major
that King Ferdinand and Queen Isabella are said to have
received Columbus on his return from his first voyage to
America in 1493. Inside, the Spanish Inquisition once sat
in the Saló del Tinell, exploiting the local myth that should
any prisoner lie, the stones on the ceiling would move.
Today, the hall functions as an exhibition area.

On the north side of the square is the chapel of Santa
Agata (also part of the royal palace), which contains a
precious 15th-century altarpiece by Jaume Huguet. On the
opposite side of the square, the Palau de Lloctinent (Palace
of the Deputy) was built in 1549 for the Catalan represen-
tative of the king in Madrid. The strenuous climb to the top
of its five-storey lookout tower (the Mirador del Rei Marti)
is well rewarded by sweeping views of the old town.

Did you know?

Catalonia's national folk dance, the sardana, *is performed during summer, either in Plaça Sant Jaume (Sunday, 6–8PM) or in the Plaça de la Seu (Sunday, 10–midday, Wednesday 7–9PM). The dancers are accompanied by an instrumental group* (cobla), *which includes tenor and soprano oboes, a* flabiol *(long flute) and a* tambori *(drum).*

PLAÇA REIAL   ✪✪

This sunny porticoed square, just off the Ramblas, with its tall palm trees, decorative fountain and buskers was constructed in 1848. Some of the façades are decorated with terracotta reliefs of navigators and the discoverers of America, and the two tree-like central lampposts mark Gaudí's first commission in Barcelona.

Keep a close watch on your belongings here – the square has a reputation for shady characters and pickpockets, hence the discreet but constant police presence. On Sunday mornings a coin and stamp market is held here.

✚ 62B2
🍴 Plenty (£–££)
🚇 Liceu
↔ Ciutat Vella (➤ 38–39)

PLAÇA SANT JAUME   ✪

Once the hub of Roman Barcelona, this impressive square today represents the city's political heart, and is dominated by two buildings; the neoclassical and Gothic **Casa de la Ciutat** (Town Hall) and, directly opposite, the Renaissance **Palau de la Generalitat de Catalunya** (Government of Catalonia).

The origins of Barcelona's municipal authority date back to 1249, when Jaume I granted the city the right to elect councillors, giving rise to the creation of the Consell de Cent (Council of One Hundred). The famous Saló de Cent (Chamber of One Hundred) and the black marble Saló de las Cronicas (Chamber of the Chronicles) are among the architectural highlights of the Town Hall.

✚ 41B1
🍴 Cafés (£)
🚇 Jaume I
↔ Plaça del Rei (➤ 68), Catedral (➤ 16)

Casa de la Ciutat
☎ 93 402 70 00
🕐 Sun 10–1:30

Palau de la Generalitat de Catalunya
☎ 93 402 46 00
🕐 Open for guided tours 23 Apr; 10–1 2nd and 4th Sun of each month
💷 Free

POBLE ESPANYOL (➤ 22, TOP TEN)

Detail on the Palau de la Generalitat in Plaça Sant Jaume

The Waterfront

Start on Moll de les Drassanes near the Columbus Monument (▶ 50), then head along Passeig del Moll de la Fusta by the water's edge.

Raised on stilts above the yacht basin, the Passeig de Colom was Barcelona's most stylish promenade when it opened in 1987, with designer restaurants and bars and a giant rooftop lobster sculpture (▶ 74). These days many of the trendier restaurants have closed down and most of the action has moved to Port Vell (▶ 72) and the Port Olímpic, but it still makes an interesting scene.

Continue walking northeast until Plaça d'Antoni López.

This busy square is dominated by the main post office (Correos y Telegrafos) and a notable mosaic sculpture by Roy Lichtenstein (▶ 74).

Above: *Lichtenstein's colourful mosaic sculpture,* Barcelona Head, *enlivens the waterfront*
Right: *Barcelona's waterfront was a stylish place to be seen in the heady days of the early 1990s*

Leave the square via the arcaded walkway of Passeig d'Isabel II, past the Stock Exchange and the famous '7 Doors' (Set Portes) restaurant (➤ 95), and turn right at Pla de Palau. Cross the main road into La Barceloneta (➤ 33) and continue along the waterfront, past the Palau de Mar (➤ 58) with its fish restaurants, until you reach Passeig de Joan de Borbó.

Note the wide variety of architectural styles here, especially No 43, which is one of the best examples of 1950s architecture in Barcelona. To your right, the clock tower by the harbour was originally a lighthouse, and the Torre de Sant Sebastià on Moll Nou once carried cable-cars, via the Jaume I Tower, to Montjuïc.

On reaching the seafront, turn left on to Passeig Marítim, which runs parallel to the beach all the way to the Port Olímpic, heralded by a massive, gleaming fish sculpture by Frank Gehry (➤ 33).

Distance
3 km

Time
2–3 hours (excluding visits)

Start point
Monument a Colom
✚ 29E3
🚇 Drassanes

End point
Port Olímpic
✚ 47D1
🚇 Ciutadella

Lunch break
Emperador (£££) (➤ 95)
✉ Palau de Mar, Plaça Pau Vila
☎ 93 221 02 20

PORT VELL ✪✪

Although Barcelona was founded on sea-going tradition, for many years its seafront was in decay, until a major redevelopment prior to the 1992 Olympics reintegrated the Port Vell (Old Port) into the city by transforming it into a lively new entertainment venue. The Rambla de Mar, a series of undulating wooden walkways and bridges, acts as an extension of La Rambla, connecting the city to Port Vell's many new attractions.

Maremagnum, Port Vell's biggest crowd puller, is a covered shopping and entertainment centre with smart boutiques, expensive restaurants, trendy bars, discos and fast-food joints. Adjacent to the conventional cinema complex, IMAX (➤ 110), the 'cinema of the future', shows spectacular films in three dimensions, with state-of-the-art wrap-around screens and sound. Near by, the Aquarium (➤ 110), one of the biggest and best in Europe, always proves popular with children.

Take a **Golondrina** (pleasure boat) for a different perspective of the new harbour developments. The luxurious leisure marina, with over 400 berths, in the previously derelict dockyard area is rapidly becoming one of the Mediterranean's most exclusive anchorages. Although the big ferries to the Balearics still depart from here, most commercial activity now takes place in the modern port further down the coast.

LA RAMBLA (➤ 23, TOP TEN)

SAGRADA FAMÍLIA (➤ 24–25, TOP TEN)

SANTA MARIA DEL MAR (➤ 26, TOP TEN)

Above: *Port Vell Marina –
one of the top
anchorages of the
Mediterranean*

TIBIDABO AND SERRA DE COLLSEROLA ✪✪

The 550m-high Mont Tibidabo forms the northwestern boundary of Barcelona and, on exceptionally clear days, Mallorca.

At its summit, and topped by a huge statue of Christ, stands the modern Church of the Sacred Heart (Sagrat Cor), whose style is probably best described as 'neo-Gothic fantasy'. Near by, the 'Magic Mountain' Amusement Park (➤ 111) cleverly balances traditional rides with high-tech attractions on several levels of the mountaintop, and is always a fun day out for the family. Tibidabo is just one of the mountains of the Collserola range, a wonderful 6,550ha nature reserve with extensive woodlands full of wildlife. It is best reached by FGC train to Baixador de Vallvidrera. From here, it is a 10-minute walk uphill to the **information centre**, where details of clearly marked itineraries for walkers and cyclists are available.

➕ 47D5
🍴 Cafés, snack bars (£–££)
🚇 FGC Avinguda Tibidabo then Tramvia Blau to Plaça Doctor Andreu followed by the Tibidabo Funicular
🚶 Free
↔ Museu de la Ciència (➤ 110–11)

Amusement Park
✉ Parc d'Atraccions del Tibidabo, Plaça Tibidabo 3–4
☎ 93 211 79 42
🕐 Call for opening times. Closed mid-Sep to Mar
🚋 Funicular del Tibidabo
🎫 Expensive

Collserola Mountains Information Centre
✉ Centre d'Informacio, Parc de Collserola
☎ 93 280 35 52
🕐 Daily 9:30–3. Closed 1 & 6 Jan, 25–26 Dec
🚇 Baixador de Vallvidrera
🚶 Free

The 'Magic Mountain': Tibidabo's amusement park

VILA OLÍMPICA ✪

The 1992 Olympic Games triggered a major renovation of Barcelona's maritime façade. Just behind the Port Olímpic, the rundown district of Poble Nou was developed into the Vila Olímpica – home to 15,000 competitors during the games, and now a high-tech corridor of apartment blocks, shops and offices.

➕ 47D2
✉ Vila Olímpica
🍴 Plenty (£–£££)
🚇 Ciutadella
🚌 36, 41, 71, 92
↔ Museu d'Art Modern (➤ 54)

73

In the Know

If you only have a short time to visit Barcelona and would like to get a real flavour of the city, here are some ideas:

10
Ways to Be a Local

Dress appropriately for Spain's most stylish city.
Learn a few words of Catalan and show interest in the regional culture.
Promenade on La Rambla (➤ 23).
Take a siesta.
Join Barcelonans for a *tertulia* (discussion) in a local café .
At weekends, visit a park or stroll along the waterfront promenades.
Follow the locals' time schedule.
Show interest in 'Barça', (➤ 54, 55).
Join in the *sardana* regional dance (➤ 69).
Develop a taste for *pa amb tomàquet* (➤ 100, panel) and *allioli* (➤ 52).

Try some tapas *beside Frank Gehry's* Fish *sculpture*

10
Top Street Sculptures

Fish, by Frank Gehry ✉ Hotel Arts, Passeig Marítim, Port Olímpica (➤ 33).
Barcelona Head, a giant mosaic sculpture by Roy Lichtenstein ✉ Passeig de Colom
Drac de la Font, Gaudí's famous 'Dragon of the Fountain' ✉ Parc Güell (➤ 21)
'La Ferralla' ('Scrap Iron'), the nickname given to the sculptural highlight of the Vila Olímpica ✉ Avinguda Icària
Gambrinus, a giant fibreglass lobster (➤ 70) by Xavier Mariscal ✉ Moll de la Fusta, Passeig de Colom
Landscape Sculptures by Beverly Pepper ✉ Parc de l'Estació del Nord
Wall by Richard Serra ✉ Plaça de la Palmera

Sardana Dancers outside the former Montjuïc Funfair ✉ Avinguda de Miramar
Dona i Ocell (Woman and Bird), in Parc Joan Miró (➤ 66) ✉ C. Tarragona
Núvol i Cadira (Cloud and Chair) on the roof of Fundació Antoni Tàpies (➤ 44) ✉ C. Aragó 255

10
Top *Tapas* Dishes

Mandonguilles (meatballs)
Boquerones and anxoves (fresh and salted anchovies)
Calamarsos amb la sevtinta (small squid cooked in their ink)
Croquetes de pollastre, or ***de bacallá*** (croquettes with chicken or salt cod)
Empanats and ***empanadillas*** (pies and deep-fried pasties with tuna filling)

La Boqueria just off La Rambla (➤ 49)

Gambas al ajillo (prawns with garlic)
Faves a la Catalana (broad beans, onions and *botifarra* – blood sausage – cooked in white wine)
Pa amb tomàquet (white bread with tomato and olive oil)
Pescaditos (deep-fried whitebait)
Pops a la gallega (octopus with paprika and olive oil)

10
Top Markets

La Boqueria – fruit and vegetables market
🕐 Mon–Sat 7AM–8PM. Closed Sun 🚇 Liceu
(➤ 49)

Concepció – flowers, fruit and vegetables in the Eixample ✉ C. Aragó
🕐 Mon 8–3, Tue–Sat 8–8, Sat 8–4 🚇 Girona
Craft market
✉ Avinguda Pau Casals
🕐 First Sun of month from 10AM 🚇 Hospital Clinic
Els Encants – flea market
✉ Plaça de les Glòries
🕐 Mon, Wed, Fri, Sat 9–5
Festa de Sant Ponç – annual market of honey, herbs, natural products
✉ Carrer Hospital 🕐 11 May 🚇 Liceu
Plaça del Pi; honey, herbs, cheeses 🕐 first and third Fri, Sat and Sun of month 10AM–10PM 🚇 Liceu

Plaça Reial – coins, stamps 🕐 Sun 10–2 🚇 Liceu
Plaça Sant Josep Oriol – art 🕐 Sat 11AM–10PM, Sun 10–3 🚇 Liceu
La Rambla – afternoon and evening craft market 🕐 Weekends only 🚇 Drassanes
Ronda Sant Antoni – coins, books, postcards and video games 🕐 Sun 9–2:30 🚇 Universitat

5
Top Rides

Bus Turístic – a good way to see the main sights if time is limited (➤ 121).
Un Cotxe Menys – city tours by bicycle ✉ C. Esparteria 3 ☎ 93 268 21 05 🕐 Tours: Sat & Sun 10AM–12:30, Tue and Sat 8.30PM–midnight (for groups of 8 or more). Booking required.
Golondrinas – cruises around the harbour and the Olympic Port (➤ 72).
Telefèric – cable-car ride to Castell de Montjuïc (➤ 18). 🕐 Summer, daily; winter, weekends.
Tramvia Blau – Barcelona's last remaining tram grinds up the hill towards Tibidabo (➤ 73).

5
Top Views

Casa Milà rooftop terrace (➤ 37)
Columbus Monument (➤ 50)
Parc Güell (➤ 21)
Sagrada Família (➤ 24–25)
Torre de Collserola ☎ 93 406 93 54 🕐 Wed–Sun 11–6

Passeig Colom from the Monument

Barcelona Metro map showing stations including:

BARCELONA METRO

1 Feixa Llarga, Avinguda del Carrilet, Bellvitge, Rambla Just Oliveras, Can Serra, Florida, Torrassa, Santa Eulàlia, Mercat Nou — Gavarra, Sant Ildefons, Can Boixeres, CanVidalet, Pubilla Cases, Collblanc, Badal — 5 Cornellà — 3 Zona Universitària — Terrassa, Sabadell-Rambla & Universitat Autonoma — Vallvidrera Superior — Tibidabo — Plaça del Funicular — Peu del Funicular — FGC Reina Elisenda — Avinguda del Tibidabo — Sarrià, El Putxet, Pàdua, Pl.Molina — Les Tres Torres, La Bonanova, Muntaner, Sant Gervasi — Palau Reial, Maria Cristina, Les Corts, Plaça del Centre — Gràcia — Plaça de Sants, Sants-Estació, Hospital Clínic, Entença, Provença — Hostafrancs, Tarragona, Espanya, Rocafort, Urgell — Bellvitge — El Prat de Llobregat — Poble Sec, Sant Antoni, Universitat — C1 Barcelona Prat International Airport — Parc de Montjuïc, Castell — Paral.Lel 2, Low Station, Intermediate Station, High Station, Drassanes

©TCS UDN.2

Barcelona's Metro

Barcelona has an impressive and efficient underground rail system, enabling you to visit most places of interest either by metro or by FGC train (➤ 121). Useful stations include Catalunya (for La Rambla), Barceloneta and Drassanes (for the waterfront), Jaume I (for the old city, the cathedral and Museu Picasso), Ciutadella (for the Olympic port and village), and Passeig de Gràcia (for L'Eixample).

Maçanet - Massanes

3 Canyelles

under construction

3 Montbau   5 Horta   Trinitat Nova 4

Vall d'Hebron   Vilapicina   under construction

Penitents   Virrei Amat   Roquetes 4   Fondo 1

Vallcarca   Llucmajor   Santa Coloma

Lesseps   Baró de Viver

Guinardó   Maragall   Trinitat Vella

Fontana   Joanic   Alfons X   Congrés   Torras i Bages   2
PepVentura

Diagonal   Sagrada Família   Hospital de Sant Pau   Sant Andreu

Verdaguer   Camp de l'Arpa   Fabra i Puig ⇌   Gorg

Girona   Monumental   Cartagena   Sagrera   Sant Roc

Tetuan   Navas   Joan XXIII

Passeig de Gràcia ⇌   Clot ⇌   Verneda

El Clot-Aragó   La Pau 4

Urquinaona   Glòries   Sant Martí

Marina   Besòs

Catalunya FGC ⇌   Arc de Triomf ⇌   Bac-de-Roda

Jaume I   Besòs Mar

Ciutadella-Villa Olimpica   Llacuna   Selva de Mar

Barceloneta

Liceu   Bogatell   Poblenou

MEDITERRANEAN SEA

User No: 9C02117

If you intend to use public transport frequently, buy one of several travelcards from any metro station or at any branch of La Caixa. The metro runs Mon–Thu 5AM–11PM; Fri, Sat and the evening before holidays 5AM–2AM; Sun 6AM–midnight. The FGC operates Mon–Thu 5:50AM–11PM; Fri–Sun 5:55AM–12:39AM. Some metro stations do not have escalators and may involve lengthy walks.

Exploring Catalonia

It would be a shame to visit Barcelona without also seeing something of Catalunya (Catalonia). Despite being an autonomous province of Spain, this unique region feels in many ways like a separate country, with its own language and deeply rooted traditions, culture and cuisine. Its geographical location makes it the gateway to Spain. Over the centuries the passage of many peoples and civilisations has shaped the region, leaving magical cities such as Girona and Tarragona brimming with historical monuments, while its beautiful landscapes have provided inspiration for such artists as Gaudí, Miró, Dalí and Picasso.

The Catalan landscape is easy to tour, and offers a wide variety of scenery, from the dramatic, snow-capped peaks of the Pyrenees and the secret bays and bustling fishing ports of the Costa Brava, north of Barcelona, to the acclaimed Penedès vineyards and long golden beaches of the Costa Daurada to the south.

'...the king, who had the sun for his hat (for it always shines in some part of his dominion), has nothing to boast of equal to Catalonia.'

PHILIP THIELENESSE,
A Year's Journey through France and Spain, 1789.

———————●———————

The magnificent Catedral – pride of Tarragona

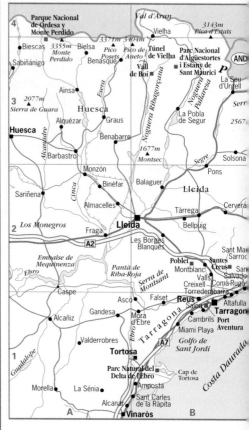

FIGUERES ✪✪

The main claim to fame of Figueres, two hours' drive northwest of Barcelona and just 17km from the Franco-Spanish border, is that the great Surrealist painter Salvador Dalí was born here in 1904 and gave his first exhibition in the town when he was just 14. In 1974, he inaugurated his remarkable **Teatre-Museu Dalí**, located in the old municipal theatre, and to this day it remains the most visited museum in Spain after the Prado in Madrid. It is the only museum in Europe that is dedicated exclusively to his works.

The building, topped with a massive metallic dome and decorated with egg shapes, is original and spectacular – in keeping with Dalí's powerful personality. Its galleries are housed in a number of enclosed, circular tiers around a

✚ 81D3

🏠 Plaça del Sol ☎ 972 50 31 55

🍽 Plenty (£–££)

↔ Girona (► 82)

Teatre-Museu Dalí

✉ Plaça Gala-Salvador Dalí 5

☎ 972 67 75 00

🕐 Oct–Jun Tue–Sat 10:30–5:45; Jul–Sep daily 9–7:45. Closed 1 Jan and 25 Dec

♿ None

✋ Very expensive

CATALUNYA

Golfo de Léon

Portbou
San Pere de Rodes
Cap de Creus
Cadaqués
Roses
Golfo de Rosas
Empúries-Ampurias
L'Escala
L'Estartit
Peralada
Figueres
Besalú
Girona
Banyoles
Ter **Girona**
Palafrugell
Begur
Peratallada
Pare Natural del Montseny
Palamós
Sant Feliu de Guixols
Tossa de Mar
Lloret de Mar
Blanes
Sant Pol de Mar
Arenys de Mar
Costa Brava

uigcerda
Camprodón
el Cadí
Ripoll **Olot**
Manlleu
Vic
Berga
Llobregat
Cardona **Barcelona**
Manresa
1712m
Caldes de Montbui
Terrassa
gualada
Granollers
Montserrat
Sant Sadurní d'Anoia
Sabadell
Mataró
Badalona
BARCELONA
Vilafranca del Penedès
L'Hospitalet de Llobregat
Sitges
Castelldefels
Vilanova i la Geltrú
Castellfollit de la Roca

F

| 0 | 20 | 40 | 60 km |

C   D

central stage and a courtyard containing a 'Rainy Taxi' and a tower of car tyres crowned by a boat and an umbrella. The galleries contain paintings, sculptures, jewellery, drawings and other works from his private collection along with weird and wonderful constructions from different periods of his career, including a bed with fish tails, skeletal figures and even a complete life-sized orchestra. Dalí died in Figueres in 1989, leaving his entire estate to the Spanish State. His body lies behind a simple granite slab inside the museum.

Other sights in Figueres include over 3,000 exhibits in the famous **Museu de Juguets** (Toy Museum), set inside the old Hotel Paris, and the **Museu de l'Empordà** (Art and History), which provides an informative overview of the region's art and history.

Museu de Juguets
✉ La Rambla
☎ 972 50 45 85
🕐 Tue–Sat 10–1, 4–7, Sun and hols 11–1:30. Closed Mon
💶 Moderate

Museu de l'Empordà
✉ La Rambla 2
☎ 972 50 23 05
🕐 Tue–Sat 11–7, Sun 11–2. Closed Mon
💶 Free

✚ 81D3
ℹ️ Rambla de la Llibertat 1
☎ 972 22 65 75
🍽 Plenty (£–££)
↔ Figueres (► 80–81)

Catedral
✉ Plaça de la Catedral
☎ 972 21 44 26
🕐 Daily 10–2, 4–6
♿ Good   🔲 Free

Museu Arqueològic
✉ Esglesia Sant Pere de Galligans
☎ 972 20 26 32
🕐 Summer Tue–Sun 10:30–1:30, 4–7; winter: Tue–Sun 10–2, 4–6. Closed Mon
🔲 Cheap

Banys Arabs
✉ Carrer Ferran Catolic
☎ 972 21 32 62
🕐 Summer Tue–Sun 10–7. Closed Mon; winter: Tue–Sun 10–2
🔲 Cheap

Above: *Girona is a little-known gem of Catalonia*

GIRONA ✪✪✪

Just 1½ hours by car or train from Barcelona, the beautiful, walled city of Girona is one of Catalonia's most characterful cities, with an admirable collection of ancient monuments. The old city, built on a steep hill and known for its lovely stairways, arcaded streets and sunless alleys, is separated from modern Girona by the River Onyar. The medieval, multicoloured houses overhanging the river are a photographer's dream, especially when seen from the iron footbridge designed by Eiffel. Most of the main sights are in the old city. Make sure you also allow time to shop along the beautiful Rambla de la Llibertat and to enjoy a drink in the arcaded Plaça de la Independencia.

At the heart of the old city, centred around Carrer de la Força, El Call, the old Jewish quarter, is one of the best preserved in Western Europe and is particularly atmospheric by night, with its street lanterns and intimate restaurants. Another splendid sight is the **Catedral**, with its impressive staircase leading up to a fine Baroque façade, a magnificent medieval interior and the widest Gothic vault in Europe. Housed inside another church, the **Museu Arqueològic** (Archaeological Musuem) outlines the city's history, and provides access to the Passeig Arqueològic, a panoramic walk around the walls of the old city. Near by, the 13th-century **Banys Arabs** (Arab Bathhouse), probably designed by Moorish craftsmen following the Moors' occupation of Girona, is the best preserved of its kind in Spain after the Alhambra, particularly striking for its fusion of Arab and Romanesque styles.

MONTSERRAT

Fifty-six kilometres northwest of Barcelona, at the summit of Catalonia's 1,200m-high holy mountain, Montserrat – named after its strangely serrated rock formations (*mont*, mountain; *serrat*, sawed – is one of the most important pilgrimage sites in the whole of Spain. Thousands travel here every year to venerate a medieval statue of the Madonna and Child called *La Moreneta* (The Black Virgin), blackened by the smoke of millions of candles over the centuries. The statue is said to have been made by St Luke and brought to the area by St Peter, and is displayed above the altar of the monastery church.

The spectacularly sited monastery, founded in 1025, is also famous for its choir, *La Escolania*, one of the oldest and best-known boys' choirs in Europe, dating from the 13th century. The choir sings daily at 1PM in the **Basilica**, a striking edifice containing important paintings including works by El Greco and Caravaggio.

Montserrat is clearly signposted by road from Barcelona, although the most enjoyable way to get there is by FGC train from Plaça d'Espanya, followed by a thrilling cable-car ride up to the monastery.

81C2

Plaça de la Creu, Montserrat

93 877 77 77

Limited choice of bars and restaurants

Basilica

Monestir de Montserrat

Jul–Sep 7:30–8:30; Oct–Jun 8–6:30

Free

Museu de Montserrat

Mar–Dec 10–6; Jan–Feb 10–4:45

Moderate

One of Spain's principal pilgrimage destinations – within easy reach of Barcelona

Alt Penedès

Distance
105km

Time
3–3½ hours (without stops)

Start point
Vilafranca del Penedès
✚ 81C2

End point
Sant Sadurní d'Anoia
✚ 81C2

Lunch break
🍴 Sant Jordi/Ca La Katy (££)
✉ 8½ km outside Vilafranca del Penedès
☎ 93 899 13 26

Vilafranca del Penedès
✚ 81C2
ℹ Carrer Cort 14
☎ 93 892 03 58
🍴 Plenty (£–££)

Sant Martí Sarroca
✚ 81B2
ℹ Plaça de l'Ajuntament 1
☎ 93 891 12 12
🍴 Limited choice (££)

The monastery of Santes Creus nestles among vineyards

The main attraction of this drive is its magnificent scenery. Leave Vilafranca del Penedès on the BP2121 past Mas Tinell, Romagosa Torné and Torres wineries (➤ 85), until you reach Sant Martí Sarroca after 9km.

This agricultural village contains an important Romanesque church with a splendid Gothic altarpiece, and a 9th-century castle.

Continue on to Torrelles de Foix, with its tiled church dome. The road then climbs through barren scrub up to Pontons. Continue up past the Romanesque church of Valldossera, through Els Ranxox, over the Coll de la Torreta, to Santes Creus.

Santes Creus, founded in 1158 alongside the Gaia river, is one of three exceptional former Cistercian monasteries in the region (the others are Poblet and Vallbona de les Monges). Following its deconsecration, it grew into a small village in 1843 when a group of families moved into the abandoned buildings and monks' residences.

Turn right at the main road (TP2002) to El Pont d'Armentera. Join the T213 to Igualada. After 22km of breathtaking mountain scenery, turn right to La Llacuna, then left through farmland to Mediona. Continue to St Pere Sacarrera then turn right at the main road to St Quintí de Mediona. Several kilometres later, turn left to Sant Pere de Riudebitlles.

Mediona is noted for its medieval church and ruined castle, while St Pere de Riudebitlles boasts a splendid Gothic manor house – the Palace of the Marquis of Lo.

The same road eventually leads to Sant Sadurní (➤ 85).

PENEDÈS WINERIES – VILAFRANCA AND SANT SADURNÍ D'ANOIA ✪

The Alt Penedès is one of Spain's most respected wine-producing areas, producing Catalonia's best-known wines and all of its *cava* (sparkling wine). Since ancient times, viticulture has been the main economic activity of its two main towns, Sant Sadurní d'Anoia and Vilafranca del Penedès.

Only half an hour's drive from Barcelona, Sant Sadurní is the centre of Catalonia's *cava* industry, with 66 *cava* firms dotted throughout the town. The largest, Codorníu, produces around 40 million bottles a year and its magnificent *Modernista* plant is open to visitors daily. Tours last 1½ hours and include a tasting.

Near by, Vilafranca del Penedès, the region's capital town, has more character than Sant Sadurní, with its fine arcaded streets and medieval mansions. In the Gothic quarter, surrounded by squares, palaces and churches, the **Museu del Vi** is the only museum in Catalonia to be wholly dedicated to wine. Current methods of production can be observed at Vilafranca's three top wineries – **Mas Tinell, Romagosa Torné** and **Miguel Torres** – all located just outside the town centre on the BP2121 to Sant Martí Sarroca.

Museu del Vi

✉ Plaça Jaume I, 1 and 3, Vilafranca del Penedès
☎ 93 890 05 82
🕐 Tue–Fri 10–2, 4–7, Sat 10–2, 4–8, Sun and hols 10–2. Closed Mon
💶 Cheap

Penedès Wineries

☎ Codorníu: 93 818 32 32; Caves Romagosa Torné: 93 899 13 53; Mas Tinell: 93 817 05 86; Miguel Torres: 93 817 74 87
🕐 Opening times vary. Phone individual wineries for details

> ### *Did you know?*
>
> *Penedès produces good red (negra or tinto), white (blanc) and rosé (rosat) wines. Of the many labels, René Barbier and Miguel Torres (the region's largest, most famous producer) are reliable, and dry Bach whites are also popular. Catalan cava is labelled according to quality and sweetness –* Brut Nature, Brut, Sec, *and* Semi-Sec *which, despite its name, is very sweet and the cheapest.*

Above: *the Museu del Vi in Vilafranca*

*Museu Maricel de Mar
houses an eclectic
collection of Catalan
treasures*

SITGES ●●

Sitges, 40km south of Barcelona, is one of Spain's oldest bathing resorts and has long been the weekend and holiday playground of Barcelonans. It was once a sleepy fishing port and, although it has now developed into a thriving seaside destination, the old town still retains its ancient charm, with narrow streets, whitewashed cottages and flower-festooned balconies. It also boasts several appealing *Modernista* buildings.

It was artist and writer Santiago Rusinyol who first put Sitges on the map, bringing it to the attention of artists such as Manuel de Falla, Ramon Casas, Nonell, Utrillo and Picasso. Rusinyol's house, **Cau Ferrat**, is today a museum, containing works by El Greco and Picasso amongst others. Neighbouring **Museu Maricel de Mar** houses an interesting collection of medieval and baroque artefacts, including Catalan ceramics, and the nearby **Museu Romàntic** provides a fascinating insight into 18th-century patrician life in Sitges.

Sitges is famous for its beautiful Platja d'Or (Golden Beach), which stretches southwards for 5km from the baroque church of Sant Bartomeu i Santa Tecla. Its palm-fringed promenade is dotted with beach bars, cafés, and some of the coast's finest fish restaurants. However, the resort is perhaps best-known for its vibrant nightlife, drawing a young cosmopolitan crowd throughout the summer season. It is also a popular gay holiday destination. From October to May, Sitges is considerably quieter, except during *Carnaval* in mid-February when the town once more comes alive with wild parties and showy parades, drawing spectators from afar.

The Costa Daurada

The Costa Daurada (Golden Coast) takes its name from its long sandy beaches. This short drive starts in Tarragona and covers its northernmost stretch.

Leave Tarragona on the N340 coast road towards Barcelona. A few kilometres later you will arrive at the resorts of Altafulla and Torredembarra.

These two thriving holiday resorts attained great prosperity in the 18th century as a result of the wine trade with the American colonies. Note the Renaissance-style castle at Torredembarra.

Continue on the N340 for 6km. Turn left to Creixell.

The hilltop village of Creixell boasts a ruined medieval castle and a church with a striking *Modernista* belltower.

Return to the N340. After 2km, the road skirts the 2nd-century Roman Arc de Bara then continues to Coma–Ruga and Sant Salvador.

Coma-Ruga was once an area of marshland with mineral-water springs. At the turn of the 19th century two spas were established around which this bustling resort developed. The local speciality, *xató* – a scrumptious cold fish salad, with a dressing similar to *romesco* (➤ 53) – must be sampled. At Sant Salvador, the cellist Pau Casals had his summer residence; today it is a museum.

From the Museu Pau Casals, the coast road leads to Calafell, where fishing boats are launched straight from the sand. Join the N246 here (direction Barcelona) and follow signs to Vilanova i la Geltrú.

The busy commercial centre of Vilanova is also a popular resort, thanks to its sandy beach, its palm-lined seafront, and its many appealing restaurants.

Continue on the N246 to Sitges (➤ 86).

Distance
63km

Time
1 hour (without stops)

Start point
Tarragona
✚ 80B1

End point
Sitges
✚ 81C2

Lunch break
🍴 Casa Victor (££)
✉ Passeig Maritim 23, Coma-Ruga
☎ 977 68 14 73

Long sandy beaches characterise the Costa Daurada

80B1
Plenty (£–££)
Carrer Major 39
977 24 52 03

Tarragona

This agreeable city is surprisingly undiscovered by most foreign visitors to the region, even though it contains the largest ensemble of Roman remains in Spain, the remarkable architectural legacy of Roman Tarraco, capital of an area that once covered half the Iberian peninsula. Originally settled by Iberians and then Carthaginians, it later became the base for the Roman conquest of Spain and the main commercial centre on this stretch of the coast until Barcelona and Valencia overshadowed it, after the Christian reconquest of Spain in the early 12th century.

The town is sited on a rocky hill, sloping down to the sea. The ancient upper town contains most of the Roman ruins, some interesting museums and an attractive medieval quarter with a grand cathedral. Below the Old Town lies the modern shopping district, centred on the Rambla Nova with its smart boutiques and restaurants, and a daily fruit and vegetable market in Plaça Corsini. Below the main town, the chief attraction of the lower part of the city is the maritime district of El Serrallo with its colourful fishing fleet, traditional *Lonja* (fish auction), and dockside restaurants that serve fish fresh from the nets. The rocky coastline beyond conceals a couple of beaches, notably Platja Arrabassada and Platja Llarga.

Catalan flags hanging in a Tarragona street

What to See in Tarragona

Carrer Oleguer
977 24 25 79
Tue–Sat Apr–Jun
10–1:30, 3:30–6:30;
Jul–Sep 9–9; Oct–Mar
10:30–1:30, 3:30–5:30.
Closed Mon. Sun
Summer 9–3; Winter
10–2
None
Moderate (combined
ticket)

AMFITEATRE ROMA ✪✪

Built into the hillside overlooking the Mediterranean, the Amfiteatre Roma (Roman Amphitheatre) was where the Romans held their public spectacles, including combats between gladiators and wild animals before an audience of some 12,000 people. During the 12th century the Romanesque church of Santa Maria del Miracle was built on the site, giving the beach below its name – El Miracle. You can visit the Amfiteatre, Passeig Arqueològic, Museu d'Història, Circ Romà (▶ 90) and Casa Museu de Castellarnau (▶ 90) on a combined ticket.

Pause a while in the cool cathedral to admire its many treasures

CATEDRAL ✪

Tarragona's grandiose Catedral – a magnificent Romanesque-Gothic building, in the form of a cross – was built as the centrepiece of the *ciutat antigua* (old city).

🕇 80B1
✉ Plaça de la Seu
☎ 977 23 86 85
🕐 Mon–Sat 10–1, 4–7; winter 10–2

MUSEU ARQUEOLÒGIC AND MUSEU D'HISTÒRIA ✪

The fascinating Museu Arqueològic (Archeological Museum) includes a section of the old Roman wall, statues of emperors, several sarcophagi and some interesting mosaics. Near by stands the Praetorium and the vaults of the 1st-century Roman Circus. The Praetorium is the site of the Museu d'Història (Tarragona History Museum), which traces the origins and history of the city through such treasures as the sarcophagus of Hipolitus, a masterpiece that was rescued from the sea in 1948.

🕇 80B1
✉ Plaça del Rei
☎ 977 23 62 09
🕐 Museu Arqueològic: Tue–Sat 10–1, 4:30–7 (8 in summer), Sun 11–2. Museu d'Història: Tue–Sat 10–5:30, Sun 10–3
🖐 Moderate (combined ticket)

MUSEU I NECROPOLIA PALEOCRISTIANS ✪✪

Tarragona's most treasured Roman remains are housed in the Museu i Necropolia Paleocristians (Paleo-Christian Museum), in what was once an ancient necropolis, a 20-minute walk west of the city centre. It includes a valuable collection of mosaics, pottery, metalwork, glass and ivory.

🕇 80B1
✉ Passeig de la Independència s/n
☎ 977 21 11 75
🕐 Seasonal variations. Call for times
🖐 Moderate

PASSEIG ARQUEOLÒGIC ✪✪

For an overview of the old city and the flat hinterland of the Camp de Tarragona, walk the Passeig Arqueològic, a promenade which encircles the northernmost half of the old town, around the Roman walls, of which 1km of the original 4km remains. Seven defence towers and gates still stand, giving access to the city.

🕇 80B1
✉ Passeig Arqueològic
☎ 977 24 57 96
🕐 As Amfiteatre Roma
🖐 Moderate

Around Tarragona's Old Town

Distance
1½ km

Time
1 hour (without visits)

Start/end point
Ajuntament, Plaça de la Font
➕ 80B1

Coffee-break
🍴 Can Peret (£)
✉ Plaça de la Font 6
☎ 977 23 76 25

An ancient well in fascinating Tarragona

Start in Plaça de la Font. Take Carrer del Cós del Bou, at the opposite end to the Ajuntament building, up to the Circ Romà.

These ruins are all that remain of Tarragona's Roman Circus, which once occupied the Plaça de la Font.

Continue up Baixada de la Peixateria, turn right into Carrer de l'Enrajolat and immediately left into Plaça del Rei.

The Museu Arqueològic and the Museu d'Història (➤ 89) provide a useful overview of the early history of Tarragona.

A small unmarked street beside the Museu Arqueològic leads to Plaça dels Angels. From here go left, then first right along Carrer Santa Anna as far as Plaça del Forum.

Of particular interest here is a section of wall and the ruins of the Roman Forum, currently under excavation.

Take Carrer Merceria past the Gothic arches, then climb the steps to the Catedral (➤ 89). Circle this magnificent building anticlockwise. In Plaça de Palau, steps lead down to Carrer Claustre and the entrance to the Cathedral and the cloister.

The medieval cloisters here, bathed in light filtered through arches and trees, provide an atmospheric retreat from the city.

Return to Plaça de Palau. Turn left down Carrer de la Guitarra, through Plaça Sant Joan, along Baixada del Roser (alongside the old city wall) and left into Plaça del Paillol. Follow the road round into Carrer dels Cavalers past Casa Castellarnau (one of Tarragona's finest medieval mansions). A right turn into Carrer Major swings round into Baixada Misericordia and brings you back to the main square, Plaça de la Font.

Where To...

Above: *La Rambla by night*
Right: *Gaudí wall plaque at the entrance to Parc Güell*

Barcelona

Prices

Restaurant prices are approximate, based on a three-course meal for one without drinks and service. All the cafés and *tapas* bars fall under the (£) category unless marked to the contrary.

£ = €12
££ = €12–24
£££ = over €24

Most restaurants offer a fixed price meal (*menú del día*) of around €6 – usually including a choice of appetiser, main course, dessert and wine – which is great value but restrictive. Eating *à la carte* is more expensive but it enables you to try some of the unusual dishes. Usually the price on the menu includes VAT (IVA). If not, it should be clearly displayed on the menu. After the meal, leave a tip of about 10 per cent of the total bill, depending on quality and service.

Restaurants

Old City

Abac (£££)

The elegance, spaciousness and minimalism of Abac's stylish cream-and-orange dining room provides a perfect backdrop for the fine Spanish haute cuisine of local chef Xavier Pellicier.
✉ **Carrer Rec 79–89** ☎ **93 319 66 00** 🕐 **Closed Mon lunch and Sun** Ⓜ **Barceloneta**

Agut d'Avignon (£££)

Hidden up an alleyway off Calle d'Avinyó at the heart of the Barri Gòtic, with classic Catalan cuisine that attracts politicians, artists, and even the King of Spain.
✉ **Carrer Trinitat 3** ☎ **93 302 60 34** Ⓜ **Jaume I**

Amaya (£££)

Popular Basque restaurant, featuring *angulas* (baby eels) and *besugo* (sea bream). Wash it down with one of the many regional wines.
✉ **La Rambla 20–24** ☎ **93 302 10 37** Ⓜ **Liceu**

Biocenter (£)

The best-known of Barcelona's very few vegetarian restaurants, the Biocenter serves a range of delicious soups, casseroles and copious quantities of salad.
✉ **Carrer Pintor Fortuny 25** ☎ **93 301 45 83** 🕐 **Mon–Sat 9AM–11PM** Ⓜ **Catalunya**

Brasserie Flo (££)

Famous French-founded brasserie in a handsomely converted textile warehouse. House specialities include *foie gras* and Alsatian-style ham with *choucroute* (sauerkraut).
✉ **Carrer Jonqueres 10** ☎ **93 319 31 02** Ⓜ **Urquinaona**

Café de l'Academia (££)

One of Barcelona's best-value restaurants, with generous helpings of delicious Mediterranean cuisine in the heart of the old city.
✉ **Carrer Lledó 1** ☎ **93 315 00 26** 🕐 **Closed weekends** Ⓜ **Jaume I**

Can Culleretes (££)

One of the oldest restaurants in the city, founded in 1786, and traditionally decorated with wrought-iron chandeliers and signed photographs of visiting celebrities. Among the highlights of the Catalan cuisine on the menu is *perdiz* (partridge).
✉ **Carrer Quintana 5** ☎ **93 317 30 22** 🕐 **Lunch: Tue–Sun 1:30–4; dinner: Tue–Sat 9–11PM** Ⓜ **Liceu**

Ca l'Isidre (£££)

Sophisticated bistro offering exceptional Catalan cuisine and an extensive wine list.
✉ **Carrer Les Flors 12** ☎ **93 441 11 39** 🕐 **Closed Sun and hols** Ⓜ **Paral.lel (best by taxi)**

Los Caracoles (££)

Popular with both tourists and locals, and particularly famous for its robust, country-style cuisine, especially the spit-roasted chicken, and its namesake, snails.
✉ **Carrer Escudellers 14** ☎ **93 302 31 85** Ⓜ **Drassanes, Liceu**

Casa Leopoldo (£££)

Family-run seafood restaurant, in seedy location in the Barri Xinés. Arrive by taxi!

Its *tapas* bar is also hugely popular, with its barnacles, cuttlefish and baby eels.

✉ **Carrer Sant Rafael 24** ☎ 93 441 30 14 🕐 Closed Sun and holiday eves and Mon 🚇 Liceu

La Cuineta (££)

Well-established restaurant in the Barri Gòtic, serving authentic dishes from northeastern Spain.Good-value fixed-price menu.

✉ **Carrer Paradis 4** ☎ 93 315 01 11 🚇 Jaume 1

Egipto (££)

This small restaurant on La Rambla serves good-value, hearty Catalan cuisine such as cod in a cream sauce, shellfish gratin or stuffed aubergine. Try to save room for the homemade ice cream.

✉ **La Rambla 79** ☎ 93 317 95 45 🚇 Liceu

L'Eucaliptus (£)

A two-storey, traditional tiled brasserie, offering a simple menu of *torradas* (toasted open sandwiches) and *escalivada* (traditional pepper and aubergine dish) just off La Rambla.

✉ **Carrer Bonsuccés 4** ☎ 93 302 18 24 🕐 Closed Sun eves and Mon 🚇 Catalunya

La Fonda (£–££)

One of Ciutat Vella's most popular restaurants, with good, yet affordable Catalan food in stylish - surroundings. Be prepared to queue.

✉ **Carrer Escudellers 10** ☎ 93 301 75 15 🚇 Liceu

La Gardunya (£)

Impressive seafood platters and an excellent-value *menú del día* makes this the Boqueria market's most celebrated restaurant.

✉ **Carrer Jerusalem 18** ☎ 93 302 43 23 🕐 Closed Sun 🚇 Liceu

Govinda (£)

An Indian vegetarian restaurant near La Rambla.

✉ **Plaça Vila de Madrid 4–5** ☎ 93 318 77 29 🕐 Lunch: daily 1–4; dinner: Tue–Sat 8:30–11:45 🚇 Catalunya

El Gran Café (££)

Classic restaurant, serving French and Catalan cuisine in grand turn-of-the-19th-century surroundings.

✉ **Carrer d'Avinyó 9** ☎ 93 318 79 86 🕐 Closed Sun 🚇 Liceu

Hofmann (£££)

Interpretations of regional dishes by Mey Hofmann, one of Spain's most talented chefs, who also runs a world-renowned cookery school on the premises (including short courses for visitors).

✉ **Carrer Argenteria 74–78** ☎ 93 319 58 89 🕐 Closed Sat, Sun and Aug 🚇 Jaume I ❓ Phone for details of special two-day cookery courses

Nou Celler (£)

Good service and wholesome, value-for-money Catalan cooking at this rustic *bodega* near the Picasso Museum.

✉ **Carrer de la Princesa 16** ☎ 93 310 47 73 🕐 Closed Sat 🚇 Jaume 1

L'Ou com Balla (££)

Hidden down a back street of La Ribera near Santa Maria del Mar, the friendly staff at this cosy, candlelit restaurant promise a night to remember with their sensational culinary delights, including a variety of regional dishes.

✉ **Carrer Banys Vells 20** ☎ 93 310 53 78 🚇 Jaume I

El Paraguayo (££)

Specialities from Paraguay and Argentina, including barbecued meat served on wooden boards for

Opening Times

The restaurants on these pages are all open for lunch and dinner daily unless otherwise stated. Most establishments serve lunch from around 1 to 3:30 or 4. Dinner normally starts at 8:30 or 9, and is often served until midnight or the early hours of the morning. Many cafés and *tapas* bars remain open from early morning until late at night. It is advisable to book in most restaurants, especially at weekends. Nearly all restaurants close briefly for annual holidays (dates not listed) so phone first to avoid disappointment.

Where Should We Go?

In the Old City and Gràcia, you will find small, generally reasonably priced restaurants. The Eixample is more up-market, but it also has a smattering of cheaper eateries, fast-food joints and some excellent *tapas* bars. For seafood, try La Barceloneta for traditional atmosphere or, for something more sophisticated, the Port Olímpic.

Dinner in La Barceloneta

'There is an undeniable charm in the *chiringuitos* (seafood restaurants) lining the beach like dominoes at the sea's edge… and the crowds on seemingly perpetual vacation strolling to and fro… one goes to La Barceloneta as much for the ambience as the food.' (*Llorenç Torrado, local journalist*)

carnivores, and salads and pastas for vegetarians.
✉ **Carrer Parc 1** ☎ 93 302 14 41 ⊘ **Closed Mon** ⊜ **Drassanes**

La Perla Nera (££)
Authentic flavours, perfect pastas and an attractive dining room, brimming with fresh flowers are the trademark of this deservedly well-respected Italian restaurant.
✉ **Via Laietana 32–4** ☎ 93 310 56 46 ⊜ **Jaume I**

El Pintor (££)
Serving traditional Catalan cuisine, fine regional wines, El Pintor is housed in a cosy, brick-vaulted interior with crisp white linen and candlelight.
✉ **Carrer St Honorat 7** ☎ 93 301 40 65 ⊜ **Jaume I**

Pitarra (£)
An old-fashioned Spanish restaurant in the Barri Gòtic, named after the 19th-century Catalan playwright who lived and wrote his plays and poetry here. They serve a particularly good Valencian paella.
✉ **Carrer d'Avinyó 56** ☎ 93 301 16 47 ⊘ **Closed Sun and Aug** ⊜ **Liceu**

Els Quatre Gats (££)
Many famous artists and intellectuals used to gather in this popular *Modernista* café in the early 1900s. Even the menu was designed by Picasso.
✉ **Carrer Montsió 3 bis** ☎ 93 302 41 40 ⊜ **Catalunya**

Les Quinze Nits (££)
Under the same management as La Fonda (► 93), this wood-panelled restaurant with an attractive terrace serves an excellent Catalan style *civet de conill* (rabbit stew) and an impressive *parillada de peix* (seafood mixed grill).

✉ **Plaça Reial 6** ☎ 93 317 30 75 ⊜ **Liceu**

Quo Vadis (£££)
One of Barcelona's finest restaurants, near the Boqueria market, serving time-tested recipes from all over Spain.
✉ **Carrer Carme 7** ☎ 93 302 40 72 ⊘ **Closed Sun** ⊜ **Liceu**

La Rioja (£–££)
This bright, white-tiled restaurant offers a splendid selection of Riojan dishes and wines, and a good-value *menú del día*.
✉ **Carrer Duran i Bas 5** ☎ 93 301 22 98 ⊘ **Closed Sat eve, Sun and Aug** ⊜ **Catalunya**

Sushi-Ya (££)
Small Japanese restaurant, serving the usual *sushi, sashimi, tempura* and *miso soup*.
✉ **Carrer Quintana 4** ☎ 93 412 72 49 ⊜ **Liceu**

Taxidermista (££)
Buzzy designer restaurant in an old taxidermist's studio, offering modern Mediterranean dishes such as lamb couscous or duck breast with truffle vinaigrette.
✉ **Plaça Reial 8** ☎ 93 412 45 36 ⊘ **Closed Mon** ⊜ **Liceu**

Seafront
Agua (££)
Located right on the Barceloneta beach, near the Port Olímpic (► 33). The menu is creative, yet also offers excellent traditional Barceloneta fare, with the emphasis on rice-based dishes.
✉ **Passeig Marítim de la Barceloneta 30** ☎ 93 225 12 72 ⊜ **Ciutadella**

Cal Pinxo (£££)
This former beach bar has been transformed into a fashionable seafood restaurant facing Barceloneta

beach, where paella and fish dishes can be enjoyed on a large terrace in summer.

✉ **Carrer Baluard 124** ☎ **93 221 44 60** 🚇 **Barceloneta**

El Cangrejo Loco (££)

Popular fish restaurant at the far end of the Port Olímpic but worth the walk for its extensive *pica-pica* starters and delicious main dishes – try the *fideua*, cod fried in honey.

✉ **Moll de Gregal 29–30, Port Olímpic** ☎ **93 221 05 33** 🚇 **Ciutadella**

Can Majó (£££)

The city's top seafood restaurant, in La Barceloneta. The *suquet de peix* (mixed fish casserole), *arrozes* (black rice) with *bacalao* (salt cod) or lobster, and *centollos* (crabs from the north coast) are truly delicious.

✉ **Carrer Almirall Aixada 23** ☎ **93 221 58 18** 🕔 **Closed Sun eve and Mon** 🚇 **Barceloneta**

Emperador (£££)

One of the best of the new harbourside restaurants in the extremely fashionable Palau de Mar (➤ 58), with outdoor tables and a variety of fresh fish and seafood dishes.

✉ **Palau de Mar, Plaça Pau Vila 1** ☎ **93 221 02 20** 🚇 **Barceloneta**

El Passadís d'el Pep (£££)

There's no menu as such here, just some of the best fish in town. Choose from bream, bass, oysters, shellfish or the catch of the day.

✉ **Pla del Palau 2** ☎ **93 310 10 21** 🕔 **Closed Sun and hols** 🚇 **Barceloneta**

El Petit Miau (££)

Popular, *Modernista*-inspired Catalan restaurant on the waterfront in Maremagnum (➤ 72), with beautiful stained-glass skylights, and paintings by up-and-coming local artists.

✉ **Moll d'Espanya 105 – Port Vell** ☎ **93 225 81 10** 🚇 **Drassanes**

Planet Hollywood (£–££)

A branch of the worldwide celebrity chain of restaurants, serving the usual Californian-style cuisine in a spectacular beach setting.

✉ **Carrer Marina 19–21, Marina Village** ☎ **93 221 11 11** 🚇 **Ciutadella**

San Fermín (££)

A rustic Basque restaurant by the Port Olímpic. You'll find cider poured from the barrel and huge T-bone steaks cooked on an outdoor grill.

✉ **Moll de Gregal 22** ☎ **93 221 05 43** 🚇 **Ciutadella**

Set Portes (£££)

One of Barcelona's most historic restaurants, with waiters in long white aprons, serving excellent Catalan cuisine in traditional surroundings. It has always attracted an illustrious clientele.

✉ **Passeig de Isabel II, 14** ☎ **93 319 30 33** 🚇 **Barceloneta**

Eixample & Gràcia
Asador de Burges (£££)

A traditional Castilian roast house where lamb and suckling pig are cooked in a brick oven until they are tender to the touch. Another speciality is *cocido castellano*, a hearty stew of meat, sausages and chickpeas.

✉ **Carrer Bruc 118** ☎ **93 207 31 60** 🕔 **Closed Sun** 🚇 **Verdaguer**

Beltxenea (£££)

Barcelona's premier Basque restaurant is set

Tapas

The term *tapas* is thought to come from the habit of having a snack with a pre-meal drink to *tapar el apetito* ('put a lid on the appetite'). *Tapas* consist of small portions of fish, meat or vegetables, whereas *raciones* are bigger portions and usually enough for a light meal.

95

A Sweet Tooth

Catalan desserts are often uninspiring – a choice between *gelat* (ice cream), *flam* (crème caramel), *crèma catalana* (crème brulée), *macedonia* (fruit salad) or *formatge* (cheese). But look out for *mel i mató* (curd cheese with honey), *postre de músic* (spiced fruit cake), *panellets* (marzipans), *torrons* (nougats) and *cocas* (pastries sprinkled with sugar and pine-nuts).

---

in an elegant 19th-century *Modernista* building and features a pretty interior garden terrace.

✉ **Carrer Mallorca 275** ☎ **93 215 30 24** Ⓣ **Closed Sat lunch, all day Sun, Aug and public hols** Ⓜ **Diagonal, Passeig de Gràcia**

Botafumeiro (£££)

This Galician seafood restaurant serves fish (flown in daily from Galicia) with regional wines and Catalan *cavas*. The *mariscos Botafumeira* (seafood platter) is a sight to behold.

✉ **Carrer de Gran de Gràcia 81** ☎ **93 218 42 30** Ⓜ **Fontana**

El Caballito Blanco (£)

The 'Little White Horse' is a cheerful, good-value, traditional restaurant, always packed with locals.

✉ **Carrer Mallorca 196** ☎ **93 453 10 33** Ⓣ **Closed Sun eve, Mon and Aug** Ⓜ **Hospital Clinic**

Casi Casi (£)

An Andalusian restaurant in Gracia. Try the excellent gazpacho or *ajoblanco* (cold garlic soup) to start, followed by the daily catch *a la Andaluza*.

✉ **Carrer Laforja 8** ☎ **93 415 81 94** Ⓜ **Gràcia**

Citrus (££)

Recently opened, this first-floor restaurant serves seasonal Mediterranean cuisine.

✉ **Passeig de Gràcia 44** ☎ **93 487 23 45**

La Dama (£££)

The French cuisine of this Michelin star-rated restaurant rivals that of the top restaurants of Paris. An added bonus is the exceptional *Modernista* setting.

✉ **Avinguda Diagonal 423** ☎ **93 202 06 86** Ⓜ **Provença**

FrescCo (£)

Eat-as-much-as-you-want from the self-service salads, pasta, pizza, ice cream, bread and beverages. Take-away service also available. Founded by Jordi Arrese, silver medallist in the Barcelona Olympics. Also at Ronda Universitat 29.

✉ **Carrer València 263** ☎ **93 488 10 49** Ⓜ **Passeig de Gràcia**

El Glop (£)

Crowded restaurant serving chargrilled meat and seasonal vegetables at reasonable prices, washed down with Catalan wines.

✉ **Carrer Sant Lluís 24 (also at Carrer Casp 21 and Rambla Catalunya 65)** ☎ **93 213 70 58** Ⓣ **Closed Mon** Ⓜ **Joanic**

Jean Luc Figueras (£££)

Exquisite culinary delights served in striking surroundings of tangerine and pale-green ceramics, and enhanced by original art deco silverware.

✉ **Carrer Santa Teresa 10** ☎ **93 415 28 77** Ⓣ **Closed Sat lunch, Sun** Ⓜ **Diagonal**

Madrid-Barcelona (££)

Charming café-restaurant in a converted railway station. Dishes are served *a la brasa* – cooked on a coal-fired range.

✉ **Carrer d'Aragó 282** ☎ **93 215 70 26** Ⓣ **Closed Sun** Ⓜ **Passeig de Gràcia**

El Racó d'en Freixa (£££)

Highly original cooking makes this one of the city's most popular Sunday-lunch haunts. Save room for the puddings which come in threes – bananas, fried, baked and caramelised, or a trio of iced, warm and hot chocolate delights.

✉ **Carrer Sant Elies 22** ☎ **93 209 75 59** Ⓣ **Closed Mon, Sun eve & Aug** Ⓜ **Plaça Molina/Sant Gervasi**

Suburbs

La Balsa (£££)
International cuisine served at the top of this circular tower, originally built as a water cistern.
✉ Carrer Infanta Isabel 4, Sant Gervasi ☎ 93 211 50 48 ☻ Closed Sun and Mon 🚇 Tibidabo

La Bodeguita del Poble (££)
One of several theme restaurants in the Poble Espanyol (► 22), this one offers Cuban market cooking such as pork, beans and rice.
✉ Poble Espanyol ☎ 93 426 38 45 🚌 13, 50, 61

Can Cortada (££)
One of Barcelona's most distinguished restaurants is housed in 11th-century buildings.
✉ Avinguda de l'Estatut de Catalunya s/n, Horta ☎ 93 427 23 15 🚇 Montbau, Horta

Can Travinou (£££)
Set in a beautiful 18th-century masìa (farmhouse) and garden, on a hill above Horta. The wine list extends to 500 wines and cavas.
✉ Carrer Jorge Manrique s/n ☎ 93 428 03 01 ☻ Closed Sun eve 🚇 Montbau

Casa Calvet (£££)
Gaudí's first apartment building in Barcelona is now a sumptuous, formal restaurant offering sophisticated French and Catalan cuisine.
✉ Carrer Casp 48 ☎ 93 412 40 12 ☻ Closed Sun 🚇 Urquinaona

Gaig (£££)
A famous family-run restaurant, founded in 1869 as a café for cart drivers. It is now one of Barcelona's most upmarket eateries.
✉ Passeig Maragall 402 ☎ 93 429 10 17 ☻ Closed Sun, Mon eve 🚇 Vilapicina

Neichel (£££)
This stylish restaurant boasts the talents of Alsace-born chef Jean-Louis Neichel, who has been described as 'the most brilliant ambassador French cuisine has ever had within Spain'.
✉ Carrer Beltrán í Rózpide 16 bis ☎ 93 203 84 08 ☻ Closed Sat lunch, Sun, Aug and hols 🚇 Palau Reial

La Parra (£–££)
Country cooking in an old coaching inn with hearty portions of lamb, rabbit, steak and spare ribs cooked on a giant wood-fired grill, and served on wooden slabs with lashings of homemade allioli (► 52).
✉ Carrer Joanot Martorell 3, Hostafranca ☎ 93 332 51 34 ☻ Closed Mon, Tue and Fri lunch and Sun eve 🚇 Hostafranca

La Venta (£££)
The conservatory and terrace, and the light, imaginative menu, make for perfect spring lunches and relaxing summer evenings.
✉ Plaça Dr Andreu, Sant Gervasi ☎ 93 212 64 55 ☻ Closed Sun 🚇 Avinguda Tibidabo then Tramvia Blau

Cafés and Tapas Bars

Old City

Ambos Mundos
Pleasant cerveceria (beer bar) in Plaça Reial serving wholesome tapas in terracotta dishes. Has a popular terrace for buskers.
✉ Plaça Reial 9–10 ☎ 93 317 01 66 ☻ Closed Tue 🚇 Liceu

Bar del Pi
Simple but hugely popular, despite its small tapas selection, in one of Barcelona's most atmospheric squares.
✉ Plaça Sant Josep Oriol 1 ☎ 93 302 21 23 🚇 Liceu

'Cafè Sol, Per Favor'
Start the day with a cafè amb llet (a large milky coffee). After mid-morning, drink a tallat (a small coffee with a dash of milk), a cafè sol (espresso) or a cafè americano. Descafeinado is widely available but order it de máquina (espresso-style). After dinner, why not try a carajillo (a sol with a shot of brandy)?

Bodegas, Cervecerias and Orxaterias

There are bars on every second street in Barcelona – cosy, old-fashioned *bodegas*, serving wine from the barrel, and *cervecerias* or beer bars, offering both local beer on draught (*una cana*) and pricier imported beers. Or visit an *orxateria* and try *orxata*, the refreshing, milk-like drink made from crushed *chufa* nuts, and unique to Spain.

El Bosc de les Fades

An extraordinary café-cum-magic fairy world, decorated with fountains, toadstools and fairytale princesses.

✉ Passatge de la Banca, La Rambla 4–6 ☎ 93 317 26 49 🚇 Drassanes

Cafè de l'Òpera

This original 19th-century café is one of Barcelona's favourites, and the best terrace-café along the Ramblas.

✉ La Rambla 74 ☎ 93 302 41 80 🚇 Liceu

Café Zurich

Popular bar and meeting place at the top of La Rambla. A great place for people-watching and soaking up the atmosphere.

✉ Plaça Catalunya 1 ☎ 93 317 91 53 🚇 Catalunya

Celta

A Galician bar near the port, known for its fried *rabas* (squid) and its *patatas bravas*, (potatoes in a spicy mayonnaise), serving Galician white wine in traditional white ceramic cups.

✉ Carrer Mercè 16 ☎ 93 315 00 06 🕐 Closed Sun 🚇 Drassanes, Barceloneta

Ceveceria Naviera

Although the concept of *tapas* on La Rambla sounds dear, this is good value.

✉ La Rambla de Canaletas 127 ☎ 93 301 92 25 🚇 Catalunya

Dulcinea

The most famous chocolate shop in town. Try *melindros* (sugar-topped sponge fingers) dipped in very thick hot chocolate.

✉ Carrer Petritxol 2 ☎ 93 302 68 24 🚇 Liceu

Forn de Betlem

A bright orange, trendy café and cake shop near the Museum of Contemporary Art (▶ 50), one of very few places around the museum for a coffee or a snack.

✉ Carrer Joaquín Costa 34 🚇 Universitat

Hard Rock Café

The latest addition to the world-famous chain.

✉ Plaça de Catalunya 21 ☎ 93 270 23 05 🚇 Catalunya

Hivernacle

Elegant café inside the Parc de la Ciutadella's beautiful 19th-century greenhouse. Occasional live jazz or classical music.

✉ Parc de la Ciutadella ☎ 93 295 40 17 🚇 Arc de Triomf

Mesón del Café

Join locals at the bar for a coffee or hot chocolate while exploring the Barri Gòtic.

✉ Carrer de la Libreteria 16 ☎ 93 315 07 54 🕐 Closed Sun 🚇 Jaume I

La Plata

One of several *tascas* (traditional bars) on this narrow medieval street, specialising in whitebait, anchovies, and tomato and onion salads.

✉ Carrer Mercè 28 ☎ 93 315 10 09 🚇 Barceloneta

Sagardi

A spacious new bar, popular with the young pre-dinner crowd, or for those wishing to make a meal out of their large, tasty portions of *tapas*.

✉ Carrer Argenteria 62 ☎ 93 319 99 93 🕐 Closed Sat 🚇 Jaume I

Tèxtil Cafè

Delicious quiches and salads, in the courtyard of the medieval palace which houses the Museu Tèxtil.

✉ Carrer Montcada 12 ☎ 93 268 25 98 🚇 Jaume I ❓ No need to pay museum entrance

La Vinya del Senyor

A modern, stand-up wine bar beside Santa Maria del Mar.
✉ **Plaça Santa Maria 5** ☎ **93 310 33 79** 🚇 **Jaume I**

Seafront
Can Ramonet

This is a stand-up *tapas* bar in one of La Barceloneta's top fish restaurants. It is worth trying their mussels, 'from the beach'.
✉ **Carrer Maquinista 17** ☎ **93 319 30 64** 🕐 **Closed Sun eve** 🚇 **Barceloneta**

Goyescas

An eye-popping choice of *tapas* on the first floor of the Hotel Arts, overlooking the Port Olímpic.
✉ **Hotel Arts, Carrer de Marina 19** ☎ **93 221 10 00** 🚇 **Ciutadella**

El Rey de la Gamba

The 'King of Prawns' serves seafood and cured hams, and is busy at weekends.
✉ **Passeig Joan de Borbó 53 (also Moll Mistral, Port Olímpic)** ☎ **93 221 73 06** 🚇 **Barceloneta**

El Vaso del Oro

One of very few *cervecerias* (beer bars) that brews its own beers.
✉ **Carrer Balboa 6** ☎ **93 319 30 98** 🚇 **Barceloneta**

Eixample & Gràcia
Ba-Ba-Reeba

The *tapas* selection here includes prawns wrapped in bacon and sea urchins filled with melted cheese.
✉ **Passeig de Gràcia 28** ☎ **93 301 43 02** 🚇 **Passeig de Gràcia**

Bodega Sepúlveda

Boquerones (fresh anchovies) are the speciality at this genuine locals' bar.
✉ **Carrer Sepúlveda 173 bis** ☎ **93 323 59 44** 🕐 **Closed Sun** 🚇 **Universitat**

La Bodegueta

An old wine tavern, well known for its Catalan *charcuterie*, accompanied by a wide selection of local wines and vermouths,
✉ **Rambla de Catalunya 100** ☎ **93 215 48 94** 🕐 **Closed Sun lunch** 🚇 **Provença**

Ciudat Condal Cerveceria

A popular meeting-place in the centre of town for breakfast or coffee.
✉ **Rambla de Catalunya 18** ☎ **93 318 19 97** 🚇 **Catalunya**

Flash-Flash Tortilleria (£)

This is the place for cheap, healthy Spanish fast food – *tortillas* (omelettes) and salad.
✉ **Carrer Granada del Penedes 25** ☎ **93 237 09 90** 🚇 **Diagonal**

Pla de la Garsa

A former 16th-century stables and dairy near the Picasso Museum (▶ 20), Pla de la Garsa is now a beautiful bar-restaurant, known for its excellent cheeses, pâtés and hams.
✉ **Carrer Assaonadors 13** ☎ **93 315 24 13** 🕐 **Closed Sun lunch** 🚇 **Jaume I**

Qu-Qu (Quasi Queviures)

A delicatessen-cum-*tapas* bar, specialising in salads, cheeses and Catalan sausage meats.
✉ **Passeig de Gràcia 24** ☎ **93 317 45 12** 🚇 **Passeig de Gràcia**

Tapa Tapa

This *cerveceria* is the in-place in town to meet for *tapas* and a beer. Specials include snails, fried pig snout, black squid and octopus.
✉ **Passeig de Gràcia 44** ☎ **93 488 33 69** 🚇 **Passeig de Gràcia**

Regional Cuisine

Barcelona boasts restaurants to suit all tastes, budgets and occasions. Contrary to what many visitors assume, there is no such thing as 'Spanish national cuisine' but rather a wide variety of regional styles, such as Galician, Basque, Castilian and Andalucian, all to be found in Barcelona.

Catalonia

Pa amb Tomàquet
No Catalan meal is complete without *pa amb tomàquet* – a hearty slice (*llesque*) of white country bread rubbed with a ripe tomato, with a drizzle of olive oil and a pinch of salt. There are even restaurants called *llesqueria*, which specialise solely in '*pa-amb-t*' with a variety of toppings.

Restaurants and Cafés/Bars

Girona

L'Arcada (£)
Chic café bar-cum-restaurant underneath Rambla Llibertat's handsome arcade.
✉ **Rambla Llibertat 38** ☎ **972 20 10 15**

Cipresaia (££)
Smart, sophisticated restaurant, at the heart of the old Jewish quarter.
✉ **Carrer General Fornas 2** ☎ **972 22 24 49**

El Pou de Call (££)
Local cuisine in traditional surroundings. Excellent-value *menú del diá* and wine list.
✉ **Carrer de la Força 14** ☎ **972 22 37 74** ⏰ **Closed Sun eve**

Montserrat

Abat Cisneros (££)
Montserrat's top restaurant. The 16th-century stone dining-room used to contain the monastery stables.
✉ **Hotel Abat Cisneros** ☎ **93 877 77 01**

Sitges

Chiringuito (£)
A traditional-style *tapas* bar in a wooden hut on the seafront, specialising in fresh sardines and salads
✉ **Passeig de la Ribera** ☎ **93 894 75 96**

Mare Nostrum (££)
Smart waterfront restaurant. Try the *Xato de Sitges* (grilled fish with a local variant of *romesco* sauce, ➤ 53), or monkfish and prawns with garlic mousseline.
✉ **Passeig de la Ribera 60–62** ☎ **93 894 33 93** ⏰ **Closed Wed**

Tarragona

Bodega Celler Gras (£)
A good place to join the locals for *tapas* specialities – pâtés, cheeses and *charcuterie*, including spicy *xoriço* and Mallorquin *sobrassada*.
✉ **Carrer Governadir Gonzalez 8** ☎ **977 23 48 20** ⏰ **Closed Sun eve**

Can Llesques (£)
A small restaurant in the old town with low stone arches giving it a decidedly rustic feel. Ceramic pitchers, for serving the wine, add to this pleasantly bucolic ambience.
✉ **Carrer Natzaret 6, Plaça del Rei** ☎ **977 22 29 06**

Estació Maritima (£££)
This is one of the best of the many fish restaurants and tapas bars that line the waterfront in the fishermen's district of Serralló.
✉ **Moll de Costa Tinglade 4** ☎ **977 22 74 18** ⏰ **Closed Sun eve and Mon**

Sol-Ric (££)
This excellent fish restaurant is located on the outskirts of town near Platja Rembassada.
✉ **Via Augusta 227** ☎ **977 23 20 32** ⏰ **Closed Sun eve**

Vilafranca del Penedès

Cal Ton (££)
It may come as a surprise to find such a smart, modern restaurant in an otherwise traditional town. Try the mouth-watering pancakes filled with a seafood and *cava* sauce.
✉ **Carrer del Casal 8** ☎ **93 890 37 41** ⏰ **Closed Sun eve and Mon, Easter week, 2 August**

Barcelona

Arts Barcelona (£££)
Barcelona's most fashionable hotel provides state-of-the-art, unabashed luxury beside the sea (► panel).
✉ Carrer de la Marina 19–21
☎ 93 221 10 00;
www.ritzcarlton.com
🚇 Ciutadella/Vila Olímpica

Barcelona Hilton (£££)
High-amenity hotel, 15 minutes from the airport, at the heart of the city's commercial and financial district.
✉ Avinguda Diagonal 589–591
☎ 93 495 77 77;
www.hilton.com 🚇 Maria Cristina

Citadines (££)
A 3-star 'aparthotel' on the Ramblas, with a rooftop terrace overlooking part of the Old City (► 102).
✉ La Rambla 122 ☎ 93 270 11 11; www.citadines.com
🚇 Catalunya/Liceu

Claris (£££)
Just off the exclusive Passeig de Gràcia, this impressive hotel features modern accommodation furnished in marble, glass and works of art. Several restaurants, a roof terrace with pool, a fitness centre, a Japanese garden and even a museum of priceless Egyptian antiques.
✉ Carrer Pau Claris 150
☎ 93 487 62 62;
www.derbyhotels.es
🚇 Passeig de Gràcia

Colón (££–£££)
Old-fashioned, family-friendly hotel, opposite the cathedral. Country-home feel rather than that of a busy city hotel.
✉ Avenida de la Catedral 7
☎ 93 301 14 04;
www.hotelcolon.es 🚇 Jaume I/ Urquinaona

Condes De Barcelona (£££)
Stylish hotel in Barcelona's main shopping district. Elegant public rooms, and bedrooms furnished in *Modernista* style.
✉ Passeig de Gràcia 73–75
☎ 93 467 47 80;
www.condesdebarcelona.es
🚇 Diagonal

Duques De Bergara (££)
Contemporary elegance in a turn-of-the-19th-century building. Four stars.
✉ Carrer Bergara 11 ☎ 93 301 51 51; www.hotels-catalonia.es 🚇 Catalunya

Gallery (£££)
You'll get a warm welcome and relaxing stay at this lovely hotel. Ask for their leaflet with five city strolls.
✉ Carrer Rosselló 249
☎ 93 415 99 11;
www.galleryhotel.com
🚇 Diagonal

Gaudí (££)
Facing Palau Güell, one of Gaudí's masterworks, this modern 3-star hotel has 73 well-equipped rooms and a Gaudí-inspired reception area.
✉ Carrer Nou de la Rambla 12
☎ 93 317 90 32;
www.hotelgaudi.es
🚇 Drassanes/Liceu

Gran Hotel Barcino (£££)
Modern luxury and tasteful rooms await you here in the heart of the Barri Gòtic.
✉ Carrer Jaume I, 6 ☎ 93 302 20 12; www.gargallo-hotels.com 🚇 Jaume I

Granvía (£)
It is easy to imagine how splendid this reasonably priced hotel must have been in its heyday, with its old-world gilt, balustraded

Prices
Prices are based on the cost of a double room per night (excluding breakfast and tax).

£££ = over €180
££ = €110–180
£   = under €110

Symbol of Perfection
Hotel Arts Barcelona, the highest building in Spain and Barcelona's only waterfront hotel, towers above the entrance to the Port Olímpic. Its post-Modern interior is filled with modern Catalan art and on its waterfront terraces a vast copper fish designed by Frank Gehry (► 74) has become a new symbol of the city.

Hotel Construction
Several hotels have recently been constructed at the top of La Rambla, in an attempt to revitalise this famous street. The apartment-style Citadines, designed by Esteve Bonnell, is one of the more attractive (▶ 101).

staircase and chandeliers.
✉ **Gran Via de les Cortes Catalanes 642** ☎ 93 318 19 00; www.nnhotels.es 🚇 **Catalunya**

Gravina (££)
This charming 3-star hotel has a prime location near the bustling Plaça de Catalunya. Totally refurbished.
✉ **Carrer Gravina 12** ☎ 93 301 68 68 🚇 **Universitat**

Jardí (£)
A small, friendly hotel with clean, simple rooms overlooking two of the Barri Gòtic's prettiest squares, Plaça Sant Josep Oriol and Plaça del Pi.
✉ **Plaça Sant Josep Oriol 1** ☎ 93 301 59 00 🚇 **Liceu**

Méson Castilla (£)
A quiet, characterful family-run hotel on the edge of the old town, with 56 rooms furnished in traditional Castilian style.
✉ **Carrer Valldonzella 5** ☎ 93 318 21 82; www.husa.es 🚇 **Universitat**

Oriente (££)
The Oriente was once *the* place to stay in Barcelona. Restored but still traditionally furnished, it draws those seeking a taste of history.
✉ **La Rambla 45** ☎ 93 302 25 58; www.husa.es 🚇 **Liceu**

Rey Juan Carlos I Conrad International (£££)
A member of the 'Leading Hotels of the World' group, set in private gardens and with extensive views of the city. First-rate facilities.
✉ **Avinguda Diagonal 661–671** ☎ 93 364 40 40; www.hrjuancarlos.com 🚇 **Zona Universitària**

Rialto (£)
The cosy atmosphere and bedrooms stylishly furnished with Catalan flair makes this 3-star hotel in the Barri Gòtic an excellent choice.
✉ **Carrer Ferran 42** ☎ 93 318 52 12; www.gargallo-hotels.com 🚇 **Jaume I**

Ritz (£££)
Part of the 'Leading Hotels of the World' group, this hotel has gracious old-world charm, solicitous staff and a reputation for excellent cuisine and service.
✉ **Gran Via de les Corts Catalanes 668** ☎ 93 318 52 00; www.rtizbcn.com 🚇 **Passeig de Gràcia**

Rivoli Rambla (£££)
Opened in 1989, this hotel immediately established itself as one of the best. Behind the dignified *Modernista* façade, the interior contains murals, art deco furnishings and many antiques. A rooftop terrace overlooks the smarter end of La Rambla.
✉ **La Rambla 128** ☎ 93 302 66 43; www.rivolihotels.com 🚇 **Catalunya**

Roma Reial (£)
Excellent, cheap accommodation overlooking the Plaça Reial. Service is friendly and all rooms have bathroom and phone.
✉ **Plaça Reial 11** ☎ 93 302 03 66 🚇 **Liceu**

Sant Agustí (£)
Just off La Rambla, and near Boqueria market, this smart, modern 3-star hotel offers excellent value in a quiet yet central location.
✉ **Plaça Sant Agustí 3** ☎ 93 318 16 58; www.hotelsa.com 🚇 **Liceu**

Catalonia

Figueres

Ampurdan (££)

This stylish hotel, just north of Figueres, was the birthplace of the new Catalan cuisine and is still a place of pilgrimage for food-lovers.

✉ Antiga Carretera de França
☎ 972 50 05 62

Hotel Durán (££)

This popular hotel also has a highly regarded restaurant, that serves hearty traditional cuisine with a modern touch and was a favourite lunchtime haunt of Salvador Dalí and friends.

✉ Carrer Lasuaca 5 ☎ 972 50 12 50; wwwhotelduran.com

Girona

Bellmirall (£)

Characterful hotel, housed inside the ancient buildings of the Jewish quarter and near to the cathedral. Feels more like a country dwelling.

✉ Carrer Bellmirall 3 ☎ 972 20 40 09

Carlemany (£££)

Smart, modern hotel between the station and the old town, and brimful of modern art. Its restaurant is one of the best in town.

✉ Plaça Miquel Santaló
☎ 972 21 12 12;
www.carlemany.es

Montserrat

Abat Cisneros (££)

The name of this 3-star hotel, set in Montserrat's main square, is derived from a title given to the head of Benedictine monasteries during the Middle Ages. It has cheap, basic rooms in the former monks' cells.

✉ Plaça de Monestir, 08199 Montserrat ☎ 93 877 77 01; www.abadiamontserrat.net

Sitges

Capri-Veracruz (£–££)

Excellent value just off the seafront, this family-run hotel consists of two houses which sandwich a small garden with an outdoor pool, Jacuzzi and terrace.

✉ Avinguda Sofia 13–17
☎ 93 811 02 67

Celimar (£–££)

A recently renovated 3-star *Modernista* hotel, with 26 rooms just a stone's throw from the beach. Ask for one with a balcony.

✉ Passeig de Ribera 20
☎ 93 811 01 70;
www.hotelcelimar.com

El Xalet (£)

A discreet hotel in a beautiful *Modernista* villa, with just 10 well-furnished rooms, restaurant, pool and garden.

✉ Carrer Isla de Cuba 35
☎ 93 811 0070

Tarragona

Fòrum (£)

Simple, clean rooms overlooking Plaça de la Font in the Old Town, above a jolly *bodega*-style restaurant.

✉ Plaça de la Font 37 ☎ 977 23 17 18

Imperial Tarraco (££)

Tarragona's top hotel (4-star), centrally situated and overlooking both the sea and the Amfiteatre Romà (► 88).

✉ Passeig de Palmeres
☎ 977 23 30 40; www.husa.es

Urbis (£)

Reasonably priced, friendly 3-star hotel in the town centre, just off the Rambla Nova and near the daily fruit market.

✉ Carrer Reding 20 bis
☎ 977 24 01 16

Hotel Choices

It is advisable to make reservations in advance throughout Catalonia, especially in the cities and the coastal regions. Two types of accommodation are available – hotels (H) and pensions (P). Hotels are classified from 1- to 5-star, while pensions have 1 or 2 stars. As hotel standards vary considerably, view the room before committing yourself.

Clothes, Jewellery & Accessories

Department Stores and Malls

El Corte Inglés is the city's foremost department store, with several different locations (Plaça Catalunya, Plaça Francesc Macià, Avinguda Diagonal 617–6 and 471–3, and Avinguda Portal de l'Angel 19–21), and particularly strong fashion sections for men, women and children. Fashion malls include La Avenida, a small arcade of luxury shops (✉ Rambla de Catalunya 121), and Bulevard Rosa (✉ Passeig de Gràcia 55). Look out for mega-malls, Barcelona Glòries and L'Illa (✉ Diagonal 208 and 545-557) and Maremagnum, Moll d'Espanya s/n.

Adolfo Domínguez

One of Spain's most famous designers, Adolfo Domínguez is renowned for introducing linen suits in the 1980s with the slogan 'wrinkles are fashionable'. He also designed this shop.

✉ **Passeig de Gràcia 89**
☎ **93 215 13 39** Ⓜ **Passeig de Gràcia**

Alea

Splendid showcase for up-and-coming Catalan jewellers in the newly trendy district of La Ribera.

✉ **Carrer Argenteria 66**
☎ **93 310 13 73** Ⓜ **Jaume I, Barceloneta**

Antonio Miró

Antonio Miró is Spain's brightest young fashion star. Although best known for his men's fashions, he also designs women's and children's clothes, shoes, spectacles and furniture.

✉ **Carrer Consell de Cent 349–351** ☎ **93 487 06 70**
Ⓜ **Passeig de Gràcia**

Argenters

Small, chic jewellery shop near the Picasso Museum featuring work in gold, silver, platinum and steel from four young Spanish designers.

✉ **Carrer Montcada 25** ☎ **93 319 43 18** Ⓜ **Jaume I**

Bagués

Run by an old family of gold and silversmiths, this shop on the ground floor of Casa Amatller (► 36) contains priceless works by Masriera, the sole creator of the *Modernista* style in the Spanish jewellery trade.

✉ **Passeig de Gràcia 41**
☎ **93 216 01 74** Ⓜ **Passeig de Gràcia**

Bóboli

A leading Spanish brand for children and teens clothing. Comfortable, stylish and sporty.

✉ **Carrer Gran de Gràcia 98**
☎ **93 237 56 70** Ⓜ **Gràcia**

Carles Galindo

Stylish shop-cum-showroom featuring local designer Carles Galindo's striking collection of accessories for both sexes – handbags, belts and jewellery often made from unusual materials.

✉ **Carrer Verdi 56** ☎ **93 416 07 04** Ⓜ **Lesseps**

Corbata Barcelona

An astonishing range of ties are on sale in this tiny shop at Port Vell.

✉ **Moll d'Espanya s/n, Maremagnum** ☎ **93 225 81 32**
Ⓜ **Barceloneta, Drassanes**

Cristina Castaner

All the latest trends in women's footwear, plus handbags and other accessories.

✉ **Carrer Mestre Nicolau 23**
☎ **93 414 24 28** Ⓜ **Muntaner**

Joaquín Berao

Jewellery by Joaquín Berao, celebrated for his unusual combinations of materials and avant-garde chunky designs.

✉ **Rosselló 277** ☎ **93 218 61 87** Ⓜ **Provença, Diagonal**

Lydia Delgado

Delgado is one of Barcelona's most distinctive local designers of easy-to-wear women's fashions. Her collections are sold in this shop alone.

✉ **Carrer Minerva 21** ☎ **93 415 99 98** Ⓜ **Gràcia, Diagonal**

Loewe
One of the most celebrated leather-goods companies in the world, located in Domènech i Montaner's *Modernista* Lleó-Morera building.
✉ **Passeig de Gràcia 35**
☎ **93 216 04 00** 🚇 **Passeig de Gràcia**

Mango
This chainstore brims with cheap, trendy designs for the truly fashionable. Several branches around Barcelona, include a particularly large one at Passeig de Gràcia 65 and another inside the L'Illa Diagonal shopping mall.
✉ **Avinguda Portal de l'Àngel 5** ☎ **93 317 69 85** 🚇 **Catalunya**

La Manual Alpargatera
This shop has been making traditional Spanish espadrilles, with esparto soles, by hand since 1910. Their footwear has been worn by celebrities as diverse as Michael Douglas, Jack Nicholson and the Pope.
✉ **Carrer Avinyó 7** ☎ **93 301 01 72** 🚇 **Jaume I, Liceu**

Mokuba
A specialist shop which seems dominated by the rows and rows of ribbons and braids. It must be every haberdasher's dream to come to a place like this!
✉ **Carrer Consell de Cent 329** ☎ **93 488 12 77** 🚇 **Universitat**

Muxart Chic
This is a vibrant shop showcasing shoes by Barcelonan shoe designer, Muxart.
✉ **Carrer Roselló 230**

☎ **93 488 10 64** 🚇 **Provença, Diagonal**

Noel Barcelona
All the latest trends in footwear, from thigh boots to not-very-sensible-but-fun platform trainers.
✉ **Carrer Pelai 46** ☎ **93 317 86 38** 🚇 **Catalunya**

Pedro Alonso
This small shop with its gloves, fans and imitation jewellery, once catered mainly for stage performers, but today has a more diverse clientele.
✉ **Carrer Santa Anna 27** ☎ **93 317 60 85** 🚇 **Catalunya**

La Perla Gris
Lingerie, swimwear and corsetry from all the best brands.
✉ **Rambla Catalunya 112** ☎ **93 218 07 96** 🚇 **Diagonal, Provença**

Regia
This is Barcelona's prime perfumery and it even has its own small 'Perfume Museum' at the back of the shop, which may be visited by appointment.
✉ **Passeig de Gràcia 39** ☎ **93 216 01 21** 🚇 **Passeig de Gràcia**

Sole
Shoes, boots and sandals made of fine Moroccan and Spanish leather, including Spanish cowboy boots.
✉ **Carrer Ample 7** ☎ **93 301 69 84** 🚇 **Drassnes**

Zara
A nationwide chain of trendy fashion stores, popular with young shoppers.
✉ **Carrer Pelai 58** ☎ **93 301 09 78** 🚇 **Catalunya**

Streetwise
Barcelona has two main shopping areas. The Ciutat Vella contains many traditional shops as well as more off-beat boutiques. Try Carrer Banys Nous for arts and antique shops; Carrer Petritxol for home accessories and gift ideas; Carrer Portaferrissa and Carrer Portal de l'Angel for fashion and shoes. The Eixample's three main streets – Passeig de Gràcia, Rambla de Catalunya and the Diagonal – are a showcase for the latest in fashion and design.

Art, Crafts, Gifts & Design

Museum Shops

Barcelona's museum shops stock a high-quality selection of goods such as designer items, gifts and arty souvenirs. Fundació Miró or Museu Picasso both offer a large array of fine products devoted to these artists; La Pedrera shows *Modernista* jewellery and other Gaudí-inspired gifts; and MACBA is one of the main outlets for the quality 'Made in Barcelona' range of gifts and souvenirs.

Ajupa't

Hidden through a low, arched doorway, this small shop is a veritable treasure trove of original gift ideas, including chunky local jewellery, handicrafts, papier mâché and paper goods.

✉ **Carrer València 261** ☎ **93 488 24 13** Ⓜ **Passeig de Gràcia**

Art Escudellers

Huge emporium selling Spanish pottery and ceramics, from factory pieces to arty individual designs. In the basement are a wine cellar, delicatessen and wine bar where you can sample the local products.

✉ **Carrer Escudellers 23** ☎ **93 412 68 01** 🕐 **Daily 11–11** Ⓜ **Liceu, Drassanes**

Aspectos

Fascinating design gallery featuring weird and wonderful furniture and ornaments from Spanish designers.

✉ **Carrer Rec 28** ☎ **933 19 52 85** Ⓜ **Jaume I**

Atalanta Manufactura

Just behind Santa Maria del Mar, a husband-and-wife team from Madrid paint the most beautiful silk scarves, often inspired by local art and architecture. They also undertake personalised designs upon request.

✉ **Passeig del Born 10** ☎ **93 268 37 02**

BD Ediciones de Diseno

Winner of several awards for its state-of-the-art furniture and household design, beautifully displayed in a striking *Modernista* house by Domènech i Montaner.

✉ **Carrer Mallorca 291** ☎ **93 458 69 09** Ⓜ **Diagonal**

Centre Catal d'Artesania

The impressive centre of Catalan handicrafts contains some of the finest ceramics, jewellery, textiles, sculptures and glassware of the region.

✉ **Passeig de Gràcia 55** ☎ **93 467 46 60** Ⓜ **Passeig de Gràcia**

Cereria Subirà

The oldest shop in the city, founded in 1761, selling candles ancient and modern, religious and profane.

✉ **Baixada Llibreteria 7** ☎ **93 315 26 06** Ⓜ **Jaume I**

Coses de Casa

Handmade patchwork quilts and fabrics, including the distinctive Mallorcan *roba de llengües* (literally 'cloth of tongues'), striking for its red, blue or green zigzag patterns.

✉ **Plaça Sant Josep Oriol 5** ☎ **93 302 73 28** Ⓜ **Jaume I**

Germanes Garcia

Wickerwork of all shapes and sizes tumbles out of this village-style shop into the streets of the Old City.

✉ **Carrer Banys Nous 15** ☎ **93 318 66 46** Ⓜ **Liceu**

Ici et La

Interesting, exotic shop stocking new furniture, lighting and accessories by young Spanish designers.

✉ **Plaça Santa Maria del Mar 2** ☎ **93 268 11 67** Ⓜ **Diagonal**

D Barcelona

A wide choice of gifts and avant-garde household items, together with temporary exhibitions presenting the work of young designers as well as some of the more established names.

✉ **Avinguda Diagonal 367**
☎ 93 216 03 46 🚇 Diagonal

Dos I Una
The first design shop in Barcelona – a tiny treasure trove of gadgets and unusual gift ideas.
✉ **Carrer Rosselló 275** ☎ 93 217 70 32 🚇 Diagonal

Galeria Maeght
Come to these specialists in 20th-century art, design and photography for posters, prints and other graphic works. Upstairs is a prestigious art gallery.
✉ **Carrer Montcada 25** ☎ 93 301 42 54 🚇 Liceu, Jaume I

El Ingenio
Children adore this old-fashioned magic shop, where carnival masks and costumes are created in a workshop at the back. Come here for free magic shows on Thursday afternoons.
✉ **Carrer Rauric 6** ☎ 93 317 71 38 🚇 Liceu

Itaca
Folk pottery and crafted glassware from all parts of Spain, Mexico and Morocco.
✉ **Carrer Ferran 24–26** ☎ 93 301 30 44 🚇 Liceu

La Manual Alpargatera
All kinds of handmade, straw woven items, including hats, bags and their speciality, espadrilles.
✉ **Carrer Avinyá 7** ☎ 93 301 01 72 🚇 Liceu, Jaume I

Museu Picasso
One of Barcelona's many notable museum shops reflecting the city's connections with this major 20th century artist (➤ 106, panel).

✉ **Carrer Montcada 15** ☎ 93 319 63 10 🚇 Jaume I

Pilma
This is an expensive store specialising in top-name furniture, textiles, household items and accessories.
✉ **Avinguda Diagonal 403** ☎ 93 416 13 99 🚇 Diagonal

Poble Espanyol
Over 60 art and craft shops in a reproduction 'Spanish Village' (➤ 22) selling traditional wares from all corners of Spain (➤ panel).
✉ **Carrer Marques de Comillas s/n** ☎ 93 325 78 66 🚇 13, 61

Puzzlemanía
Over a thousand different jigsaw puzzles.
✉ **Carrer Diputació 225** ☎ 93 451 58 03 🚇 Universitat

El Rey de la Màgica
Stepping inside this extraordinary magic shop, founded in 1881 and the oldest in Spain, is like entering another world.
✉ **Carrer la Princessa 11** ☎ 93 319 73 93 🚇 Jaume I

Sala Parés
Barcelona's finest gallery – specialist in 19th- and 20th-century paintings, drawings and sculptures.
✉ **Carrer Pextritxol 5** ☎ 93 318 70 20 🚇 Catalunya

Vinçon
This design 'department store' is Barcelona's answer to Terance Conran. Trendy yet practical household articles at accessible prices. Won the National Design Prize in 1995.
✉ **Passeig de Gràcia 96** ☎ 93 215 60 50 🚇 Passeig de Gràcia

Poble Espanyol
This purpose-built 'Spanish Village' (➤ 22), with its methodically numbered shops and studios demonstrating local craft-making skills, offers a comprehensive range of Spanish and Mallorçan souvenirs. On sale are fine glassware, wood-carvings, Lladro porcelain, decorative goldware and jewellery together with flamenco costumes, guitars, fans and castanets.

Antiques, Books & Music

Local Alternative to St Valentine's Day

To celebrate the day of Sant Jordi (St George), Catalonia's patron saint, couples express their love by exchanging gifts: roses for the woman and a book for the man. The Ramblas are lined with temporary bookstalls, and half of Catalonia's annual book sales take place on this day.

Angel Batlle

Antiquarian books, old maps, prints and nautical charts are in abundance here.

✉ **Carrer Palla 23** ☎ **93 301 58 84** Ⓜ **Liceu**

L'Arca de l'Avia

An Aladdin's cave of antique cottons, linens, silks. Beautiful, albeit pricey, patchwork eiderdowns and beaded bags.

✉ **Carrer Banys Nous 20** ☎ **93 302 15 98** Ⓜ **Liceu**

Artur Ramon Anticuario

Two adjacent premises displaying a wide array of antique paintings, sculpture and decorative arts.

✉ **Carrer de la Palla 23–25** ☎ **93 302 59 70** Ⓜ **Jaume I**

Born Subastas

This auction house holds sales every other week, but it's always an interesting place in which to browse.

✉ **Carrer Bonaire 5** ☎ **93 268 34 55** Ⓜ **Jaume I, Barceloneta**

Bulevard dels Antiquaris

Spacious mall containing over 70 shops for art-lovers and antique collectors. Don't miss Ivan's (☎ **93 215 94 09**), with its porcelain doll collection, or Turn of the Century (☎ **93 215 94 63**) for decorative *Modernista* pieces.

✉ **Passeig de Gràcia 55** ☎ **93 215 44 99** Ⓜ **Passeig de Gràcia**

Casa Beethoven

Founded in 1915, this shop carries scores and sheet music. Specialising in pieces by Spanish and Catalan composers.

✉ **La Rambla 97** ☎ **93 301 48 26** Ⓜ **Liceu**

Castelló

A chain of record shops. Carrer Tallers 3 has a huge selection of pop, rock, jazz, blues and soul. No 7 is devoted to classical music.

✉ **Carrer Tallers 3 & 7** ☎ **93 302 59 46** Ⓜ **Catalunya**

FNAC

A book megastore inside El Triangle shopping mall. Two floors of books, videos, CDs, computers, PlayStations, video games and magazines from all over the world.

✉ **Plaça Catalunya** ☎ **93 344 18 00** Ⓒ **Mon–Sat 10–10** Ⓜ **Catalunya**

Jordi Capell – Cooperative d'Arquitectes

Specialist bookshop for architecture and design, in the basement of the College of Architects.

✉ **Plaça Nova 5** ☎ **93 481 35 60** Ⓜ **Jaume I, Liceu**

Laie

The best selection of English-language books in Barcelona, including travel maps and guides. Has a café upstairs.

✉ **Carrer Pau Claris 85** ☎ **93 318 17 39** Ⓒ **Café: Mon– Sat 9–1** Ⓜ **Urquinaona**

Musical Emporium

A small shop (despite its grand name) that specialises in stringed musical instruments, especially classical guitars.

✉ **La Rambla 129** ☎ **93 317 63 38** Ⓜ **Catalunya**

Norma Comics

Barcelona's largest comic shop sells a huge variety of comics from many different genres.

✉ **Carrer Rosello 237** ☎ **93 237 40 56** Ⓜ **Diagonal**

Food & Drink

Brunells Pastisseria

Appears in the *Guinness Book of Records* for making Spain's biggest Easter egg. Try the *torró* (traditional almond fudge), *roques de Montserrat* (meringues) and *carquinyolis* (soft almond biscuits).

✉ **Carrer Princesa 22** ☎ **93 319 68 25** 🚇 **Jaume I**

Casa Gispert

Dried fruits, spices, cocoa, coffee, and nuts which are toasted daily in a traditional oak-fired oven.

✉ **Carrer Sombrerers 23** ☎ **93 319 75 35** 🚇 **Jaume I**

Colmado Quillez

Barcelona's most famous traditional grocery store, selling an exceptional array of tinned foods, preserves, cold meats and wines.

✉ **Rambla de Catalunya 63** ☎ **93 215 23 56** 🚇 **Passeig de Gràcia**

Escribà Patisseries

Many important *Modernista* artists collaborated on the design of this shop. Celebrated for its monumental chocolate cakes.

✉ **La Rambla 83** ☎ **93 301 60 27** 🚇 **Liceu**

Formatería Cirera

A little out of the way but worth a visit, this specialist cheese store sells many unusual Spanish cheeses.

✉ **Carrer Cera 45** ☎ **93 441 07 59** 🚇 **Sant Antoni**

Forn de Pa Sant Jordi

The long queue outside this bakery is testimony to its excellence. Be sure to taste their *tortellet de cabell d'angel*, a crumbly tart filled with 'angel's hair' (spun candied fruit).

✉ **Carrer Llibreteria 8** ☎ **93 310 40 16** 🚇 **Jaume I**

Jamón Jamón

As the name suggests, this shop sells hams and other cold cuts (▶ panel). There is also a restaurant upstairs.

✉ **Carrer Mestre Nicolau 4** 🚌 **41**

Mel Viadiu

Just about every product in this shop is made with honey from the Caldes de Montbui, near Barcelona.

✉ **Carrer Comtal 20** ☎ **93 317 04 23** 🚇 **Urquinaona**

Murrià

This *Modernista* store first opened in 1898, and today sells a wide assortment of cheeses, *charcuterie* and other delicacies.

✉ **Carrer Roger de Llúria 85** ☎ **93 215 57 89** 🚇 **Passeig de Gràcia**

Planelles-Donat

Specialists in Spanish nougats, made by artisanal methods. Try the home-made ice creams, too.

✉ **Avinguda Portal de l'Àngel 25 and 27** ☎ **93 317 34 39** 🚇 **Catalunya**

Vins i Caves La Catedral

Wines from all over Spain, with a particularly strong selection from Catalonia.

✉ **Plaça de Ramon Berenguer el Gran 1** ☎ **93 319 07 27** 🚇 **Jaume I**

Xampany

The only shop devoted solely to the sale of *cava* (sparkling wine). More than 100 varieties to choose from.

✉ **Carrer València 200** ☎ **93 453 93 38** 🚇 **Passeig de Gràcia**

Jamón Jamón

Spain is famous for its hams, its cured and smoked meats and its sausages. The quality of ham varies considerably. Expect to pay up to €84 a kilo for the best, traditionally cured *jamón Jabugo*. Look out also for the classic, cheaper haunches of *jamón serrano* and *jamón Iberico*, and be sure to try *salchichón*, piquant *chorizo*, Catalan *botifarra* and spicy Mallorcan *sobresada* sausages.

Children's Attractions

Parks for Children

Most city parks have attractions for children: Parc de l'Espanya Industrial (► 65) has a giant dragon slide and a small boating lake; Parc del Laberint (► 66–67) has a topiary maze; Turó Parc holds puppet shows at noon on Sundays in summer; Parc del Castell de l'Oreneta offers miniature train and pony rides on Sunday mornings in summer; Parc de la Ciutadella (► 64) contains several play areas, a small boating lake and a zoo.

L'Aquàrium

One of Barcelona's most recent children's attractions, and the largest aquarium in Europe. As well as the aquatic life on display, the highlight for most children is the impressive 80m-long tunnel which runs straight through the middle of the shark tank (► 72).

✉ Moll d'Espanya, Port Vell
☎ 93 221 74 74 🕐 Jul–Aug 9:30AM–11PM; Jun–Sep weekends 9:30AM–9:30PM; rest of the year 9:30AM–9PM 🔗 Good
🚇 Barceloneta, Drassanes
💰 Very expensive

Beaches

With so much to see and do, it is easy to forget the city's 4km of clean, sandy beaches with playgrounds, palm-lined promenades and shower facilities. There is also very good access for people with disabilities.

✉ Platja de Barceloneta, Nova Icària, Bogatell and La Nova Mar Bella 🚇 Ciutadella, Selva de Mar

Bus Turístic

A circuit around the city on the Bus Turístic with 18 stops at key points of interest is an enjoyable way for children to see the sights. There are two routes, the northern (red) and southern (blue), and you can hop on and off and change routes as often as you like. The ticket also gives discounts to various attractions as well as the Golondrinas pleasure boats (► below) and the Tibidabo tram.

✉ Plaça de Catalunya (or any of its 18 stops) 🕐 First bus leaves Plaça de Catalunya at 9AM 🚇 Catalunya
❓ Tickets for 1 day or 2 days.

Golondrinas (Pleasure Boats, ► 72)

A pleasure boat tour of the old harbour or the Port Olímpic is fun for all the family and provides a breath of fresh sea air. The most fun is a trip out to the breakwater on one of the old wooden 'swallow boats', which have been operating since 1888.

✉ Moll de les Drassanes Plaça Portal de la Pau
☎ 93 442 31 06
🕐 Harbour trips operate regularly in summer and once an hour on winter weekends. Trips to the Port Olímpic in a modern covered vessel take place throughout the year, several times daily from Easter to October. 🚇 Drassanes
💰 Moderate

Illa de Fantasia

Europe's largest water park is just north of Barcelona on the coast near Mataró. Daily bus from Estació de Sants and Plaça Universitat (☎ 93 451 27 72 for bus details).

✉ Carrer Vilassar de Dalt
☎ 93 751 45 53 🕐 Jun to mid-Sep 10–7 💰 Very expensive

IMAX Cinema

Older children will enjoy the nature films on IMAX's giant 3-D screen (► 72).

✉ Moll d'Espanya, Port Vell
☎ 93 225 11 11
🚇 Barceloneta, Drassanes

Museu de la Ciència

The Museu de la Ciència (Science Museum) is one of Barcelona's most popular museums, and the most important science museum in Spain. Among the attractions, children can lift a hippopotamus, ride on a human gyroscope, feel an earthquake and watch the world turn. Special one-hour guided sessions are given daily. Phone for details.

✉ Carrer Teodor Roviralta 55 ☎ 93 212 60 50 🕐 Tue–Sun 10AM–8PM. Closed Mon. Planetarium shows: Tue–Fri 1, 6; weekends every 45 mins starting at 11.15 ♿ Good 🚇 Avinguda Tibidabo 🚌 17, 22, 58, 60, 73, 85 🚌 Moderate

Museu de la Cera
The Waxwork Museum is ideal for a rainy day. Pinocchio, Superman and other heroes are all here and don't miss the horror hall!

✉ Passeig de la Banca, 7 ☎ 93 317 26 49 🕐 Jul–Sep daily 10–10. Oct–Jun Mon–Fri 10–1:30, 4–7:30; weekends & hols 11–2, 4:30–8 🚇 Drassanes, Liceu 🚌 Expensive

Museu del Futbol Club Barcelona (► 55)
A must for all children who are keen on football at this holiest of shrines to the glorious game.

✉ Nou Camp – Gate 7 or 9 Carrer Aristides Maillol ☎ 93 496 36 00 🕐 Mon–Sat 10–6:30; Sun and hols 10–2 🍴 Café (£)

Parc Zoològic
Spain's top zoo boasts over 7,000 animals of 500 different species including its main celebrity, Copito de Nieve (Snowflake), the world's only captive albino gorilla. There is also a zoo for the under-fives, where children can stroke farm animals and pets, and a dolphinarium which stages spectacular shows (🕐 Mon–Fri 11:30, 1:30, 4, Sat, Sun and hols 12, 1:30, 4).

✉ Parc de la Ciutadella ☎ 93 225 67 80 🕐 Summer daily 9:30AM–7:30PM; Winter daily 10–5 ♿ Good 🚇 Ciutadella 🚌 Very expensive

Poble Espanyol (► 22)
Children enjoy this open-air 'museum', especially on *festa* days.

Port Aventura
Catalonia's answer to Disneyland, and reputedly one of Europe's biggest and best theme parks (► panel) has recently been taken over by Universal Studios. Part of their revamped attractions is the introduction of cartoon characters and a ride called *Sea Odyssey*, a graphic simulated underwater journey with computer animation.

✉ Port Aventura, near Salou ☎ 902 20 22 20 🕐 Mar–Oct Mon–Fri 10–7, Sat and Sun 10–10; mid-June to mid-Sep daily 10–2AM ♿ Good 🚈 Port Aventura 🚌 Expensive

Tibidabo Amusement Park
The charm of this recently renovated fairground, nicknamed *La Muntanya Màgica* (The Magic Mountain), is its authentic, old-fashioned funfair atmosphere with carousels, bumper cars, a hall of mirrors and a breathtaking open ferris wheel (► 73). Getting there, on the ancient Tramvia Blau tramline and then by funicular, is exciting in itself.

✉ Parc d'Atraccions del Tibidabo, Plaça Tibidabo 3–4 ☎ 93 211 79 42 🕐 Call for opening times. Closed mid-Sep to Mar 🚈 Funicular del Tibidabo 🚌 Moderate

Port Aventura
This spectacular theme park south of Barcelona on the Costa Daurada promises an entertaining day out for all the family with special shops, restaurants, shows and fairground rides in exotic Mexican, Chinese, Polynesian, Wild Western and Mediterranean settings. Top attractions are the 'typhoon' corkscrew ride and the eight 360° loops of the Dragon Khan, Europe's largest roller-coaster.

Bars, Clubs & Live Music

When in Spain ...
Barcelonans are night owls, especially on Thursdays, Fridays and Saturdays. The evening begins around 8:30PM with a *passeig* (promenade), followed by *tapas* in a local bar, then dinner at around 10:30PM. Opera, ballet and concerts usually start at 9PM, and the theatre at 10PM. After midnight, music bars become crowded. Around 3AM, clubs and discos fill up and the famous Barcelonan night movement – *la movida* – sweeps across the city until dawn.

Bikini
One of Barcelona's best night spots, with a popular rock/disco club, a Latin-American salsa room and a classy cocktail lounge.
✉ **Carrer Deu i Mata 105** ☎ **93 322 08 00** 🕓 **Tue–Sat from midnight** 🚇 **Les Corts**

La Bolsa
An unusual bar which lets you play the market at 'The Stock Exchange', where the drink prices fluctuate according to a drink's popularity that night.
✉ **Carrer Tuset 17** ☎ **93 202 26 35** 🚇 **Gràcia**

Buena Vista
Barcelona's most authentic salsa club, with free classes on Wed and Thu at 10:30PM and dancing partners at weekends to take you through the cha-cha-cha.
✉ **Carrer Rosselló 217** ☎ **93 237 65 28** 🕓 **Wed–Thu 10:30PM–4AM, Fri and Sat 11PM–5:30 AM, Sun 8PM–1AM** 🚇 **Diagonal**

La Cova del Drac
The city's top jazz venue.
✉ **Carrer Vallmajor 33** ☎ **93 200 70 32** 🕓 **Closed Sun and Mon** 🚇 **Muntaner**

Estadi Olímpic
Main venue for mega-star pop concerts. Tickets best bought through record shops.
✉ **Passeig Olímpic** ☎ **93 425 49 49** 🚇 **61**

Harlem Jazz Club
Small, but very atmospheric jazz club – has long been a favourite of jazz aficionados.
✉ **Carrer Comtessa de Sobradiel 8** ☎ **93 310 07 55** 🕓 **Tue–Sun 8PM–4AM** 🚇 **Jaume I**

Jamboree
A choice nightspot for blues, soul, jazz, funk and occasional hip-hop live bands. Upstairs is Los Tarantos, a laid-back bar with predominantly Spanish music.
✉ **Plaça Reial** ☎ **93 301 75 64** 🕓 **Daily from 11PM** 🚇 **Liceu**

Marsella
In stark contrast to Barcelona's many design bars, this unspoiled, traditional bar in the Barri Xines has been run by the same family for five generations and still serves locally made absinthe (*absenta*).
✉ **Carrer Sant Pau** ☎ **No phone** 🕓 **Mon–Thu 9PM–2:30AM, Fri–Sun 5PM–3:30AM** 🚇 **Liceu**

Nayandei Boîte
The biggest of the discos on the roof terrace of the Maremagnum complex. The Nayadei Boîte is always teeming with teenagers.
✉ **Maremagnum, Port Vell** ☎ **93 225 80 10** 🕓 **Mon–Sat 9PM–5AM, Sun 6PM–5AM** 🚇 **Barceloneta, Drassanes**

Nick Havanna
One of Barcelona's most talked-about bars, thanks to its sensational design. Go late.
✉ **Carrer Rosselló 208** ☎ **93 215 65 91** 🕓 **Daily 11PM–4AM (5AM Fri and Sat)** 🚇 **Diagonal**

Nitsa
Young clubbers flock to this kitsch 70s-style club at weekends, to dance to the non-stop techno-thump of top international DJs on a revolving steel dance-floor, or to relax in the salsa-playing

lounge bar upstairs.

✉ Plaça Joan Llongueres 1–3
☎ 93 458 62 50 ⏰ Thu–Sat
midnight–6AM 🚇 17, 39, 45, 57,
59, 64

Otto Zutz

One of the smartest clubs in
town, and a *tour de force* of
design, with its clever
lighting and metal staircases
and galleries. Dress smartly
and arrive after midnight.

✉ Carrer Lincoln 15 ☎ 93
238 07 22 ⏰ Wed–Sun
midnight–6AM 🚇 Fontana,
Passeig de Gràcia

La Paloma

Foxtrots, tangos and boleros
are still *de rigueur* at the
city's famous dance hall.

✉ Carrer Tigre 27 ☎ 93 317
79 94 ⏰ Thu– Sun 6–9:30PM,
11:30PM–5AM 🚇 Universitat

Partycular

With its restaurant, disco,
beautiful terrace café and
rambling gardens on the
slopes of Tibidabo, this
sophisticated establishment
is a favourite summer venue,
despite the lengthy uphill
trek from the station.

✉ Avinguda Tibidabo 61
☎ 93 211 62 61 ⏰ Tue–Sun
7PM–3AM 🚇 Tibidabo

Pastis

Small, dimly lit bohemian
bar. Sip *pastis* accompanied
by Edith Piaf songs played
on a phonograph.

✉ Calle Santa Mònica 4 ☎
93 318 79 80 ⏰ Mon, Wed–Sun
7:30PM–2:30AM (Fri till 3:30AM);
closed Tue 🚇 Drassanes

La Terrazza

Summertime open-air club
on Montjuïc mountain,
behind Poble Espanyol. Gets
crowded around 3 or 4AM.

✉ Avinguda Montanyans,
Montjuïc ☎ 93 423 12 85
⏰ Fri–Sat midnight–6AM
🚇 61

Torres de Ávila

Design-bar in the Poble
Espanyol. Trance-techno
discos are staged here at
weekends and, in summer,
the rooftop terrace bars are
particularly magical.

✉ Avinguda Marquès de
Comillas, Poble Espanyol,
Montjuïc ☎ 93 424 93 09
⏰ Fri, Sat and Sun from 11PM
🚇 Espanya

Tres Torres

Beautiful gardens and an
elegant courtyard create a
sophisticated background for
a moneyed clientele. On
Thursday nights there is
often live jazz or blues.

✉ Via Augusta 300 ☎ 93 205
16 08 ⏰ Mon–Sat 7PM–3AM
🚇 Tres Torres

Up And Down

Barcelona's most exclusive
nightclub. 'Up'stairs, an
affluent, black-tie, post-opera
crowd dance, while
'down'stairs, their well-
dressed offspring enjoy
contemporary club music.

✉ Carrer Numància 179
☎ 93 205 51 94 ⏰ Disco:
Tue–Sat 12AM–5:30 or 6AM
🚇 Sants Estació ❓ Men
must wear a tie

Xampanyería Casablanca

Catalan champagne bar near
the Passeig de Gràcia
serving four kinds of house
cava by the glass as well as
a wide range of tasty *tapas*
snacks (➤ panel).

✉ Carrer Bonavista 6
☎ 93 237 63 99 ⏰ Thu–Sat
8PM–2:30AM; (3AM Fri & Sat)
🚇 Passeig de Gràcia

Barcelona's 'Bubbly'

Over 50 Spanish
companies produce
champagne. Look out for
Gramona, Mestres and
Torello labels. Catalan
champagne is called *cava*,
and champagne bars are
known as *xampanyerías*.
Most serve a limited
selection of house *cavas*
by the glass, *brut* or *brut
nature* (*brut* is slightly
sweeter), accompanied by
tapas. Xampanyet
(✉ Carrer Montcada 22),
Xampanyería Casablanca
and La Bodegueta del
Xampú (✉ Gran Via de
les Corts Catalanes 702)
are among the most
popular.

Theatre, Cinema, Music & Dance

Listings
For entertainment listings, the best source of local information is the magazine *Guía del Ocio*, which previews *La Semana de Barcelona* (This Week in Barcelona). Available from any newsstand, it gives full details (in Spanish) of film, theatre and musical events, and lists bars, restaurants and nightlife. *Informatiu Musical* and the monthly magazine *Barcelona en Música*, available free from tourist offices and record shops, are useful sources of concert information.

Auditori
Barcelona's auditorium was designed by the Spanish architect Rafael Moneo and opened in 1999 as the home of the city's symphony orchestra.
✉ **Carrer Lepant 150** ☎ **93 247 93 00** Ⓜ **Marina**

Centre Artesà Tradicionàrius
The Centre for Traditional Arts is devoted to the study, teaching and performance of traditional Catalan music and dance.
✉ **Travessera de Sant Antoni 6–8** ☎ **93 218 44 85** Ⓜ **Fontana**

Centre Cultural De La Fundació 'La Caixa'
Classical concerts in the splendid *Modernista* setting of Casa Macaya, designed by Puig i Cadalfach in 1901.
✉ **Passeig de Sant Joan 108** ☎ **93 458 89 07** Ⓜ **Verdaguer**

Filmoteca de la Generalitat De Catalunya
Barcelona's official film theatre shows three films a day. These are usually in VO (original version) ie, not in Spanish. There is also a children's programme at 5PM on Sundays.
✉ **Cinema Aquitania, Avinguda de Sarrià 31–33** ☎ **93 410 75 90** ⏲ **Performance: 5, 7:30 and 10PM. Closed hols and Aug** Ⓜ **Hospital Clinic**

Fundació Joan Miró
The Foundation Joan Miró is Spain's main centre for the development of contemporary music and stages a series of concerts (*Nit de Música* – Music Nights) during the summer.
✉ **Plaça Neptú, Parc de Montjuïc** ☎ **93 329 19 08** ⏲ **Jun–Sep** 🚌 **61**

Gran Teatre del Liceu
Gutted by fire in 1994 this opera house reopened in 1999. World-famous singers, including the Catalan diva Montserrat Caballé, have performed here.
✉ **La Rambla 51–59** ☎ **93 485 99 00** Ⓜ **Liceu**

IMAX Cinema (➤ 110)

Mercat de les Flors
Innovative dance, drama and music productions.
✉ **Carrer Lleida 59** ☎ **93 426 18 75** Ⓜ **Espanya**

Palau de la Música Calatána
Barcelona's main venue for classical music (➤ 59).
✉ **Carrer Sant Francesc de Paula 2** ☎ **93 268 10 00** ⏲ **Box office: Mon–Fri 10–9; Sat 3–9**

El Tablao de Carmen
Highly rated flamenco cabaret at the Poble Espanyol. Booking in advance is recommended.
✉ **Carrer Arcs 9, Poble Espanyol, Montjuïc** ☎ **93 325 68 95** ⏲ **Tue–Sun 8PM–1AM (2–3AM at weekends)** 🎭 **Shows Tue–Sun 9:30 . Also 11:30PM on Sat and Sun**

Teatre Nacional de Catalunya
Designed by local architect Ricard Bofill as the centrepiece of a new arts district, this theatre is a showcase for contemporary Catalan dance.
✉ **Plaça de les Arts 1** ☎ **93 306 57 06** Ⓜ **Glòries**

Sport

Spectator Sports

American Football
Estadi Olímpic
The 'Barcelona Dragons' play against other teams in the World League on Sundays, April–June. Buy tickets on the day at the stadium.
✉ **Passeig Olímpic 17–19**
☎ **93 425 49 49** 🚌 **61**

Basketball
Joventut
Joventut play league games on Sunday evenings, and European and Spanish Cup matches midweek, September–May. Book tickets in advance.
✉ **Avinguda Alfons XIII-Carrer Ponent 143–161, Badalona**
☎ **93 460 20 40** Ⓜ **Gorg**

Bullfighting
Plaça De Toros Monumental
The Bullring and its museum (▶ 56) are open only during the bullfighting season (Apr–Sep). Reserve tickets in advance (☎ 93 453 38 21).
✉ **Grand Via de les Corts Catalanes 749** ☎ **93 245 58 04** Ⓜ **Monumental**

Football
Nou Camp – FC Barcelona
No visit to Barcelona is complete without a visit to Nou Camp, Europe's largest stadium (seating 120,000), and its museum (▶ 55).
✉ **Avinguda Aristides Maillol. Museum: Gate 7 or 9** ☎ **93 496 36 00** Ⓜ **Collblanc, Maria Cristina**

Ice Hockey
FC Barcelona Pista de Gel
Barcelona's only professional ice-hockey team. On non-match days, the rink is open

to the public.
✉ **Avinguda de Joan XXIII**
☎ **93 496 36 30** Ⓜ **Maria Cristina, Collblanc**

Participatory Sports

Cycling
Un Cotxe Menys
Escorted daytime and evening cycle tours around the city (▶ 75).
✉ **Carrer Esparteria 3** ☎ **93 268 21 05** Ⓜ **Jaume 1**

Golf
El Prat Golf Club
Just 15km outside Barcelona. You will need to present a membership card of a nationally federated club before you can play here. Phone or write in advance.
✉ **Apartado de Correus 10, 08820 El Prat de Llobregat**
☎ **93 379 02 78**

Horse riding
Hípica Severino de Sant Cugat
Riding lessons and treks through the countryside around Sant Cugat and the Sierra de Collserola.
✉ **Carrer Princep, Sant Cugat del Vallès** ☎ **93 674 11 40**

Sailing
Centre Municipal de Vela
Short weekend courses in sailing and windsurfing.
✉ **Moll de Gregal, Port Olímpic** ☎ **93 222 14 99**
Ⓜ **Ciutadella**

Tennis
Vall Parc Club
Fourteen open-air tennis courts on Tibidabo. Racquets (not balls) for hire.
✉ **Carretera Sant Cugat s/n**
☎ **93 212 67 89** 🚌 **A6**

Tickets
Purchase tickets from the relevant box office or from several ticket offices and booths (*taquillas*) throughout the city. The Centre d'Informació (✉ Palau de la Virreina, Rambla Sant Josep 99 ☎ 902 10 12 12 🕐 Mon–Thu 8–2:30, Fri 8–2:30, 4:30–7:30) sells tickets for all Ajuntament-sponsored performances. Credit card bookings can be made by phone at other times. The booth on the corner of Carrer Aribau and Gran Via (🕐 Mon-Sat 10:30–1:30, 4–7:30) sells tickets for major pop concerts and most theatre productions.

What's On When

Giants & Big Heads

Dancing giants, dragons, *capgrossos* (big heads) and demons play an important part in traditional Catalan folklore. They feature in many *festes*, especially *La Mercè*, with its eccentric *Ball de Gegants*, a dance of costumed 5m-high giants and grinning papier-mâché 'big heads' which is performed from Drassanes to Ciutadella, and the *Corre Foc* (Fire-Running), when devils and dragons scatter firecrackers in the Ciutat Vella.

January

Reis Mags (5–6 Jan): the Three Kings arrive by boat, then tour the city, showering the crowds with sweets.

February

Santa Eulàlia (12–19 Feb): a series of musical events in honour of one of the city's patron saints.
Carnestoltes: one week of pre-Lenten carnival celebrations and costumed processions come to an end on Ash Wednesday with the symbolic burial of a sardine.

March

Sant Medir de Gràcia (3 Mar): procession of traditionally dressed horsemen from Gràcia who ride over Collserola to the Hermitage of Sant Medir (Saint of Broad Beans) for a bean-feast.

March/April

Setmana Santa: religious services and celebrations for Easter Week include a solemn procession from the church of Sant Augustì on Good Friday. Easter celebrations are particularly important in the areas of the city settled by Spaniards from Andalucia and southern Spain.

April

Sant Jordi (23 Apr): the Catalan alternative to St Valentine's Day (➤ 108, panel).

May

Festa de la Bicicleta (one Sun in May): join the Mayor and 15,000 others on a cycle-ride around the city, in an effort to encourage fewer cars.

June

Midsummer (23–24 June) is a good excuse for huge-scale partying and spectacular fireworks.
Trobada Castellera (mid-June): displays of human-tower building.
International Film Festival (last two weeks)
Flamenco Festival (last two weeks).
Festival del Grec; arts festival (end Jun–Aug).

July

Aplec de la Sardana, Olot; the biggest *Sardana* dancing festival in Catalonia.

August

Festa Major de Gràcia (3rd week of Aug): a popular festival of music, dancing and street celebrations in the Gràcia district (➤ 44–45).

September

Diada de Catalunya (11 Sep): Catalonia's National Day does not mark a victory, but the taking of the city by Felipe V in 1714.
La Mercè (20–24 Sep): boisterous parades and spectacles featuring giants, devils, dragons, big heads and musically choreographed fireworks (➤ panel).
Festa Major de la Barceloneta (1–15 Oct): one of the liveliest district *festes*, with processions and dancing on the beach every night.

October

International Jazz Festival.

December

Christmas festivities include a craft fair outside the cathedral (6–23 Dec) and a crib in Plaça Sant Jaume.

Practical Matters

Above: *a busy bus stop in Plaça de Catalunya*
Below: *the* Bus Turístic *connects the major attractions*

TIME DIFFERENCES

GMT 12 noon	Barcelona 1PM	Germany 1PM	USA (NY) 7AM	Netherlands 1PM	Spain 1PM

BEFORE YOU GO

WHAT YOU NEED

- ● Required
- ○ Suggested
- ▲ Not required

	UK	Germany	USA	Netherlands	Spain
Passport/National Identity Card	●	●	●	●	●
Visa	▲	▲	▲	▲	▲
Onward or Return Ticket	▲	▲	▲	▲	▲
Health Inoculations	▲	▲	▲	▲	▲
Health Documentation (► 123)	●	●	●	●	●
Travel Insurance	○	○	○	○	○
Driving Licence (national with Spanish translation or International)	●	●	●	●	●
Car Insurance Certificate (if own car)	●	●	●	●	●
Car registration document (if own car)	●	●	●	●	●

WHEN TO GO

Barcelona

| ■ High season |
| □ Low season |

14°C	15°C	17°C	19°C	22°C	25°C	29°C	29°C	27°C	23°C	18°C	15°C
JAN	FEB	MAR	APR	MAY	JUN	JUL	AUG	SEP	OCT	NOV	DEC

Wet   Cloud   Sun   Sunshine & showers

TOURIST OFFICES

In the UK
Spanish Tourist Office
22–23 Manchester Square
London W1M 5AP
☎ (020) 7486 8077
Fax: (020) 7486 8034
Brochureline:
(0900) 669920

In the USA
Tourist Office of Spain
666 Fifth Avenue (35th floor)
New York
NY 10103
☎ (212) 265-8822
Fax: (212) 265-8864

Tourist Office of Spain
8383 Wilshire Boulevard
Suite 960
Beverley Hills
CA 90211
☎ (323) 658-7192
Fax: (323) 658-1061

CITY POLICE (POLICÍA MUNICIPAL) 092

NATIONAL POLICE (POLICÍA NACIONAL) 091

FIRE (BOMBEROS) 080

AMBULANCE (AMBULÀNCIA) 061

WHEN YOU ARE THERE

ARRIVING

Spain's national airline, Iberia, has scheduled flights to Barcelona's El Prat de Llobregat Airport from major Spanish and European cities. The city is served by over 30 international airlines including BA, Delta, KLM, Lufthansa and Virgin Express, and has direct flights to more than 80 international destinations.

El Prat de Llobregat Airport Kilometres to city centre	Journey times
	🚇 20 minutes
	🚌 40 minutes
12 kilometres	🚗 30 minutes

Estacio de França Railway Station Near Barceloneta	Journey times
	🚇 available
	🚌 available
Near centre	🚗 available

MONEY

The euro is the official currency of Spain.
Euro banknotes and coins were introduced in January 2002. Spain's former currency, the peseta, went out of circulation in early 2002.
Banknotes are in denominations of 5, 10, 20, 50, 100, 200 and 500 euros; coins are in denominations of 1, 2, 5, 10, 20 and 50 cents, and 1 and 2 euros.
Euro traveller's cheques are widely accepted, as are major credit cards. Credit and debit cards can also be used for withdrawing euro notes from ATMs.

TIME

 Like the rest of Spain, Catalonia is one hour ahead of Greenwich Mean Time (GMT+1), except from late March to late October, when summer time (GMT+2) operates.

CUSTOMS

 YES
From another EU country for personal use (guidelines)
800 cigarettes, 200 cigars, 1 kilogram of tobacco
10 litres of spirits (over 22%)
20 litres of aperitifs
90 litres of wine, of which 60 litres can be sparkling wine
110 litres of beer

From a non-EU country for your personal use, the allowances are:
200 cigarettes OR
50 cigars OR 250 grams of tobacco
1 litre of spirits (over 22%)
2 litres of intermediary products (eg sherry) and sparkling wine
2 litres of still wine
50 grams of perfume
0.25 litres of eau de toilette
The value limit for goods is 175 euros

Travellers under 17 years of age are not entitled to the tobacco and alcohol allowances.

 NO
Drugs, firearms, ammunition, offensive weapons, obscene material, unlicensed animals.

UK
93 366 62 00

Germany
93 292 100 0

USA
93 280 22 27

Netherlands
93 410 62 10

France
93 270 30 00

WHEN YOU ARE THERE

TOURIST OFFICES

Turisme de Barcelona
- Plaça de Catalunya 17
  ☎ 906 30 12 82 (local) or
  93 368 97 30 (international)
  ⏰ Daily 9–9

The main tourist office is situated beneath Plaça de Catalunya. Services include hotel reservations, currency exchange, walking tours and theatre and concert tickets.

There are branches of the city tourist office on the ground floor of the city hall and at the Sants railway station.

- Plaça Sant Jaume I
  ⏰ Mon–Sat 10–8, Sun 10–2
- Sants Railway Station (Estació de Sants)
  ⏰ Mon–Fri 8–8, Sat–Sun 8–2

There are also tourist information offices in the airport arrival halls, open daily 9–9.

Turisme de Catalunya
- Palau Robert
  Passeig de Gràcia 105
  ☎ 93 238 40 00
  ⏰ Mon–Sat 10–7, Sun 10–2

In summer, information booths can be found at Sagrada Família and La Rambla. In the Barrí Gòtic, you may also come across uniformed tourist officials, known as 'Red Jackets'.

NATIONAL HOLIDAYS

J	F	M	A	M	J	J	A	S	O	N	D
2		1(2)	(2)	(1)1	(1)1		1	2	1	1	4

1 Jan	New Year's Day
6 Jan	Three Kings
19 Mar	Sant Josep
Mar/Apr	Good Friday, Easter Monday
1 May	Labour Day
May/Jun	Whit Monday
24 Jun	St John
15 Aug	Assumption
11 Sep	Catalan National Day
24 Sep	Our Lady of Mercy
12 Oct	Hispanitat
1 Nov	All Saints' Day
6 Dec	Constitution Day
8 Dec	Feast of the Immaculate Conception
25 Dec	Christmas
26 Dec	Sant Esteve

OPENING HOURS

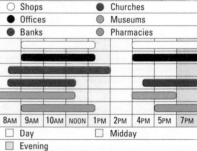

- ○ Shops
- ● Offices
- ● Banks
- ● Churches
- ◐ Museums
- ◐ Pharmacies

| 8AM | 9AM | 10AM | NOON | 1PM | 2PM | 4PM | 5PM | 7PM |

- ☐ Day
- ☐ Midday
- ☐ Evening

Large department stores and supermarkets may open outside these times, especially in summer. Business hours also vary depending on the season, with many companies working *horas intensivas* in summer, from 8–3. Banks generally close on Saturdays, although some main branches open in the morning 8:30–12:30. Outside banking hours, money-exchange facilities are available at the airport and Sants railway station. Some *barris* (districts) also have their own separate feast days, when some shops and offices may close.

DRIVE ON THE
RIGHT

TOILETS
FREE

PUBLIC TRANSPORT

Metro The metro is the easiest and fastest way of moving around the city. There are two different underground train systems, the Metro with its five lines identified by number and colour, and the FGC (☎ 93 205 15 15) with two lines in Barcelona and four more lines going to nearby towns.

Buses Barcelona has an excellent bus network; pick up a free plan from any tourist office. Timetables are also shown at individual bus stops. Buses run 5:30AM–11PM. At night there is a *Nitbus* with routes centred on Plaça de Catalunya. Throughout the year the *Bus Turistic*, a hop-on-hop-off service, circuits the main city sights.

Trains The Spanish railway system, RENFE, runs trains from Barcelona to all the major cities in Spain and some outside. Many main-line trains stop at the underground stations at Passeig de Gràcia and Plaça de Catalunya. There are two main railway stations: Estació de Sants and Estació de França near Barceloneta.

Boat Trips The best way to admire the port and coastline is from the sea. Golondrinas offer frequent 35-minute harbour tours or 2-hour voyages to the Port Olímpic (➤ 33). Although Barcelona is the biggest port in the Mediterranean, the only regular passenger services are to the Balearic islands.

Cable cars, Funiculars and the Tramvia Blau A cable car connects the lower city with Montjuïc castle and links with the funicular railway. To reach Tibidabo, take the Tramvia Blau (Blue Tram), then the Funicular del Tibidabo to the Amusement Park at the top of the hill.

CAR RENTAL

The leading international car rental companies have offices at Barcelona airport and you can book a car in advance (essential in peak periods) either direct or through a travel agent. Local companies offer competitive rates and will usually deliver a car to the airport.

TAXIS

Pick up a black and yellow taxi at a taxi rank or hail one if it's displaying a green light and the sign *Lliure/Libre* (free). Fares are not unduly expensive but extra fees are charged for airport trips and for baggage. Prices are shown on a sticker inside.

DRIVING

Speed limit on motorways (*autopistas*): **120kph**

Speed limit on main roads : **100kph** On minor roads: **90kph**

Speed limit in towns (*Poblaciones*): **50kph**

Seat belts must be worn in front seats at all times and in rear seats where fitted.

Blood alcohol limit: 8 milligrams per millilitre.

Fuel (*gasolina*) is available as: *Super Plus* (98 octane), *Super* (96 octane), unleaded or *sin plomo* (90 octane) and *gasoleo* or *gasoil* (diesel). Petrol stations are normally open 6AM–10PM, and closed Sundays, though larger ones are open 24 hours. Most take credit cards.

If you break down driving your own car and are a member of an AIT-affiliated motoring club, you can call the Real Automóvil Club de Catalunya (☎ 93 228 50 00). If the car is hired, follow the instructions given in the documentation; most of the international rental firms provide a rescue service.

PERSONAL SAFETY

The Policía Municipal (navy-blue uniforms) keep law and order in the city. For a police station ask for *la comisaría*.

To help prevent crime:

- Do not carry more cash than you need
- Beware of pickpockets in markets, tourist sights or crowded places
- Avoid walking alone in dark alleys at night, in the Barri Xines, especially in the Barri Xines.
- Leave valuables and important documents in the hotel or apartment safe.

City Police assistance:
☎ **092** from any call box

ELECTRICITY

The power supply is usually 220 volts but a few old buildings are still wired for

125 volts. Sockets accept two-round-pin-style plugs, so an adaptor is needed for most non-Continental appliances and a transformer for appliances operating on 110–120 volts.

TELEPHONES

Public telephones (*teléfono*) still take 25, 100 and 500 peseta coins. They are to be converted to take euros . A phonecard (*credifone*) is available from post offices and tobacconists (*estancs*) for €6.01 or €12.02.

International Dialling Codes	
From Spain to:	
UK:	00 44
Germany:	00 49
USA & Canada:	00 1
Netherlands:	00 31
France:	00 33

Reduced prices apply to calls made between 10PM and 8AM and on Saturdays after 2PM

POST

Most post offices (*correos*) open Mon–Fri, 8:30–2 but some also open in the afternoon and on Saturday morning. The main post office (*Oficina Central*) at Via Laietana 1 is open Mon–Sat 8:30AM–9PM, Sun 8AM–2PM, and the Eixample post office at Carrer Aragó 282 is open Mon–Fri 8AM–9PM and Sat 9–2. You can also buy stamps at any tobacconist (*estanc*).

TIPS/GRATUITIES

Yes ✓ No ✗		
Restaurants (if service not inc.)	✓	10%
Cafés/Bars (if service not inc.)	✓	change
Tour Guides	✓	€1
Hairdressers	✓	change
Taxis	✓	10%
Chambermaids/Porters	✓	€1
Theatre/cinemas usherettes	✓	change
Cloakroom attendants	✓	change
Toilets	✗	

What to photograph: *Modernista* buildings, colourful markets, busy street scenes, the Ramblas, the waterfront and sweeping city views from Montjuïc and Tibidabo.

When to photograph: the Spanish summer sun can be powerful at the height of the day, making photos taken at this time appear 'flat'; it is best to photograph in the early morning or late evening.

Where to buy film: film and camera batteries are readily available from specialist shops and *drouguerías*.

HEALTH

Insurance
Nationals of EU and certain other countries can get medical treatment in Spain with the relevant documentation (Form E111 for Britons), although private medical insurance is still advised and is essential for all other visitors.

Dental Services
Dental treatment is not usually available free of charge as all dentists practise privately. A list of *dentistas* can be found in the yellow pages of the telephone directory. Dental treatment should be covered by private medical insurance.

Sun Advice
The sunniest (and hottest) months are July and August, with an average of 11 hours sun a day and daytime temperatures of 29°C. Particularly during these months you should avoid the midday sun and use a strong sunblock.

Drugs
Prescription and non-prescription drugs and medicines are available from pharmacies (*farmàcias*), distinguished by a large green cross. They are able to dispense many drugs that would be available only on prescription in other countries.

Safe Water
Tap water is generally safe though it can be heavily chlorinated. Mineral water is cheap to buy and is sold as *con gaz* (carbonated) and *sin gaz* (still). Drink plenty of water during hot weather.

CONCESSIONS

Students Holders of an International Student Identity Card (ISIC) may be able to obtain some concessions on travel, entrance fees etc. Most museums offer 50 per cent discount to students, and many are free on the first Sunday of each month. There are several IYHF youth hostels in the city, with accommodation in multi-bed dormitories. Expect to pay around €6–10 per person.

Senior Citizens Barcelona is a popular destination for older travellers, especially during winter. Most museums and galleries offer a 50 per cent discount for retired people.

CLOTHING SIZES

Spain	UK	Europe	USA	
46	36	46	36	Suits
48	38	48	38	
50	40	50	40	
52	42	52	42	
54	44	54	44	
56	46	56	46	
41	7	41	8	Shoes
42	7.5	42	8.5	
43	8.5	43	9.5	
44	9.5	44	10.5	
45	10.5	45	11.5	
46	11	46	12	
37	14.5	37	14.5	Shirts
38	15	38	15	
39/40	15.5	39/40	15.5	
41	16	41	16	
42	16.5	42	16.5	
43	17	43	17	
36	8	34	6	Dresses
38	10	36	8	
40	12	38	10	
42	14	40	12	
44	16	42	14	
46	18	44	16	
38	4.5	38	6	Shoes
38	5	38	6.5	
39	5.5	39	7	
39	6	39	7.5	
40	6.5	40	8	
41	7	41	8.5	

WHEN DEPARTING

- Remember to contact the airport on the day before leaving to ensure the flight details are unchanged.
- Spanish customs officials are usually polite and normally willing to negotiate.

LANGUAGE

In Barcelona, there are two official languages, Catalan and Spanish, both coming from Latin but both sounding quite different. Everybody can speak Spanish, although Catalan is most commonly spoken. At most tourist attractions you will always find someone who speaks English, and many restaurants have polyglot menus. However, it is advisable to try to learn at least some Catalan, since English is not as widely spoken as in other European countries. Here is a basic vocabulary to help you with the most essential words and expressions.

	hotel	*hotel*	chambermaid	*cambrera*
	bed and breakfast	*llit i berenar*	bath	*bany*
	single room	*habitació senzilla*	shower	*dutxa*
	double room	*habitació doble*	washbasin	*lavabo*
	one person	*una persona*	toilet	*toaleta*
	one night	*una nit*	balcony	*balcó*
	reservation	*reservas*	key	*clau*
	room service	*servei d'habitació*	lift	*ascensor*

	bank	*banc*	exchange rate	*tant per cent*
	exchange office	*oficina de canvi*	commission	*comissió*
	post office	*correos*	cashier	*caixer*
	coin	*moneda*	change	*camvi*
	banknote	*bitllet de banc*	foreign	*moneda*
	traveller's	*xec de*	currency	*estrangera*
	cheque	*viatage*	open	*obert*
	credit card	*carta de crèdit*	closed	*tancat*

	café	*cafè*	starter	*primer plat*
	pub/bar	*celler*	main course	*segón plat*
	breakfast	*berenar*	dessert	*postres*
	lunch	*dinar*	bill	*cuenta*
	dinner	*sopar*	beer	*cervesa*
	table	*mesa*	wine	*vi*
	waiter	*cambrer*	water	*aigua*
	waitress	*cambrera*	coffee	*café*

	aeroplane	*avió*	single ticket	*senzill-a*
	airport	*aeroport*	return ticket	*anar i tornar*
	train	*tren*	non-smoking	*no fumar*
	bus	*autobús*	car	*cotxe*
	station	*estació*	petrol	*gasolina*
	boat	*vaixell*	bus stop	*la parada*
	port	*port*	how do I get	*per anar*
	ticket	*bitllet*	to…?	*a…?*

	yes	*si*	tomorrow	*demà*
	no	*no*	excuse me	*perdoni*
	please	*per favor*	you're welcome	*de res*
	thank you	*gràcies*	how are you?	*com va?*
	hello	*hola*	do you speak	*parla*
	goodbye	*adéu*	English?	*anglès?*
	good morning	*bon dia*	I don't understand	*no ho enten*
	good afternoon	*bona tarda*	how much?	*quant es?*
	goodnight	*bona nit*	where is…?	*on és…?*
	today	*avui*		

INDEX

Acknowledgements

Teresa Fisher wishes to thank Rosemary Trigg of Hotel Arts for her assistance during the research of this book.

The Automobile Association would like to thank the following photographers, libraries, associations and individuals for their assistance in the preparation of this book:
DACS 17; MARY EVANS PICTURE LIBRARY 10b; TERESA FISHER 21b, 38b, 43b, 54, 57a, 58, 70b, 75a, 84b,122a,b,c; HULTON GETTY 14c; MUSEU PICASSO 20b, 20c; NATURE PHOTOGRAPHERS (R Bush) 13a; REX FEATURES 14b; SPECTRUM COLOUR LIBRARY 9c, 25, 27b, 52b, 53c, 87b; WORLD PICTURES 51b; www.euro.ecb.int/ 119 (euro notes).

The remaining pictures are from the Association's own library (AA PHOTO LIBRARY) and were taken by S DAY with the exception of the following:
P ENTICKNAP 5b, 13b, 19b, 23c, 61, 78, 79, 80a, 81, 82, 83, 84a, 85a, 85b, 88a, 88b, 89a, 89b, 90a, 90b, 91a, 92–116; MAX JOURDAN F/cover (c) mime artist; P WILSON F/cover (a) dragon, B/cover arch, 11b, 12b, 17b, 22b, 26b, 26c, 32, 36, 41, 49, 50b, 53b, 55, 59b, 67b, 69b, 73b, 85b, 86.

Dear Essential Traveller

Your comments, opinions and recommendations are very important to us. So please help us to improve our travel guides by taking a few minutes to complete this simple questionnaire.

You do not need a stamp (unless posted outside the UK). If you do not want to cut this page from your guide, then photocopy it or write your answers on a plain sheet of paper.

Send to: **The Editor, AA World Travel Guides, FREEPOST SCE 4598, Basingstoke RG21 4GY.**

Your recommendations...

We always encourage readers' recommendations for restaurants, nightlife or shopping – if your recommendation is used in the next edition of the guide, we will send you a *FREE* AA *Essential* **Guide** of your choice. Please state below the establishment name, location and your reasons for recommending it.

_____

_____

_____

_____

Please send me **AA *Essential*** _____

(*see list of titles inside the front cover*)

About this guide...

Which title did you buy?
   AA *Essential* _____
Where did you buy it? _____
When? m m / y y

Why did you choose an AA *Essential* Guide? _____

_____

_____

_____

_____

Did this guide meet your expectations?
   Exceeded ☐   Met all ☐   Met most ☐   Fell below ☐
   Please give your reasons_____

_____

_____

_____

continued on next page...

Were there any aspects of this guide that you particularly liked? _____

_____

_____

_____

Is there anything we could have done better? _____

_____

_____

_____

_____

About you...

Name (*Mr/Mrs/Ms*) _____

Address _____

_____

_____ Postcode _____

Daytime tel nos _____

Which age group are you in?
Under 25 ☐ 25–34 ☐ 35–44 ☐ 45–54 ☐ 55–64 ☐ 65+ ☐

How many trips do you make a year?
Less than one ☐ One ☐ Two ☐ Three or more ☐

Are you an AA member? Yes ☐ No ☐

About your trip...

When did you book? m m / y y   When did you travel? m m / y y
How long did you stay? _____
Was it for business or leisure? _____
Did you buy any other travel guides for your trip?
If yes, which ones? _____

_____

Thank you for taking the time to complete this questionnaire. Please send
it to us as soon as possible, and remember, you do not need a stamp
(*unless posted outside the UK*).

Happy Holidays!

AA All In One

Spanish
Phrasebook

AA Publishing

Contents

Introduction

● **Welcome to the AA's Spanish Phrasebook,
which contains everything you'd expect from a
comprehensive language guide. It's concise, accessible
and easy to understand, and you'll find it
indispensable on your trip abroad.**

The guide is divided into 15 themed sections and starts
with a pronunciation table which explains the phonetic
pronunciation to all the words and phrases you'll need
to know for your trip, while at the back of the book is
an extensive word list and grammar guide which will
help you construct basic sentences in Spanish.

Throughout the book you'll come across coloured
boxes with a 🕲 beside them. These are designed to
help you if you can't understand what your listener is
saying to you. Hand the book over to them and
encourage them to point to the appropriate answer to
the question you are asking.

Other coloured boxes in the book – this time without
the symbol – give alphabetical listings of themed
words with their English translations beside them.

For extra clarity, we have put all English words and
phrases in black, foreign language terms in red and
their phonetic pronunciation in italic.

This phrasebook covers all subjects you are likely to
come across during the course of your visit, from
reserving a room for the night to ordering food and
drink at a restaurant and what to do if your car breaks
down or you lose your traveller's cheques and money.
With over 2,000 commonly used words and essential
phrases at your fingertips you can rest assured that
you will be able to get by in all situations, so let the
AA's Spanish Phrasebook become your passport to a
secure and enjoyable trip!

Pronunciation table

The pronunciation provided should be read as if it were English, bearing in mind the following main points:

Vowels

Vowels in Spanish are very open

a	is like **a** in amber,	*ah*	as in **casa**	*kahsah*
e	is like **e** in egg,	*eh*	as in **esta**	*ehstah*
i	is like **ee** in seen,	*ee*	as in **isla**	*eeslah*
o	is like **o** in John,	*oh*	as in **hotel**	*ohtehl*
u	is like **oo** in room,	*oo*	as in **uno**	*oonoh*
y	is like **ee** in seen,	*ee*	as in **y**	*ee*

the diphthong **ay** is pronounced as in aisle or eye

			as in **hay**	*eye*

Consonants

Consonants are as in English, pronounced less clearly, except

b/v	are pronounced roughly the same		
		as in **vamos**	*bahmohs*
c	before e and i is soft and is like the **th** in tha**tch**		
		as in **la acera**	*lah ahthehrah*
	before a,o and u is hard		
		as in **cosa**	*kohsah*
cu	before another vowel is pronounced like **cw**		
		as in **la cuenta**	*lah kwehntah*
g	before e and i is soft and is like the Scottish **ch** in lo**ch**,		
		as in **la gente**	*lah hehnteh*
	before a, o and u is hard		
		as in **gato**	*ghahtoh*
gu	before e and i is pronounced as hard **g**		
		as in **la guía**	*geeah*
	before a, o and u is pronounced like **gw**		
		as in **guapo**	*gwahpoh*
gü	before e and i is pronounced like **gw**		
		as in **lingüística**	*leengwees-teekah*
h	is silent		
j	is like the soft **g**	as in **jarra**	*hahrrah*
ll	is like **lli** in billion	as in **llave**	*lyahbeh*
ñ	is like **ni** in onion	as in **año**	*ahnyoh*
r	is rolled as in the Scottish **r**, **rr** is a longer roll		
z	is like **th** in thought	as in **taza**	*tahthah*

The stress normally falls on the last syllable of the word (**hotel**), except that words ending in a vowel (not including **y**) or in n or s (**casa**, **casas**) are stressed on the next to the last syllable. All exceptions are indicated by a written acute accent (**Córdoba**, *kohrdohbah*).

Note: In the south, the soft **c** and the **z** are pronounced *s*. This is also true in Latin America.

Useful lists

Useful lists

.1 Today or tomorrow?

Useful lists

What day is it today? _____	¿Qué día es hoy?
	keh deeah ehs oy?
Today's Monday_____	Hoy es lunes
	oy ehs loonehs
– Tuesday_____	Hoy es martes
	oy ehs mahrtehs
– Wednesday _____	Hoy es miércoles
	oy ehs myehrkohlehs
– Thursday_____	Hoy es jueves
	oy ehs hooehbehs
– Friday_____	Hoy es viernes
	oy ehs byehrnehs
– Saturday _____	Hoy es sábado
	oy ehs sahbahdoh
– Sunday _____	Hoy es domingo
	oy ehs dohmeengoh
in January _____	en enero
	ehn ehnehroh
since February _____	desde febrero
	dehsdeh fehbrehroh
in spring_____	en primavera
	ehn preemahbehrah
in summer_____	en verano
	ehn behrahnoh
in autumn _____	en otoño
	ehn ohtohnyoh
in winter_____	en invierno
	ehn eenbyehrno
1997_____	mil novecientos noventa y siete
	meel nohbehthyentohs nohbehntah ee
	syehteh
the twentieth century _____	el siglo XX (veinte)
	ehl seegloh beheenteh
What's the date today? ____	¿Qué día es hoy?
	keh deeah ehs oy?
Today's the 24th_____	Hoy es 24 (veinticuatro)
	oy ehs beheenteekwahtroh
Monday 3 November _____	lunes 3 (tres) de noviembre de 1998 (mil
1998	novecientos noventa y ocho)
	loonehs trehs deh nohbyehmbreh deh meel
	nohbehthyehntohs nohbehntah ee ohchoh
in the morning _____	por la mañana
	pohr lah mahnyahnah
in the afternoon_____	por la tarde
	pohr lah tahrdeh
in the evening _____	por la noche
	pohr lah nohcheh
at night_____	por la noche
	pohr lah nohcheh
this morning _____	esta mañana
	ehstah mahnyahnah

this afternoon _____	esta tarde
	ehstah tahrdeh
this evening _____	esta noche
	ehstah nohcheh
tonight _____	esta noche
	ehstah nohcheh
last night _____	anoche
	ahnohcheh
this week _____	esta semana
	ehstah sehmahnah
next month _____	el mes próximo
	ehl mehs prohxeemoh
last year _____	el año pasado
	ehl ahnyo pahsahdoh
next... _____	el/la... próximo/a
	ehl/lah... prohxeemoh/ah
in...days/weeks/ _____	dentro de...días/semanas/meses/años
months/years	*dehntroh deh...*
	deeahs/sehmahnahs/mehsehs/ahnyohs
...weeks ago _____	hace...semanas
	ahthe...sehmahnahs
day off _____	día libre
	deeah leebreh

🕐 .2 Bank Holidays

● **The most important** Bank Holidays in Spain are the following:

January 1	New Year's Day (Año Nuevo)
January 6	Epiphany (Epifanía)
March 19	St. Joseph's Day (San José)
March/April	Good Friday (Viernes Santo)
March/April	Easter Monday(Catalonia) (Lunes Santo)
May 1	Labour Day (Día del Trabajo)
May/June	Corpus Christi (Corpus Christi)
July 25	St. James's Day (Santiago)
August 15	Assumption Day (Asunción)
October 12	Columbus Day (Día de las Américas)
November 1	All Saints' Day (Todos los Santos)
December 6	Constitution Day (Día de la Constitución)
December 8	Immaculate Conception (Inmaculada Concepción)
December 25	Christmas (Navidad)

There are also various regional holidays like San Fermín in Pamplona (July 6-13) and the Fallas in Valencia (March 19).

🕐 .3 What time is it?

What time is it? _____	¿Qué hora es?
	keh ohrah ehs?
It's nine o'clock _____	Son las nueve
	sohn lahs nwehbeh
– five past ten _____	Son las diez y cinco
	sohn lahs dyeth ee theenkoh
– a quarter past eleven ____	Son las once y cuarto
	sohn lahs ohntheh ee kwahrtoh
– twenty past twelve _____	Son las doce y veinte
	sohn lahs dohthe ee beheenteh

9

1

– half past one _____	Es la una y media
	ehs lah oonah ee mehdyah
– twenty–five to three _____	Son las tres menos veinticinco
	sohn lahs trehs mehnohs
	beheenteetheenkoh
– a quarter to four _____	Son las cuatro menos cuarto
	sohn lahs kwahtroh mehnohs kwahrtoh
– ten to five _____	Son las cinco menos diez
	sohn lahs theenkoh mehnohs dyehth
– twelve noon _____	Son las doce del mediodía
	sohn lahs dohtheh dehl mehdyohdeeah
– midnight _____	Son las doce de la noche
	sohn lahs dohtheh deh lah nohcheh
half an hour _____	media hora
	mehdyah ohrah
What time? _____	¿A qué hora?
	ah keh ohrah?
What time can I come _____ round?	¿A qué hora puedo pasar?
	ah keh ohrah pwehdoh pahsahr?
At... _____	A las...
	ah lahs...
After... _____	Después de las...
	dehspwehs deh lahs...
Before... _____	Antes de las...
	ahntehs deh lahs...
Between...and... _____	Entre las...y las...
	ehntreh lahs...ee lahs...
From...to... _____	De las...a las...
	deh lahs...ah lahs...
In...minutes _____	Dentro de...minutos
	dehntroh deh...meenootohs
– an hour _____	Dentro de una hora
	dehntroh deh oonah ohrah
– ...hours _____	Dentro de...horas
	dehntroh deh...ohrahs
– a quarter of an hour _____	Dentro de un cuarto de hora
	dehntroh deh oon kwahrtoh deh ohrah
– three quarters of _____ an hour	Dentro de tres cuartos de hora
	dehntroh deh trehs kwahrtohs deh ohrah
early/late _____	muy temprano/tarde
	mwee tehmprahnoh/tahrdeh
on time _____	a tiempo
	ah tyehmpoh
summer opening hours _____	horario de verano
	ohrahryoh deh behrahnoh
winter opening hours _____	horario de invierno
	ohrahryoh deh eenbyehrnoh

1 .4 One, two, three...

0 _____	cero	*thehroh*
1 _____	uno	*oonoh*
2 _____	dos	*dohs*
3 _____	tres	*trehs*
4 _____	cuatro	*kwahtroh*

10

5 _____	cinco	*theenkoh*
6 _____	seis	*sehees*
7 _____	siete	*syehteh*
8 _____	ocho	*ohchoh*
9 _____	nueve	*nwehbeh*
10 _____	diez	*dyeth*
11 _____	once	*ohntheh*
12 _____	doce	*dohtheh*
13 _____	trece	*trehtheh*
14 _____	catorce	*kahtohrtheh*
15 _____	quince	*keentheh*
16 _____	dieciséis	*dyetheesehees*
17 _____	diecisiete	*dyetheesyehteh*
18 _____	dieciocho	*dyetheeohchoh*
19 _____	diecinueve	*dyetheenwehbe*
20 _____	veinte	*beheenteh*
21 _____	veintiuno	*beheenteeoonoh*
22 _____	veintidós	*beheenteheedohs*
30 _____	treinta	*treheentah*
31 _____	treinta y uno	*treheentah ee oonoh*
32 _____	treinta y dos	*treheentah ee dohs*
40 _____	cuarenta	*kwahrehntah*
50 _____	cincuenta	*theenkwehntah*
60 _____	sesenta	*sehsehntah*
70 _____	setenta	*sehtehntah*
80 _____	ochenta	*ohchehntah*
90 _____	noventa	*nohvehntah*
100 _____	cien	*thyehn*
101 _____	ciento uno	*thyehntoh oonoh*
110 _____	ciento diez	*thyehntoh dyeth*
120 _____	ciento veinte	*thyehntoh beheenteh*
200 _____	doscientos	*dohsthyehntohs*
300 _____	trescientos	*trehsthyehntohs*
400 _____	cuatrocientos	*kwahtrohthyehntohs*
500 _____	quinientos	*keenyehntohs*
600 _____	seiscientos	*seheesthyehntohs*
700 _____	setecientos	*sehtehthyehntohs*
800 _____	ochocientos	*ohchohthyehntohs*
900 _____	novecientos	*nohbehthyentohs*
1000 _____	mil	*meel*
1100 _____	mil cien	*meel thyehn*
2000 _____	dos mil	*dohs meel*
10,000 _____	diez mil	*dyeth meel*
100,000 _____	cien mil	*thyehn meel*
1,000,000 _____	un millón	*oon meelyohn*
1st _____	primero	*preemehroh*
2nd _____	segundo	*sehgoondoh*
3rd _____	tercero	*tehrthehroh*
4th _____	cuarto	*kwahrtoh*
5th _____	quinto	*keentoh*
6th _____	sexto	*sehxtoh*
7th _____	séptimo	*sehpteemoh*
8th _____	octavo	*ohktahboh*

Useful lists

9th _____	noveno	*nohvehnoh*
10th _____	décimo	*dehtheemoh*
11th _____	undécimo	*oondehtheemoh*
12th _____	duodécimo	*doo-ohdehtheemo*
13th _____	decimotercero	*dehtheemohtehrthehroh*
14th _____	decimocuarto	*dehtheemohkwahrtoh*
15th _____	decimoquinto	*dehtheemohkeentoh*
16th _____	decimosexto	*dehtheemohsehxtoh*
17th _____	decimoséptimo	*dehtheemosehpteemoh*
18th _____	decimoctavo	*dehtheemohktahboh*
19th _____	decimonoveno	*dehtheemonobenoh*
20th _____	vigésimo	*beeheseemoh*
21st _____	vigesimoprimero	*beeheseemohpreemeroh*
22nd _____	vigesimosegundo	*beeheseemohsegoondoh*
30th _____	trigésimo	*treeheseemoh*
100th _____	centésimo	*thentehseemoh*
1,000th _____	milésimo	*meelehseemoh*

once _____	una vez	
	oonah behth	
twice _____	dos veces	
	dos behthes	
double _____	el doble	
	ehl dohbleh	
triple _____	el triple	
	ehl treepleh	
half _____	la mitad	
	lah meetath	
a quarter _____	un cuarto	
	oon kwartoh	
a third _____	un tercio	
	oon terthyoh	
a couple, a few, some _____	unos, algunos	
	oonohs, algoonohs	

2 + 4 = 6 _____	dos más cuatro, seis	
	dohs mahs kwahtroh, sehees	
4 – 2 = 2 _____	cuatro menos dos, dos	
	kwahtroh mehnohs dohs, dohs	
2 x 4 = 8 _____	dos por cuatro, ocho	
	dohs pohr kwahtroh, ohchoh	
4 ÷ 2 = 2 _____	cuatro dividido dos, dos	
	kwahtroh deebeedeedoh dohs, dohs	

odd/even _____	par/impar	
	pahr/eempahr	
total _____	(en) total	
	(ehn) tohtahl	
6 x 9 _____	seis por nueve	
	sehees pohr nwehbeh	

1.5 The weather

Is the weather going to be good/bad?	¿Hará buen/mal tiempo?
	ahrah bwehn/mahl tyehmpoh?
Is it going to get colder/hotter?	¿Hará más frío/calor?
	ahrah mahs freeoh/kahlohr?

What temperature is it going to be?	¿Cuántos grados hará?
	kwahntohs grahdohs ahrah?
Is it going to rain?	¿Va a llover?
	bah ah lyohbehr?
Is there going to be a storm?	¿Tendremos tormenta?
	tehndrehmohs tohrmehntah?
Is it going to snow?	¿Va a nevar?
	bah ah nehbahr?
Is it going to freeze?	¿Va a helar?
	bah ah ehlahr?
Is the thaw setting in?	¿Comenzará el deshielo?
	kohmehnzahrah ehl dehsyeloh
Is it going to be foggy?	¿Habrá niebla?
	ahbrah nyehblah?
Is there going to be a thunderstorm?	¿Habrá tormenta eléctrica?
	ahbrah tohrmehntah ehlehktreekah?
The weather's changing	Va a cambiar el tiempo
	bah ah kahmbyahr ehl tyehmpoh
It's cooling down	Va a refrescar
	bah ah rehfrehskahr
What's the weather going to be like today/tomorrow?	¿Qué tiempo hará hoy/mañana?
	keh tyehmpoh ahrah oy/mahnyahnah?

---

algo nublado/nublado	granizo	ola de calor
light/heavy clouds	hail	heat wave
bochornoso	...grados(bajo/sobre cero)	pesado
stormy	...degrees(above/below zero)	muggy
bueno	helada	sofocante
fine	(black) ice	scorching hot
caluroso	húmedo	soleado
hot	damp	sunny
chubasco	huracán	suave
shower	hurricane	mild
cielo cubierto	llovizna	tormenta eléctrica
overcast	drizzle	thunderstorm
desapacible	lluvia	vendaval
bleak	rain	gale
despejado	lluvioso	ventoso
clear	wet	windy
escarcha	niebla	viento
frost	fog	wind
fresco	nieve	viento leve /moderado/ fuerte
chilly	snow	light/moderate/ strong wind
frìo	nublado	tempestad
cold	cloudy	squall

13

See also 5.1 Asking for directions

Useful lists

here/there _____	aquí/allá
	ahkee/ahlyah
somewhere/nowhere _____	en alguna/ninguna parte
	ehn algoonah/neengoonah pahrteh
everywhere _____	en todas partes
	ehn tohdahs pahrtehs
far away/nearby _____	lejos/cerca
	leh<u>hos</u>/thehrkah
right/left _____	a la derecha/izquierda
	ah lah dehrehchah/eethkyehrdah
to the right/left of _____	a la derecha/izquierda de
	ah lah dehrehchah/eethkyehrdah deh
straight ahead _____	todo recto
	tohdoh rehktoh
via _____	pasando por
	pahsahndoh pohr
in _____	en
	ehn
on_____	sobre
	sohbreh
under _____	debajo de
	dehbah<u>ho</u>h deh
against _____	contra
	kohntrah
opposite_____	frente a
	frehnteh ah
next to _____	al lado de
	ahl lahdoh deh
near_____	junto a
	<u>hoontoh</u> ah
in front of_____	delante de
	dehlahnteh deh
in the centre _____	en el medio
	ehn ehl mehdyoh
forward_____	hacia adelante
	ahthyah ahdehlanteh
down_____	(hacia) abajo
	(ahthyah) ahbah<u>ho</u>h
up_____	(hacia) arriba
	(ahthya) ahrreebah
inside _____	(hacia) adentro
	(ahthya) ahdehntroh
outside _____	(hacia) afuera
	(ahthya) ahfwehrah
behind _____	(hacia) atrás
	(ahthya) ahtrahs
at the front _____	delante
	dehlahnteh
at the back_____	detrás
	dehtrahs
in the north _____	en el norte
	ehn ehl nohrteh

to the south _____	hacia el sur	
	ahthya ehl soor	
from the west _____	del oeste	
	dehl ohehsteh	
from the east _____	del este	
	dehl ehsteh	
...of _____	al...de	
	ahl...deh	

 .7 What does that sign say?

See 5.4 Traffic signs

---

abierto/cerrado **open/closed**	horario (de apertura) **opening hours**	prohibido pisar el césped
agua no potable **no drinking water**	información **information**	**keep off the grass**
alta tensión **high voltage**	liquidación (por cese)	razón aquí **inquiries**
ascensor **lift**	**closing-down sale**	rebajas **clearance**
caballeros **gents/gentlemen**	no funciona **out of order**	recepción **reception**
caja **pay here**	no tocar **please do not touch**	recién pintado **wet paint**
completo **full**	peligro **danger**	reservado **reserved**
coto privado **private (property)**	peligro de incendio **fire hazard**	saldos **sale**
cuidado con el perro **beware of the dog**	...piso **...floor**	salida **exit**
cuidado, escalón **mind the step**	primeros auxilios **first aid**	salida de emergencia/salida de socorro
entrada **entrance**	prohibido el paso **no entry**	**emergency exit**
entrada libre **free admission**	prohibido fotografiar **no photographs**	se alquila **for hire**
escalera **stairs**	prohibido fumar **no smoking**	se ruega no molestar **do not disturb**
escalera de incendios	prohibido hacer fuego	se vende **for sale**
fire escape	**no open fires**	señoras **ladies**
escalera mecánica **escalator**	prohibido para animales	servicios **toilets**
freno de emergencia **emergency brake**	**no pets allowed**	empujar/tirar **push/pull**

.8 Telephone alphabet

a _____	*ah*	de Antonio	*deh ahntohnyoh*
b _____	*beh*	de Barcelona	*deh bahr-thehlohnah*
c _____	*theh*	de Carmen	*deh kahrmehn*
ch _____	*cheh*	de chocolate	*deh chohkohlahteh*
d _____	*deh*	de Dolores	*deh dohlohrehs*

15

e _____ *eh*	de Enrique	*deh ehnreekeh*
f _____ *hefeh*	de Francia	*deh frahnthyah*
g _____ *heh*	de Gerona	*de <u>h</u>ehrohnah*
h _____ *ahcheh*	de historia	*de eestohryah*
I _____ *ee*	de Inés	*deh eenehs*
j _____ *hohtah*	de José	*deh <u>h</u>ohseh*
k _____ *kah*	de Kilo	*deh keeloh*
l _____ *ehleh*	de Lorenzo	*deh lohrehnthoh*
ll _____ *ehlyeh*	de Llobregat	*deh lyohbrehgaht*
m _____ *ehmeh*	de Madrid	*deh Mahdreedh*
n _____ *ehneh*	de Navarra	*deh nahbahrrah*
ñ _____ *ehnyeh*	de ñoño	*deh nyohnyoh*
o _____ *oh*	de Oviedo	*deh ohbyedoh*
p _____ *peh*	de París	*deh pahrees*
q _____ *koo*	de querido	*deh kehreedoh*
r _____ *ehrreh*	de Ramón	*deh rahmohn*
s _____ *ehseh*	de sábado	*deh sahbahdoh*
t _____ *teh*	de Tarragona	*deh tahrrahgohnah*
u _____ *oo*	de Ulises	*deh ooleesehs*
v _____ *oobeh*	de Valencia	*deh bahlehnthyah*
w _____ *oobehdohbleh*	de Washington	*deh wahsheengtohn*
x _____ *ehkees*	de Xiquena	*deh <u>h</u>eekehnah*
y _____ *eegryehgah*	griega	
z _____ *thehtah*	de Zaragoza	*deh thahrahgohthah*

🕐 .9 Personal details

surname _____	apellidos
	ahpehlyeedohs
christian name(s) _____	nombre
	nohmbreh
initials _____	iniciales
	eeneethyahlehs
address (street/number) ___	dirección (calle/número)
	deerehkthyohn (kahlyeh/noomehroh)
post code/town _____	código postal/población
	cohdeegoh pohstahl/pohblahthyon
sex (male/female) _____	sexo (v = varón, m = mujer)
	sehksoh (v = bahrohn, m = moo<u>h</u>ehr)
nationality _____	nacionalidad
	nahthyohnahleedahdh
date of birth _____	fecha de nacimiento
	fehchah deh nahtheemyehntoh
place of birth _____	lugar de nacimiento
	loogahr deh natheemyehntoh
occupation _____	profesión
	profehsyohn
married/single/divorced ___	casado, casada/soltero, soltera/
	divorciado, divorciada
	kahsahdoh, kahsahdah/sohltehroh,
	sohltehrah/deebohrthyahdoh,
	deebohrthyahdah
widowed _____	viuda/viudo
	byoodah/byoodoh
(number of) children _____	(número de) hijos
	(noomehroh deh) ee<u>h</u>ohs

passport/identity _____ pasaporte/carnet de identidad/permiso de
card/driving licence/ conducir/número, lugar y fecha de
number, place and date expedición
of issue *kahrneh deh eedehnteedahdh*
(pahsahpohrteh/pehrmeesoh deh
kohndootheer) noomehroh, loogahr ee
fehchah deh ehkspehdeethyohn

Courtesies

2 Courtesies

● **Female friends and relatives** kiss on both cheeks in Spain.
In shops, etc., you will hear ¡Buenos días! or just ¡Buenas!, and expect
to be addressed in Basque or Catalan in these provinces. For example
you will hear ¡Agur! instead of ¡Adiós! in the Basque Country.

2.1 Greetings

Hello, Mr Smith _____	Hola, buenos días
	ohlah, bwehnohs deeahs
Hello, Peter _____	Hola, Pedro
	ohlah, pehdroh
Hi, Helen _____	Qué hay, Elena
	keh ay, ehlehnah
Good morning, madam ____	Buenos días, señora (before 2pm)
	bwehnohs deeahs, sehnyohrah
Good afternoon, sir _____	Buenas tardes, señor (after 2pm)
	bwehnahs tahrdehs, sehnyohr
Good evening_____	Buenas tardes (before 9pm), buenas
	noches (after 9pm)
	bwehnahs tahrdehs, bwehnahs nohchehs
How are you? _____	¿Qué tal?
	keh tahl?
Fine, thank you, and you?__	Muy bien, ¿y usted?
	mwee byehn, ee oostehdh?
Very well _____	Estupendo
	ehstoopehndoh
Not very well _____	Regular
	rehgoolahr
Not too bad_____	Tirando
	teerando
I'd better be going_____	Bueno, me voy
	bwehnoh, meh boy
I have to be going. _____	Tengo que irme. Me están esperando
Someone's waiting	*tehngoh keh eermeh, meh ehstahn*
for me	*ehspehrahndoh*
Bye!_____	¡Adiós!
	ahdyohs!
Goodbye _____	Hasta luego
	ahstah lwehgoh
See you soon _____	Hasta pronto
	ahstah prohntoh
See you later _____	Hasta luego
	ahstah lwehgoh
See you in a little while ____	Hasta ahora
	ahstah ahohrah
Sleep well _____	Que descanse
	keh dehskahnseh
Good night _____	Buenas noches
	bwehnahs nohchehs
All the best _____	Que le vaya bien
	keh leh bahyah byehn
Have fun_____	Que se divierta, que lo pase bien
	keh seh deebyehrtah, keh loh pahseh byehn

Good luck _____	Mucha suerte
	moochah swehrteh
Have a nice holiday _____	Felices vacaciones
	fehleetehs bahkahthyohnehs
Have a good trip _____	Buen viaje
	bwehn byahheh
Thank you, you too_____	Gracias, igualmente
	grahthyahs, eegwahlmehnteh
Say hello to...for me_____	Recuerdos a...
	rehkwehrdohs ah...

.2 How to ask a question

Who?_____	¿Quién?
	kyehn?
Who's that? _____	¿Quién es?
	kyehn ehs?
What? _____	¿Qué?
	keh?
What's there to_____	¿Qué se puede visitar aquí?
see here?	*keh seh pwehdeh beeseetahr ahkee?*
What kind of hotel_____	¿Qué clase de hotel es?
is that?	*keh klahseh deh ohtehl ehs?*
Where?_____	¿Dónde?
	dohndeh?
Where's the toilet? _____	¿Dónde están los servicios?
	dohndeh ehstahn lohs sehrbeethyohs?
Where are you going? _____	¿A dónde va?
	ahdohndeh bah?
Where are you from? _____	¿De dónde es usted?
	deh dohndeh ehs oostehdh?
How?_____	¿Cómo?
	kohmoh?
How far is that? _____	¿A qué distancia queda?
	ah keh deestahnthyah kehdah?
How long does it take? ____	¿Cuánto dura?
	kwahntoh doorah?
How long is the trip? _____	¿Cuánto dura el viaje?
	kwahntoh doorah ehl byahheh?
How much?_____	¿Cuánto?
	kwahntoh?
How much is this?_____	¿Cuánto vale?
	kwahntoh bahleh?
What time is it? _____	¿Qué hora es?
	keh ohrah ehs?
Which? _____	¿Cuál? ¿Cuáles?
	kwahl? kwahlehs?
Which glass is mine? _____	¿Cuál es mi copa?
	kwahl ehs mee kohpah?
When? _____	¿Cuándo?
	kwahndoh?
When are you leaving? ____	¿Cuándo sale?
	kwahndoh sahleh?
Why?_____	¿Por qué?
	pohr keh?
Could you...me?_____	¿Podría...?
	pohdreeah...?

Could you help me, _____ please?	¿Podría ayudarme? *pohdreeah ahyoodahrmeh?*
Could you point that_____ out to me?	¿Me lo podría indicar? *meh loh pohdreeah eendeekahr?*
Could you come _____ with me, please?	¿Le importaría acompañarme? *leh eempohrtahreeah ahkohmpahnyahrmeh?*
Could you..._____	¿Quiere...?/¿Podría...? *kyehreh...?/pohdreeah...?*
Could you reserve some ___ tickets for me, please?	¿Me podría reservar entradas? *meh pohdreeah rehsehrbahr ehntrahdahs?*
Do you know...? _____	¿Sabe...? *sahbeh...?*
Do you know another_____ hotel, please?	¿Sabría indicarme otro hotel? *sahbreeah eendeekahrmeh ohtroh ohtehl?*
Do you know whether...?___	¿Tiene...? *tyehneh...?*
Do you have a...?_____	¿Me podría dar un(a)...? *meh pohdreeah dahr oon(ah)...?*
Do you have a _____ vegetarian dish, please?	¿Tendría un plato sin carne? *tehndreeah oon plahtoh seen kahrneh?*
I'd like... _____	Quisiera... *keesyehrah...*
I'd like a kilo of apples, ____ please.	Quisiera un kilo de manzanas *keesyehrah oon keeloh deh mahnthahnahs*
Can I...?_____	¿Puedo...?/¿Se puede...? *pwehdoh...?/seh pwehdeh?*
Can I take this?_____	¿Podría llevármelo? *pohdreeah lyehbahrmehloh?*
Can I smoke here?_____	¿Se puede fumar aquí? *seh pwehdeh foomahr ahkee?*
Could I ask you _____ something?	¿Puedo hacerle una pregunta? *pwehdoh ahthehrleh oonah prehgoontah?*

2 .3 How to reply

Yes, of course_____	Sí, claro *see, klahroh*
No, I'm sorry_____	No, lo siento *noh, loh syehntoh*
Yes, what can I do _____ for you?	Sí. ¿En qué puedo servirle? *see, ehn keh pwehdoh sehrbeerleh?*
Just a moment, please ____	Un momento, por favor *oon mohmehntoh, pohr fahbohr*
No, I don't have _____ time now	No, ahora no tengo tiempo *noh, aohrah noh tehngoh tyehmpoh*
No, that's impossible _____	No, eso es imposible *noh, ehsoh ehs eempohseebleh*
I think so _____	Creo que sí *krehoh keh see*
I agree_____	Yo también lo creo *yoh tahmbyehn loh krehoh*
I hope so too_____	Yo también lo espero *yoh tahmbyehn loh ehspehroh*
No, not at all_____	No, de ninguna manera *noh, deh neengoonah mahnehrah*
No, no-one _____	No, nadie *noh, nahdyeh*

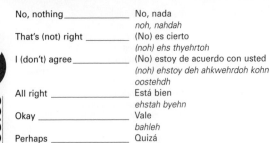

No, nothing _____	No, nada
	noh, nahdah
That's (not) right _____	(No) es cierto
	(noh) ehs thyehrtoh
I (don't) agree_____	(No) estoy de acuerdo con usted
	(noh) ehstoy deh ahkwehrdoh kohn
	oostehdh
All right _____	Está bien
	ehstah byehn
Okay _____	Vale
	bahleh
Perhaps _____	Quizá
	keethah
I don't know _____	No lo sé
	noh loh seh

2 .4 Thank you

Thank you _____	Gracias
	grahthyahs
You're welcome _____	De nada
	deh nahdah
Thank you very much _____	Muchísimas gracias
	moocheeseemahs grahthyahs
Very kind of you_____	Muy amable (de su parte)
	mwee ahmahbleh (deh soo pahrteh)
I enjoyed it very much _____	Ha sido un verdadero placer
	ah seedoh oon behrdahdehroh plahthehr
Thank you for your _____	Gracias por la molestia
trouble	*grahthyahs pohr lah mohlehstyah*
You shouldn't have _____	No se hubiera molestado
	noh seh oobyehrah mohlehstahdoh
That's all right _____	No se preocupe
	noh seh prehohkoopeh

2 .5 Sorry

Excuse me_____	Perdone
	pehrdohneh
Sorry! _____	¡Perdone!
	pehrdohneh!
I'm sorry, I didn't know...___	Perdone, no sabía que...
	pehrdohneh, noh sahbeeah keh...
I do apologise_____	Perdone
	pehrdohneh
I'm sorry_____	Lo siento
	loh syehntoh
I didn't do it on purpose,___	No ha sido a propósito; ha sido sin querer
it was an accident	*noh ah seedoh ah prohpohseetoh; ah*
	seedoh seen kehrehr
That's all right _____	No importa
	noh eempohrtah
Never mind_____	Déjelo
	deh_hehloh
It could've happened to____	Le puede pasar a cualquiera
anyone	*leh pwehdeh pahsahr ah kwahlkyehrah*

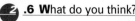

Which do you prefer?_____	¿Qué prefiere? *keh prehfyehreh?*
What do you think?_____	¿Qué te parece? *keh teh pahrehtheh?*
Don't you like dancing? ____	¿No te gusta bailar? *noh teh goostah bahylahr?*
I don't mind_____	Me da igual *meh dah eegwahl*
Well done!_____	¡Muy bien! *mwee byehn!*
Not bad!_____	¡No está mal! *noh ehstah mahl!*
Great! _____	¡Excelente! *ehxthehlehnteh!*
Wonderful! _____	¡Qué delicia! *keh dehleethyah!*
It's really nice here! _____	¡Qué bien se está aquí! *keh byehn seh ehstah ahkee!*
How nice! _____	¡Qué mono/bonito! *keh mohnoh/bohneetoh!*
How nice for you! _____	¡Cuánto me alegro por usted! *kwahntoh meh ahlehgroh pohr oostehdh!*
I'm (not) very happy_____ with...	(No) estoy muy contento con... *(noh) ehstoy mwee kohntehntoh kohn...*
I'm glad..._____	Me alegro de que... *meh ahlehgroh deh keh...*
I'm having a great time ____	Me lo estoy pasando muy bien *meh loh ehstoy pahsahndoh mwee byehn*
I'm looking forward to it ___	Me hace ilusión *meh ahtheh eeloosyohn*
I hope it'll work out_____	Espero que salga bien *ehspehroh keh sahlgah byehn*
That's ridiculous!_____	¡Qué ridículo! *keh reedeekooloh!*
That's terrible! _____	¡Qué horrible! *keh ohrreebleh!*
What a pity! _____	¡Qué lástima! *keh lahsteemah!*
That's filthy! _____	¡Qué asco! *keh ahskoh!*
What a load of rubbish! ___	¡Qué tontería! *keh tohntehreeah!*
I don't like..._____	No me gusta... *noh meh goostah...*
I'm bored to death _____	Me aburro como una ostra *meh ahboorroh kohmoh oonah ohstrah*
I've had enough_____	Estoy harto(a) *ehstoy ahrtoh(ah)*
This is no good _____	No puede ser *noh pwehdeh sehr*
I was expecting _____ something completely different	Yo me había esperado otra cosa *yoh meh ahbeeah ehspehrahdoh ohtrah kohsah*

Conversation

3 Conversation

3 .1 I beg your pardon?

I don't speak any/ _____	No hablo/hablo un poco de...
I speak a little...	*noh ahbloh/ahbloh oon pohkoh deh...*
I'm English _____	Soy inglés/inglesa
	soy eenglehs/eenglehsah
I'm Scottish _____	Soy escocés/escocesa
	soy ehskohthehs/ehskothehsah
I'm Irish _____	Soy irlandés/irlandesa
	soy eerlahndehs/eerlahndehsah
I'm Welsh_____	soy galés/galesa
	soy gahlehs/gahlehsah

Do you speak _____	¿Habla inglés/francés/alemán?
English/French/German?	*ahblah eenglehs/frahnthehs/ahlehmahn?*
Is there anyone who_____	¿Hay alguien que hable...?
speaks...?	*ay ahlgyehn ahkee keh ahbleh...?*
I beg your pardon? _____	¿Cómo dice?
	kohmoh deetheh?
I (don't) understand _____	(No) comprendo
	(noh) kohmprehndoh
Do you understand me? ___	¿Me entiende?
	meh ehntyehndeh?
Could you repeat that, _____	¿Le importa repetirlo?
please?	*leh eempohrtah rehpehteerloh?*
Could you speak more_____	¿Podría hablar más despacio?
slowly, please?	*pohdreeah ahblahr mahs dehspahthyo?*
What does that (word)_____	¿Qué significa esto/esta palabra?
mean?	*keh seegneefeekah ehstoh/ehstah pahlahbrah?*
Is that similar to/the _____	¿Es (más o menos) lo mismo que...?
same as...?	*ehs mahs oh mehnohs loh meesmoh keh...?*
Could you write that_____	¿Podría escribírmelo?
down for me, please?	*pohdreeah eskreebeermehloh?*
Could you spell that _____	¿Podría deletreármelo?
for me, please?	*pohdreeah dehlehtrehahrmehloh?*
(See 1.8 Telephone alphabet)	
Could you point that_____	¿Me lo podría señalar en esta guía?
out in this phrase book,	*meh loh pohdreeah sehnyahlahr ehn*
please?	*ehstah gheeah?*
One moment, please,_____	Espere que lo busco en la guía
I have to look it up	*ehspehreh keh loh booskoh ehn lah gheeah*
I can't find the word/the ___	No puedo encontrar la palabra/la frase
sentence	*noh pwehdoh ehnkohntrahr lah pahlahbrah/lah frahseh*
How do you say_____	¿Cómo se dice eso en...?
that in...?	*kohmoh seh deetheh ehstoh ehn...?*
How do you pronounce_____	¿Cómo se pronuncia?
that?	*kohmoh seh prohnoonthyah?*

May I introduce myself?	Permítame presentarme
	pehrmeetahmeh prehsehntahrmeh
My name's...	Me llamo...
	meh lyahmoh...
I'm...	Soy...
	soy...
What's your name?	¿Cómo se llama?
	kohmoh seh lyahmah?
May I introduce...?	Permítame presentarle a...
	pehrmeetahmeh prehsehntahrleh ah...
This is my wife/ daughter/mother/ girlfriend	Esta es mi mujer/mi hija/mi madre/mi amiga
	ehstah ehs mee moohehr/mee eehah /mee mahdreh/mee ahmeegah
– my husband/son/ father/boyfriend.	Este es mi marido/mi hijo/mi padre/mi amigo
	ehsteh ehs mee mahreedoh/mee eehoh/mee pahdreh/mee ahmeegoh
How do you do	Hola, mucho gusto
	ohlah, moochoh goostoh
Pleased to meet you	Encantado(a) (de conocerle)
	ehnkahntahdoh(ah) (deh kohnohthehrleh)
Where are you from?	¿De dónde es usted?
	deh dohndeh ehs oostehdh?
I'm from England/Scotland/ Ireland/Wales	Soy inglés/esa escocés/esa irlandés/esa galés/esa
	soy eenglehs/ehsah ehskohthehs/ehsah eerlahndehs/ehsah gahlehs/ ehsah
What city do you live in?	¿En qué ciudad vive?
	ehn keh thyoodahdh beebeh?
In..., It's near...	En...Eso está cerca de...
	ehn...ehsoh ehstah thehrkah deh...
Have you been here long?	¿Hace mucho que está aquí?
	ahtheh moochoh keh ehstah ahkee?
A few days	Unos días
	oonohs deeahs
How long are you staying here?	¿Cuánto tiempo piensa quedarse?
	kwahntoh tyehmpoh pyehnsah kehdahrseh?
We're (probably) leaving tomorrow/ in two weeks	Nos iremos (probablemente) mañana/dentro de dos semanas
	nohs eerehmohs (prohbahblehmehnteh) mahnyahnah/dehntroh deh dohs sehmahnahs
Where are you staying?	¿Dónde se aloja?
	dohndeh seh ahlohhah?
In a hotel/an apartment	En un hotel/apartamento
	ehn oon ohtehl/ahpahrtahmehntoh
On a camp site	En un camping
	ehn oon kahmpeen
With friends/relatives	En casa de amigos/parientes
	ehn kahsah deh ahmeegohs/pahryehntehs
Are you here on your own/with your family?	¿Ha venido solo(a)/con su familia?
	ah behneedoh sohloh(ah)/kohn soo fahmeelyah?

I'm on my own _____	He venido solo(a)
	eh behneedoh sohloh(ah)
I'm with my _____ partner/wife/husband	con mi pareja/mujer/marido
	kohn mee pahrehhah/moohehr/mahreedoh
– with my family _____	con mi familia
	kohn mee fahmeelyah
– with relatives _____	con unos parientes
	kohn oonohs pahryehntehs
– with a friend/friends _____	con un amigo/una amiga/unos amigos
	kohn oon ahmeegoh/oonah ahmeegah/oonohs ahmeegohs
Are you married? _____	¿Está casado/casada?
	ehstah kahsahdoh/kahsahdah?
Do you have a steady _____ boyfriend/girlfriend?	¿Tienes novio/novia?
	tyehnehs nohbyoh/nohbyah?
That's none of your _____ business.	No es asunto suyo
	noh ehs ahsoontoh sooyoh
I'm married _____	Soy casado
	soy kahsahdoh
– single _____	Soy soltero
	soy sohltehroh
– separated _____	Estoy separado
	ehstoy sehpahrahdoh
– divorced _____	Estoy divorciado
	ehstoy deebohrthyahdoh
– a widow/widower _____	Soy viuda/viudo
	soy byoodah/byoodoh
I live alone/with _____ someone	Vivo solo(a)/con otra persona
	beeboh sohloh(ah)/kohn ohtrah pehrsohnah
Do you have any _____ children/grandchildren?	¿Tiene hijos/nietos?
	tyehneh eehohs/nyehtohs?
How old are you? _____	¿Cuántos años tiene?
	kwahntohs ahnyohs tyehneh?
How old is she/he? _____	¿Cuántos años tiene?
	kwahntohs ahnyohs tyehneh?
I'm... _____	Tengo...años
	tehngoh...ahnyohs
She's/he's... _____	Tiene...años
	tyehneh...ahnyohs
What do you do for a _____ living?	¿En qué trabaja?
	ehn keh trahbahhah?
I work in an office _____	Trabajo en una oficina
	trahbahhoh ehn oonah ohfeetheenah
I'm a student/ _____ I'm at school	Estudio
	ehstoodyoh
I'm unemployed _____	Estoy en paro
	ehstoy ehn pahroh
I'm retired _____	Soy jubilado
	soy hoobeelahdoh
I'm on a disability _____ pension	Tengo una pensión de invalidez
	tehngoh oonah pehnsyohn deh eenbahleedeth
I'm a housewife _____	Soy ama de casa
	soy ahmah deh kahsah
Do you like your job? _____	¿Le gusta su trabajo?
	leh goostah soo trahbahhoh?

Most of the time _____	A veces sí, a veces no
	ah behthehs see, ah behthehs noh
I usually do, but I prefer ___ holidays	Por lo general sí, pero prefiero las vacaciones
	pohr loh hehnehrahl see, pehroh prehfyehroh lahs bahkahthyohnehs

.3 Starting/ending a conversation

Could I ask you _____ something?	¿Podría preguntarle una cosa?
	pohdreeah prehgoontahrleh oonah kohsah?
Excuse me	Perdone
	pehrdohneh
Excuse me, could you _____ help me?	¿Podría ayudarme?
	pohdreeah ahyoodahrmeh?
Yes, what's the problem? __	Sí, ¿qué pasa?
	see, keh pahsah?
What can I do for you? ____	¿En qué puedo servirle?
	ehn keh pwehdoh sehrbeerleh?
Sorry, I don't have time____ now	Lo siento, ahora no tengo tiempo
	loh syehntoh, ahohrah noh tehngoh tyehmpoh
Do you have a light? _____	¿Tiene fuego?
	tyehneh fwehgoh?
May I join you? _____	¿Le importa que me siente?
	leh eempohrtah keh meh syehnteh?
Could you take a _____ picture of me/us? Press this button.	¿Podría sacarme/sacarnos una foto? Hay que apretar este botón
	pohdreeah sahkahrmeh/sahkahrnohs oonah fohtoh? ay keh ahprehtahr ehsteh bohtohn
Leave me alone _____	Déjeme en paz
	dehhehmeh ehn pahth
Get lost_____	Váyase al diablo
	bahyahseh ahl deeahbloh
Go away or I'll scream_____	Como no se vaya, grito
	kohmoh noh seh bahyah, greetoh

.4 Congratulations and condolences

Happy birthday/many_____ happy returns	Feliz cumpleaños/felicidades
	fehleeth koomplehahnyohs/fehleetheedahdehs
Please accept my_____ condolences.	Le acompaño en el sentimiento
	leh ahkohmpahnyoh ehn ehl sehnteemyehntoh
I'm very sorry for you _____	¡Cuánto lo siento por usted!
	kwahntoh loh syehntoh pohr oostehdh!

.5 A chat about the weather

See also 1.5 The weather

It's so hot/cold today!_____	¡Qué calor/frío hace hoy!
	keh kahlohr/freeoh ahteh oy!
Nice weather, isn't it? _____	¡Qué buen tiempo hace! ¿Verdad?
	keh bwehn tyehmpoh ahteh! behrdah?

What a wind/storm! _____	¡Vaya viento/tormenta!
	bahyah byehntoh/tohrmentah!
All that rain/snow! _____	¡Cómo llueve/nieva!
	kohmoh lywehbeh/nyehbah!
All that fog! _____	¡Cuánta niebla!
	kwahntah nyehblah!
Has the weather been _____ like this for long here?	¿Hace mucho que hace este tiempo?
	ahtheh moochoh keh ahtheh ehsteh tyehmpoh?
Is it always this hot/cold ___ here?	¿Aquí siempre hace tanto calor/frío?
	ahkee syehmpreh ahteh tahntoh kahlohr/freeoh?
Is it always this dry/wet____ here?	¿Aquí siempre hace un tiempo tan seco/lluvioso?
	ahkee syehmpreh ahteh oon tyehmpoh tahn sehkoh/lyoobyohsoh?

3 .6 Hobbies

Do you have any _____ hobbies?	¿Tiene algún hobby?
	tyehneh algoon <u>h</u>ohbee?
I like painting/_____ reading/photography/ DIY	Me gusta pintar/leer/la fotografía/el bricolaje
	meh goostah peentahr/lehehr/lah fohtohgrahfeeah/ehl breekohlah<u>h</u>eh
I like music _____	Me gusta la música
	meh goostah lah mooseekah
I like playing the _____ guitar/piano	Me gusta tocar la guitarra/el piano
	meh goostah tohkahr lah gueetahrrah/ehl pyahnoh
I like going to the movies __	Me gusta ir al cine
	meh goostah eer ahl theeneh
I like travelling/_____ sport/fishing/walking	Me gusta viajar/hacer deporte/pescar/salir a caminar
	meh goostah byah<u>h</u>ahr/ahthehr dehpohrteh/pehskahr/sahleer ah kahmeenahr

3 .7 Being the host(ess)

See also 4 Eating out

Can I offer you a drink? ____	¿Le gustaría algo de beber?
	leh goostahreeah ahlgoh deh behbehr?
What would you like_____ to drink?	¿Qué quieres beber?
	keh kyehrehs behbehr?
Something non-alcoholic,__ please.	Algo sin alcohol
	ahlgoh seen ahlkohl
Would you like a _____ cigarette/cigar/to roll your own?	¿Quiere un cigarrillo/un puro/liar un cigarrillo?
	kyehreh oon theegahrreelyoh/oon pooroh/leeahr oon theegahrreelyoh?
I don't smoke _____	No fumo
	noh foomoh

Conversation

3

Are you doing anything ____ tonight?	¿Tiene algo que hacer esta noche? *tyehneh ahlgoh keh ahthehr ehstah nohcheh?*
Do you have any plans ____ for today/this afternoon/tonight?	¿Ya tiene planes para hoy/ esta tarde/esta noche? *yah tyehneh plahnehs pahrah oy/ehstah tahrdeh/ehstah nohcheh?*
Would you like to go _____ out with me?	¿Le(te) apetece salir conmigo? *leh(teh) ahpehtehtheh sahleer kohnmeegoh?*
Would you like to go _____ dancing with me?	¿Le(te) apetece ir a bailar conmigo? *leh(teh) ahpehtehtheh eer ah baylahr kohnmeegoh?*
Would you like to have ____ lunch/dinner with me?	¿Le(te) apetece comer/cenar conmigo? *leh(teh) ahpehtehtheh kohmehr/thenahr kohnmeegoh?*
Would you like to come____ to the beach with me?	¿Le(te) apetece ir a la playa conmigo? *leh(teh) ahpehtehtheh eer ah lah plahyah kohnmeegoh?*
Would you like to come____ into town with us?	¿Le apetece ir a la ciudad con nosotros? *leh ahpehtehtheh eer ah lah thyoodahdh kohn nohsohtrohs?*
Would you like to come____ and see some friends with us?	¿Le apetece ir a casa de unos amigos con nosotros? *leh ahpehtehtheh eer ah kahsah deh oonohs ahmeegohs kohn nohsohtrohs?*
Shall we dance?_____	¿Bailamos? *baylahmohs?*
– sit at the bar? _____	¿Vienes a sentarte conmigo en la barra? *byehnehs ah sehntahrteh kohnmeegoh ehn lah bahrrah?*
– get something to drink? __	¿Vamos a beber algo? *bahmohs ah behbehr ahlgoh?*
– go for a walk/drive?_____	¿Vamos a dar una vuelta? *bahmohs ah dahr oonah bwehltah?*
Yes, all right _____	Sí, vamos *see, bahmohs*
Good idea _____	Buena idea *bwehnah eedehah*
No (thank you) _____	No (gracias) *noh (grahthyahs)*
Maybe later_____	Quizá más tarde *keethah mahs tahrdeh*
I don't feel like it _____	No me apetece *noh meh ahpehtehtheh*
I don't have time _____	No tengo tiempo *noh tehngoh tyehmpoh*
I already have a date _____	Ya tengo otro compromiso *yah tehngoh ohtroh kohmprohmeesoh*
I'm not very good at_____ dancing/volleyball/ swimming	No sé bailar/jugar al vóleibol/nadar *noh seh baylahr/hoogahr ahl vohleheebohl/nahdahr*

3.9 Paying a compliment

You look wonderful! _____	¡Qué guapo/guapa está(estás)!
	keh wahpoh/wahpah ehstah(ehstahs)!
I like your car! _____	¡Qué bonito coche!
	keh bohneetoh kohcheh!
I like your ski outfit! _____	¡Qué bonito traje de esquiar!
	keh bohneetoh trahḫeh deh ehskeeahr!
You're a nice boy/girl _____	Eres muy bueno/buena
	ehrehs mwee bwehnoh/bwehnah
What a sweet child! _____	¡Qué niño tan majo/niña tan maja!
	keh neenyoh tahn mahḫoh/neenyah tahn mahḫah!
You're a wonderful _____ dancer!	Bailas muy bien
	bahylahs mwee byehn
You're a wonderful _____ cook!	Cocinas muy bien
	kohtheenahs mwee byehn
You're a terrific soccer _____ player!	Juegas muy bien al fútbol
	ḫwehgahs mwee byehn ahl footbohl

3.10 Chatting someone up

I like being with you _____	Me gusta estar contigo
	meh goostah ehstahr kohnteegoh
I've missed you so much __	Te he echado mucho de menos
	teh eh ehchahdoh moochoh deh mehnohs
I dreamt about you _____	He soñado contigo
	eh sohnyahdoh kohnteegoh
I think about you all day ___	Pienso todo el día en ti
	pyehnsoh tohdoh ehl deeah ehn tee
You have such a sweet ____ smile	Tienes una sonrisa muy bonita
	tyehnehs oonah sohnreesah mwee bohneetah
You have such beautiful ___ eyes	Tienes unos ojos muy bonitos
	tyehnehs oonohs ohḫohs mwee bohneetohs
I'm in love with you _____	Estoy enamorado/enamorada de ti
	ehstoy ehnahmohrahdoh/ehnahmohrahdah deh tee
I'm in love with you too ___	Yo también de ti
	yoh tahmbyehn deh tee
I love you_____	Te quiero
	teh kyehroh
I love you too _____	Yo también a ti
	yoh tahmbyehn ah tee
I don't feel as strongly _____ about you	Yo no siento lo mismo por ti
	yoh noh syehntoh loh meesmoh pohr tee
I already have a _____ boyfriend/girlfriend	Ya tengo pareja
	yah tehngoh pahrehḫah
I'm not ready for that_____	Yo no estoy preparado(a)
	yoh noh ehstoy prehpahrahdoh/ah
This is going too fast _____ for me	Vamos demasiado rápido
	bahmohs dehmahsyahdoh rahpeedoh
Take your hands off me ____	No me toque(s)
	noh meh tohkeh(s)
Okay, no problem _____	Vale, no importa
	bahleh, noh eempohrtah

Conversation

Will you stay with me tonight?	¿Te quedas a dormir?
	teh kehdahs ah dohrmeer?
I'd like to go to bed with you	Me gustaría acostarme contigo
	meh goostahreeah ahkohstahrmeh kohnteegoh
Only if we use a condom	Sólo si usamos condón
	sohloh see oosahmohs kohndohn
We have to be careful about AIDS	Hay que tener cuidado por lo del Sida
	ay keh tehnehr kweedahdoh pohr loh dehl seedah
That's what they all say	Eso es lo que dicen todos
	ehsoh ehs loh keh deethehn tohdohs
We shouldn't take any risks	Más vale no arriesgarse
	mahs bahleh noh ahrryehsgahrseh
Do you have a condom?	¿Llevas condones?
	lyehbahs kohndohnehs?
No? In that case we won't do it	¿No? Pues entonces no
	noh? pwehs ehntohntehs noh

3 .11 Arrangements

When will I see you again?	¿Cuándo te veo?
	kwahndoh teh behoh?
Are you free over the weekend?	¿Tiene tiempo este fin de semana?
	tyehneh tyehmpoh ehsteh feen deh sehmahnah?
What shall we arrange?	¿Cómo quedamos?
	kohmoh kehdahmohs?
Where shall we meet?	¿Dónde nos encontramos?
	dohndeh nohs ehnkohntrahmohs?
Will you pick me/us up?	¿Me/nos pasa a buscar?
	meh/nohs pahsah ah booskahr?
Shall I pick you up?	¿Lo/la paso a buscar?
	loh/lah pahsoh ah booskahr?
I have to be home by...	Tengo que estar en casa a las...
	tehngoh keh ehstahr ehn kahsah ah lahs...
I don't want to see you anymore	No quiero volver a verlo/verla
	noh kyehroh bohlbehr ah behrloh/behrlah

3 .12 Saying goodbye

Can I take you home?	¿Lo/la acompaño a su casa?
	loh/lah ahkohmpahnyoh ah soo kahsah?
Can I write/call you?	¿Puedo escribirle/llamarlo/llamarla por teléfono?
	pwehdoh ehskreebeerleh /lyahmahrloh/ lyahmahrlah pohr tehlehfohnoh?
Will you write/call me?	¿Me escribirá/llamará por teléfono?
	meh ehskreebeerah/lyahmahrah pohr tehlehfohnoh?
Can I have your address/phone number?	¿Me da su dirección/número de teléfono?
	meh dah soo deerehkthyohn/noomehroh deh tehlehfohnoh?
Thanks for everything	Gracias por todo
	grahthyahs pohr tohdoh
It was very nice	Lo hemos pasado muy bien
	loh ehmohs pahsahdoh mwee byehn

Say hello to... _____	Recuerdos a...
	rehkwehrdohs ah...
All the best _____	Te deseo lo mejor
	teh dehsehoh loh meh<u>h</u>ohr
Good luck _____	Que te vaya bien
	keh teh bahyah byehn
When will you be back? ___	¿Cuándo vuelves?
	kwahndoh bwohlbehs?
I'll be waiting for you _____	Te esperaré
	teh ehspehrahreh.
I'd like to see you again____	Me gustaría volver a verte
	meh goostahreeah bohlbehr ah behrteh
I hope we meet _____ again soon	Espero que nos volvamos a ver pronto
	ehspehroh keh nohs bohlbahmohs ah behr prohntoh
This is our address. _____ If you're ever in the UK	Esta es nuestra dirección. Si alguna vez pasa por el Reino Unido...
	ehstah ehs nwehstrah deerehkthyohn. see ahlgoonah behth pahsah pohr ehl reheenoh ooneedoh...
You'd be more than _____ welcome	Está cordialmente invitado
	ehstah kohrdyahlmehnteh eenbeetahdoh

3

Conversation

33

Eating out

Eating out

● **In Spain** people usually have three meals:
1 *El desayuno* (breakfast) approximately between 7 and 10 am.
Breakfast is light and consists of *café con leche* (white coffee), a
croissant or *suizo* (light sugary bun) or *tostadas* (toast).
2 *El almuerzo* (lunch) approx. between 2 and 4 pm, though hotels
usually serve at standard times. Lunch always includes a hot dish and
is the most important meal of the day. Office workers and
schoolchildren still lunch at home. It usually consists of four courses:
– starter (which can be a plate of greens)
– main course
– dessert
– fruit
3 *La cena* (dinner) between 9 and 11pm, 8pm in most hotels. Dinner is
usually a light, hot meal, taken with the family.
At around 6 or 7pm, a snack (*la merienda*) is often served, consisting
frequently of sandwiches with *chorizo* or *jamón serrano* and *pastas*
(biscuits) or small cakes.
Pinchos and *tapas* are often taken at bars with an apéritif, either in the
late morning or the evening.

4 .1 **O**n arrival

I'd like to book a table _____ for seven o'clock, please	¿Podría reservar una mesa para las siete? *pohdreeah rehsehrbahr oonah mehsah pahrah lahs syehteh?*
I'd like a table for two, _____ please	Quisiera una mesa para dos personas *keesyehrah oonah mehsah pahrah dohs pehrsohnahs*
We've/we haven't booked__	(No) hemos reservado *(noh) ehmohs rehsehrbahdoh*
Is the restaurant open _____ yet?	¿Ya está abierto el restaurante? *yah ehstah ahbyehrtoh ehl rehstahoorahnteh?*
What time does the _____ restaurant open/close?	¿A qué hora abre/cierra el restaurante? *ah keh ohrah ahbreh/thyehrrah ehl rehstahoorahnteh?*
Can we wait for a table? ___	¿Podemos esperar hasta que se desocupe una mesa? *pohdehmohs ehspehrahr ahstah keh seh dehsohkoopeh oonah mehsah?*
Do we have to wait long? __	¿Tenemos que esperar mucho? *tehnehmohs keh ehspehrahr moochoh?*

¿Ha reservado mesa? _____	Do you have a reservation?
¿A nombre de quién? _____	What name, please?
Por aquí, por favor. _____	This way, please
Esta mesa está reservada _____	This table is reserved
En quince minutos quedará libre _____ una mesa	We'll have a table free in fifteen minutes.
¿Le importaría esperar (en la barra)? ____	Would you like to wait (at the bar)?

Is this seat taken? _____	¿Está ocupada esta silla?
	ehstah ohkoopahdah ehstah seelyah?
Could we sit here/there? ___	¿Podemos sentarnos aquí/allí?
	pohdemohs sehntahrnohs ahkee/ahlyee?
Can we sit by the_____ window?	¿Podemos sentarnos junto a la ventana?
	pohdehmohs sehntahrnohs hoontoh ah lah behntahnah?
Can we eat outside? _____	¿Podemos comer afuera?
	pohdehmohs kohmehr ahfwehrah?
Do you have another _____ chair for us?	¿Podría traernos otra silla?
	pohdreeah trahehrnohs ohtrah seelyah?
Do you have a _____ highchair?	¿Podría traernos una silla para niños?
	pohdreeah trahehrnohs oonah seelyah pahrah neenyohs?
Is there a socket for _____ this bottle-warmer?	¿Hay un enchufe para este calentador de biberones?
	ay oon ehnchoofeh pahrah ehsteh kahlehntahdohr deh beebehrohnehs?
Could you warm up _____ this bottle/jar for me?	¿Podría calentarme este biberón/este bote?
	pohdreeah kahlehntahrmeh ehsteh beebehrohn/ehsteh bohteh?
Not too hot, please _____	Que no esté muy caliente, por favor
	keh noh ehsteh mwee kahlyehnteh pohr fahbohr
Is there somewhere I _____ can change the baby's nappy?	¿Hay algún lugar para cambiar al bebé?
	ay ahlgoon loogahr pahrah kahmbyahr ahl behbeh?
Where are the toilets? _____	¿Dónde están los servicios?
	dohnde ehstahn lohs sehrbeethyohs?

🔵4 .2 Ordering

Waiter! _____	¡Camarero!
	kahmahrehroh!
Madam!/Sir! _____	¡Oiga, (por favor)!
	oygah (pohr fahbohr)!
We'd like something to ____ eat/a drink	Quisiéramos comer/beber algo
	keesyehrahmohs kohmehr/behber ahlgoh
Could I have a quick_____ meal?	¿Podría comer algo rápido?
	pohdreeah kohmehr ahlgoh rahpeedoh?
We don't have much _____ time	Tenemos poco tiempo
	tehnehmohs pohkoh tyehmpoh
We'd like to have a _____ drink first	Antes quisiéramos beber algo
	ahntehs keesyehrahmohs behbehr ahlgoh
Could we see the_____ menu/wine list, please?	¿Nos podría traer la carta/la carta de vinos?
	nohs pohdreeah trahehr lah kahrtah/lah kahrtah deh beenohs?
Do you have a menu _____ in English?	¿Tienen menú en inglés?
	tyehnehn mehnoo ehn eenglehs?
Do you have a dish_____ of the day?	¿Tienen menú del día/menú turístico?
	tyehnehn mehnoo dehl deeah/mehnoo tooreesteekoh?
We haven't made a_____ choice yet	Todavía no hemos elegido
	tohdahbeeah noh ehmohs ehleh<u>h</u>eedoh

36

What do you _____ recommend?	¿Qué nos recomienda? *keh nohs rehkohmyehndah?*
What are the specialities ___ of the region/the house?	¿Cuáles son las especialidades de la región/de la casa? *kwahlehs sohn lahs ehspehthyahleedahdehs deh lah rehhyohn/deh lah kahsah?*
I like strawberries/olives ___	Me gustan las fresas/las aceitunas *meh goostahn lahs frehsahs/lahs ahtheheetoonahs*
I don't like meat/fish/... ___	No me gusta el pescado/la carne/... *noh meh goostah ehl pehskahdoh/lah kahrneh/...*
What's this? _____	¿Qué es esto? *keh ehs ehstoh?*
Does it have...in it? _____	¿Lleva...? *lyehbah...?*
What does it taste like? ____	¿A qué sabe? *ah keh sahbeh?*
Is this a hot or a_____ cold dish?	¿Es un plato caliente o frío? *ehs oon plahtoh kahlyehnteh oh freeoh?*
Is this sweet? _____	¿Es un plato dulce? *ehs oon plahtoh doolthe?*
Is this spicy? _____	¿Es un plato picante? *ehs oon plahtoh peekahnteh?*
Do you have anything _____ else, please?	¿Tendría otra cosa? *tehndreeah ohtrah kohsah?*
I'm on a salt-free diet_____	No puedo comer sal *noh pwehdoh kohmehr sahl*
I can't eat pork _____	No puedo comer carne de cerdo *noh pwehdoh kohmehr kahrneh deh thehrdoh*
– sugar _____	No puedo comer azúcar *noh pwehdo kohmehr ahthookahr*
– fatty foods _____	No puedo comer grasa *noh pwehdoh kohmehr grahsah*
– (hot) spices _____	No puedo comer cosas picantes *noh pwehdoh kohmehr kohsahs peekahntehs*
I'll/we'll have what those___ people are having	Lo mismo que esos señores, por favor *loh meesmoh keh ehsohs sehnyohrehs pohr fahbohr*

¿Van a tomar un aperitivo? _____	Would you like a drink first?
¿Ya han elegido? _____	Have you decided?
¿Qué van a tomar? _____	What would you like to eat?
Que aproveche _____	Enjoy your meal.
¿Quiere su bistec rojo, mediano o muy hecho?	Would you like your steak rare, medium or well done?
¿Van a tomar postre/café? _____	Would you like a dessert/coffee?

I'd like...	Para mí... *pahrah mee...*
We're not having a _____ starter	No vamos a comer primer plato *noh bahmohs ah kohmehr preemehr plahtoh*
The child will share_____ what we're having	El niño/la niña comerá de nuestro menú *ehl neenyoh/lah neenyah kohmehrah deh nwehstroh mehnoo*
Could I have some _____ more bread, please?	Más pan, por favor *mahs pahn pohr fahbohr*
– a bottle of water/wine____	Otra botella de agua/de vino, por favor *ohtrah bohtehlyah deh ahgwah/deh beenoh, pohr fahbohr*
– another helping of... ____	Otra ración de..., por favor *ohtrah rahthyohn deh..., pohr fahbohr*
– some salt and pepper ____	¿Podría traerme sal y pimienta? *pohdreeah trahehrmeh sahl ee peemyehntah?*
– a napkin ____	¿Podría traerme una servilleta? *pohdreeah trahehrmeh oonah sehrbeelyehtah?*
– a spoon ____	¿Podría traerme una cuchara? *pohdreeah trahehrmeh oonah koochahrah?*
– an ashtray ____	¿Podría traerme un cenicero? *pohdreeah trahehrmeh oon thehneethehroh?*
– some matches____	¿Podría traerme unas cerillas? *pohdreeah trahehrmeh oonahs thehreelyahs?*
– some toothpicks ____	¿Podría traerme unos palillos? *pohdreeah trahehrmeh oonohs pahleelyohs?*
– a glass of water ____	¿Podría traerme un vaso de agua? *pohdreeah trahehrmeh oon bahsoh deh ahgwah?*
– a straw (for the child) ____	¿Podría traerme una pajita (para el niño/la niña)? *pohdreeah trahehrmeh oonah pahheetah (pahrah ehl neenyoh/lah neenyah)?*
Enjoy your meal! ____	¡Que aproveche! *keh ahprohbehcheh!*
You too! ____	Igualmente *eegwahlmehnteh*
Cheers! ____	¡Salud! *sahloodh!*
The next round's on me ____	La próxima ronda la pago yo *lah prohxeemah rohndah lah pahgoh yoh*
Could we have a doggy____ bag, please?	¿Podemos llevarnos las sobras? *pohdehmohs lyehbarnohs lahs sohbrahs?*

4 .3 The bill

See also 8.2 Settling the bill

How much is this dish? ____	¿Cuánto vale este plato? *kwahntoh bahleh ehsteh plahtoh?*
Could I have the bill, ____ please?	La cuenta, por favor *lah kwehntah, pohr fahbohr*
All together ____	Todo junto *tohdoh hoontoh*

Everyone pays separately __	Cada uno paga lo suyo
	kahdah oonoh pahgah loh sooyoh
Could we have the menu __ again, please?	¿Podría traernos otra vez la carta?
	pohdreeah trahehrnohs ohtrah behth lah kahrtah?
The...is not on the bill _____	Ha olvidado apuntar el/la...
	ah olbeedahdoh ahpoontahr ehl/lah...

4 .4 Complaints

It's taking a very long time	Están tardando mucho
	ehstahn tahrdahndoh moochoh
We've been here an hour already	Ya llevamos una hora aquí
	yah lyebahmohs oonah ohrah ahkee
This must be a mistake ____	Esto tiene que ser una equivocación
	ehstoh tyehneh keh sehr oonah ehkeebohkahthyohn
This is not what I ordered	Esto no es lo que he pedido
	ehstoh noh ehs loh keh eh pehdeedoh
I ordered... _____	He pedido...
	eh pehdeedoh
There's a dish missing ____	Falta un plato
	fahltah oon plahtoh
This is broken/not clean __	Esto está roto/no está limpio
	ehstoh ehstah rohtoh/noh ehstah leempyoh
The food's cold _____	La comida está fría
	lah kohmeedah ehstah freeah
– not fresh _____	La comida no es fresca
	lah kohmeedah noh ehs frehskah
– too salty/sweet/spicy_____	La comida está muy salada/dulce/picante
	lah kohmeedah ehstah mwee sahlahdah/dooltheh/peekahnteh
The meat's not done_____	La carne está cruda
	lah kahrneh ehstah kroodah
– overdone _____	La carne está muy hecha
	lah kahrneh ehstah mwee ehchah
– tough _____	La carne está dura
	lah kahrneh ehstah doorah
– off_____	La carne está podrida
	lah kahrneh ehstah pohdreedah
Could I have something else instead of this?	¿Me podría traer otra cosa en lugar de esto?
	meh pohdreeah trahehr ohtrah kohsah ehn loogahr deh ehstoh?
The bill/this amount is not right	La cuenta/este precio está mal
	lah kwehntah/ehsteh prehthyoh ehstah mahl
We didn't have this_____	Esto no lo hemos comido/bebido
	ehstoh noh loh ehmohs kohmeedoh/behbeedoh
There's no paper in the toilet	No hay papel en el servicio
	noh ay pahpehl ehn ehl sehrbeethyoh
Do you have a complaints book?	¿Tienen libro de quejas?
	tyehnen leebroh deh kehhas?
Will you call the manager, please?	Haga el favor de llamar al jefe
	ahgah ehl fahbohr deh lyamahr ahl hehfeh

.5 Paying a compliment

That was a wonderful ____ meal	Hemos comido muy bien *ehmohs kohmeedoh mwee byehn*
The food was excellent ____	La comida ha estado exquisita *lah kohmeedah ah ehstahdoh ehxkeeseetah*
The...in particular was ____ delicious	Sobre todo nos ha gustado el/la... *sohbreh tohdoh nohs ah goostahdoh ehl/lah...*

.6 The menu

aperitivo	mariscos	postres
apéritif	seafood	sweets/dessert
aves	pastelería	primeros platos
poultry	pastry	starters
azúcar	pescados	raciones
sugar	fish	portions
bebidas alcohólicas	platos calientes	servicio incluido
alcoholic beverages	hot dishes	service included
bebidas calientes	platos combinados	sopas
hot beverages	combined dishes	soups
carta de vinos	plato del día	tapas
wine list	dish of the day	tapas
cócteles	platos fríos	venado
cocktails	cold dishes	game
cubierto	platos principales	verduras
cover charge	main courses	vegetables
entremeses variados	platos típicos	
hors d'oeuvres	regional specialities	

.7 Alphabetical list of drinks and dishes

aceituna	anís	biftec
olive	aniseed	steak
aguacate	apio	bizcocho (borracho)
avocado	celery	sponge cake(with
ajo	arenque	sherry or similar)
garlic	herring	bocadillo
albóndigas	arroz	sandwich
meat balls	rice	buey/vaca
alcachofa	asado	beef
artichoke	roast, roasted	cabrito
almejas	atún/bonito	kid
clams	tuna	café (solo/con leche)
almendras	avellana	coffee (black/white)
almonds	hazelnut	calamares (en su
ancas de rana	bacalao	tinta)
frog's legs	cod	squid (cooked in
anchoa/boquerón	batido de...	their ink)
anchovy	...milk shake	caldo
anguila	berenjena	broth
eel	aubergine	callos
		tripe

cangrejo
crab

caracoles
snails

carne
meat

carpa
carp

castaña
chestnut

cebolla
onion

cerdo
pork

cerezas
cherries

cerveza
beer

chorizo
chorizo (paprika
  flavoured salami
  sausage)

chucrut
sauerkraut

chuleta/costilla
chop

churros
fritters

ciervo
venison

cigalas
Dublin Bay prawns

ciruela
plum

cochinillo asado
roast suckling pig

cocido
boiled

codorniz
quail

col/berza
cabbage

coles de Bruselas
Brussels sprouts

coliflor
cauliflower

coñac
brandy

conejo
rabbit

copa helada/helado
ice cream

cordero
lamb

crema/nata
cream

criadillas/mollejas
sweetbreads

crudo
raw

cuba libre
rum coke

dátil
date

dulce
sweet

emperador
swordfish

en escabeche
pickled

endibia
chicory/endive

ensalada (mixta)
mixed salad

ensaladilla rusa
Russian salad

escalope
escalope

espárragos
asparagus

especies
spices

espinaca
spinach

fideos
noodles

filete
fillet

flan
cream caramel

frambuesa
raspberry

fresa
strawberry

frito
fried

fruta (del tiempo)
seasonal fruit

galleta
biscuit

gambas
prawns

garbanzos
chick peas

gazpacho andaluz
gazpacho (cold
  soup)

granizado de
  limón/café
iced drink
  (lemon/coffee)

grosellas
red/black currants

guisado
stew

guisantes
peas

habas
broad beans

harina
flour

hígado de oca
goose liver

higo
fig

huevos al plato/
  duros/revueltos
fried/hard
  boiled/scrambled
  eggs

jamón de
  York/serrano
ham (cooked/Parma
  style)

jerez (seco, dulce)
sherry (dry, sweet)

judías verdes
French beans

jugo/zumo
fruit juice

langosta
lobster

langostino
crayfish

leche
milk

lechuga
lettuce

legumbres
vegetables
  (legumes)

lengua
tongue

lenguado
sole

lentejas
lentils

licor
liqueur

liebre
hare

limón
lemon

lomo de cerdo
tenderloin of pork

maíz (mazorca)
corn (on the cob)
mantequilla
butter
manzana
apple
mazapán
marzipan
mejillones
mussels
melocotón (en
  almíbar)
peach (in syrup)
melón
melon
membrillo
quince
merluza
hake
mermelada
jam
mero
sea bass
morcilla
black pudding
mostaza
mustard
muslo de pollo
drumstick
nuez
walnut
ostras
oysters
paella
paella
pan
bread
pastel
cake
patatas fritas
chips/crisps
pato (silvestre)
(wild) duck
pechuga (de pollo)
(chicken) breast
pepino
cucumber
pepinillos
gherkins
pera
pear

perdiz
partridge
perejil
parsley
pescado
fish
picadillo de ternera
minced veal
pierna (de cordero)
leg (of lamb)
pimentón
paprika
pimienta
pepper
pimientos
green/red peppers
piña
pineapple
plancha (a la)
grilled
plátano
banana
plato principal
main course
platos típicos
regional specialities
pollo
chicken
puerro
leek
pulpo
octopus
queso
cheese
rábanos
radishes
rabo de buey
oxtail
rape
monkfish
remolacha
beetroot
riñones
kidneys
rodaballo
turbot
romana (a la)
deep fried
vino rosado
rosé wine
salchicha
sausage

salchichón
salami
salmón
salmon
salmón ahumado
smoked salmon
salmonete
red mullet
sandía
water melon
sangría
sangría
sardinas
sardines
setas
mushrooms
solomillo de buey
fillet of beef
sopa
soup
tarta helada
ice cream cake
ternera
veal
tinto
red wine
tocino
bacon
tortilla española
Spanish omelette
  (potato)
tortilla francesa
plain omelette
tortitas
waffles
trucha
trout
trufas
truffles
turrón
nougat
uvas
grapes
verduras
green vegetables
vinagre
vinegar
zanahorias
carrots
zumo de naranja
orange juice

On the road

5 **O**n the road

5.1 **A**sking for directions

Excuse me, could I ask you something?	Perdone, ¿podría preguntarle algo? *pehrdohneh, pohdreeah prehgoontahrleh ahlgoh?*
I've lost my way	Me he perdido *meh eh pehrdeedoh*
Is there a(n)... around here?	¿Sabe dónde hay un(a)...por aquí? *sahbeh dohndeh ay oon(ah)...pohr ahkee?*
Is this the way to...?	¿Se va por aquí a...? *seh bah pohr ahkee ah...?*
Could you tell me how to get to the... (name of place) by car/on foot?	¿Podría decirme cómo llegar a... (en coche/a pie)? *pohdreeah dehtheermeh kohmoh lyehgahr ah... (ehn kohcheh/ah pyeh)?*
What's the quickest way to...?	¿Cómo hago para llegar lo antes posible a...? *kohmoh ahgoh pahrah lyehgahr loh ahntehs pohseebleh ah...?*
How many kilometres is it to...?	¿Cuántos kilómetros faltan para llegar a...? *kwahntohs keelohmehtrohs fahltahn pahrah lyehgahr ah...?*
Could you point it out on the map?	¿Podría señalarlo en el mapa? *pohdreeah sehnyahlahrloh ehn ehl mahpah?*

No sé; no soy de aquí	I don't know, I don't know my way around here
Por aquí no es	You're going the wrong way
Tiene que volver a...	You have to go back to...
Allí los carteles le indicarán	From there on just follow the signs
Vuelva a preguntar allí	When you get there, ask again

todo recto	la calle	el viaducto
straight ahead	the street	the fly-over
a la izquierda	el semáforo	el puente
left	the traffic light	the bridge
a la derecha	el túnel	el paso a nivel/las
right	the tunnel	barreras
doblar	el stop	the level
turn	the `give way' sign	crossing/the boom
seguir	el edificio	gates
follow	the building	el cartel en
cruzar	en la esquina	dirección de...
cross	at the corner	the sign pointing to...
el cruce	el río	la flecha
the intersection	the river	the arrow

44

.2 Customs

● **Border documents**: valid passport, visa. For car and motorbike:
valid UK driving licence and registration document, insurance
document, green card, UK registration plate.
Import and export specifications:
– Foreign currency: no restrictions
– Alcohol: 10 litres of spirits and 90 litres of wine. Tobacco: 800
cigarettes, 200 cigars or a kilo of tobacco. Restricted to personal
consumption only.

Su pasaporte, por favor _____	Your passport, please
La tarjeta verde, por favor _____	Your green card, please
El permiso de circulación/la carta _____ gris, por favor	Your vehicle documents, please
¿Adónde va? _____	Where are you heading?
¿Cuánto tiempo piensa quedarse? _____	How long are you planning to stay?
¿Tiene algo que declarar? _____	Do you have anything to declare?
¿Puede abrir esto? _____	Open this, please

My children are entered ___ on this passport	Mis hijos están apuntados en este pasaporte *mees ee<u>h</u>ohs ehstahn ahpoontahdohs ehn ehsteh pahsahpohrteh*
I'm travelling through _____	Estoy de paso *ehstoy deh pahsoh*
I'm going on holiday to... __	Voy de vacaciones a... *boy deh bahkahthyohnehs ah...*
I'm on a business trip _____	He venido en viaje de negocios *eh behneedoh ehn byah<u>h</u>eh deh nehgohthyohs*
I don't know how long_____ I'll be staying yet	Todavía no sé cuánto tiempo me quedaré *tohdahbeeah noh seh kwahntoh tyehmpoh meh kehdahreh*
I'll be staying here for _____ a weekend	Pienso quedarme un fin de semana *pyehnsoh kehdahrmeh oon feen deh sehmahnah*
– for a few days _____	Pienso quedarme unos días *pyehnsoh kehdahrmeh oonohs deeahs*
– for a week_____	Pienso quedarme una semana *pyehnsoh kehdahrmeh oonah sehmahnah*
– for two weeks _____	Pienso quedarme dos semanas *pyehnsoh kehdahrmeh dohs sehmahnahs*
I've got nothing to_____ declare	No tengo nada que declarar *noh tehngoh nahdah keh dehklahrahr*
I've got...with me_____	Traigo... *trahygoh...*
– ...cartons of cigarettes ___	Traigo...cartones de cigarrillos *trahygoh...kahrtohnehs deh theegahrreelyohs*
– ...bottles of... _____	Traigo...botellas de... *trahygoh...bohtehlyahs deh...*

– some souvenirs _____	Traigo algunos recuerdos de viaje
	trahygoh ahlgoonohs rehkwehrdohs de
	byahheh
These are personal _____ effects	Estos son artículos personales
	ehstohs sohn ahrteekoolohs pehrsohnahlehs
These are not new _____	Estas cosas no son nuevas
	ehstahs kohsahs noh sohn nwehbahs
Here's the receipt _____	Aquí está el recibo
	ahkee ehstah ehl rehtheeboh
This is for private use _____	Esto es para uso personal
	ehstoh ehs pahrah oosoh pehrsohnahl
How much import duty _____ do I have to pay?	¿Cuánto tengo que pagar por derechos de aduana?
	kwahntoh tehngoh keh pahgahr pohr
	dehrehchohs deh ahdwahnah?
Can I go now? _____	¿Puedo seguir?
	pwehdoh sehgheer?

5 .3 Luggage

Porter! _____	¡Mozo!
	mohthoh!
Could you take this _____ luggage to...?	¿Podría llevar este equipaje a...?
	pohdreeah lyehbahr ehsteh ehkeepahheh
	ah...?
How much do I _____ owe you?	¿Cuánto le debo?
	kwahntoh leh dehboh?
Where can I find a _____ luggage trolley?	¿Dónde hay carritos para el equipaje?
	dohndeh ay kahrreetohs pahrah ehl
	ehkeepahheh?
Could you store this _____ luggage for me?	¿Podría dejar este equipaje en la consigna?
	pohdreeah dehhahr ehsteh ehkeepahheh
	ehn lah kohnseegnah?
Where are the luggage _____ lockers?	¿Dónde está la consigna automática?
	dohndeh ehstah lah kohnseegnah
	ahootohmahteekah?
I can't get the locker _____ open	No logro abrir la puerta de la consigna
	noh lohgroh ahbreer lah pwehrtah deh lah
	kohnseegnah
How much is it per item _____ per day?	¿Cuánto sale por bulto y por día?
	kwahntoh sahleh pohr booltoh ee pohr
	deeah?
This is not my bag/ _____ suitcase	Este/ésta no es mi bolso/mi maleta
	ehsteh/ehstah noh ehs mee bohlsoh/mee
	mahlehtah
There's one item/bag/ _____ suitcase missing still	Todavía falta un bulto/un bolso/una maleta
	tohdahbeeah fahltah oon booltoh/oon
	bohlsoh/oonah mahlehtah
My suitcase is damaged _____	Me han dañado la maleta
	meh ahn dahnyahdoh lah mahlehtah

.4 Traffic signs

a la derecha	ceda el paso	obras
right	give way	roadworks ahead
a la izquierda	cerrado	paso a nivel
left	closed	(sin barreras)
abierto	cruce peligroso	level crossing
open	dangerous crossing	(no gates)
altura máxima	curvas en ... km	paso de ganado
maximum height	bends for...km	cattle crossing
arcenes sin afirmar	despacio	peaje
soft verges	drive slowly	toll
¡atención, peligro!	desprendimientos	peatones
danger	loose rocks	pedestrian crossing
autopista de peaje	desvío	precaución
toll road	diversion	caution
autovía	dirección prohibida	prohibido aparcar
motorway	no entry	no parking
bajada peligrosa	dirección única	prohibido adelantar
steep hill	one-way traffic	no overtaking
calzada resbaladiza	encender las luces	puesto de socorro
slippery road	switch on lights	first aid
cambio de sentido	espere	salida
change of direction	wait	exit
cañada	estacionamiento	salida de camiones
animals crossing	reglamentado	factory/works exit
carretera comarcal	limited parking zone	substancias
secondary road	excepto...	peligrosas
carretera cortada	except for...	dangerous
road closed	fin de...	substances
carretera en mal	end of...	travesía peligrosa
estado	hielo	dangerous crossing
irregular road	ice on road	zona peatonal
surface	niebla	pedestrian zone
carretera nacional	beware fog	
main road		

 .5 The car

See the diagram on page 51.

● **The motorways in Spain** have been very well updated and expanded. Tolls, however, can be expensive.

Particular traffic regulations:
maximum speed for cars:
120km/h on toll roads
110km/h on other motorways
60km/h in town centres
– give way: all traffic from the right has the right of way, except for major roads and thoroughfares.
– towing: prohibited to private drivers.

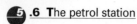

5 .6 **T**he petrol station

● **Petrol is easily available** but rather expensive in Spain.

How many kilometres to the next petrol station, please?	¿Cuántos kilómetros faltan para la próxima gasolinera? *kwahntohs keelohmehtrohs fahltahn pahrah lah prohxeemah gahsohleenehrah?*
I would like...litres of..., please	Póngame...litros de..., por favor *pohngahmeh...leetrohs deh..., pohr fahbohr*
– super	Póngame...litros de gasolina súper *pohngahmeh...leetrohs de gahsohleenah soopehr*
– leaded	Póngame...litros de gasolina normal *pohngahmeh...leetrohs deh gahsohleenah nohrmahl*
– unleaded	Póngame...litros de gasolina sin plomo *pohngahmeh...leetrohs deh gahsohleenah seen plohmoh*
– diesel	Póngame...litros de gasóleo *pohngahmeh...leetrohs deh gahsohlehoh*
I would like...pesetas' worth of petrol, please	Póngame gasolina por...pesetas *pohngahmeh gahsohleenah pohr...pehsehtahs*
Fill her up, please	Lléneme el depósito, por favor *lyehnehmeh ehl dehpohseetoh, pohr fahvohr*
Could you check...?	¿Podría controlar...? *pohdreeah kohntrohlahr?*
– the oil level	¿Podría controlar el nivel del aceite? *pohdreeah kohntrohlahr ehl neebehl dehl ahtheheeteh?*
– the tyre pressure	¿Podría controlar la presión de los neumáticos? *pohdreeah kohntrohlahr lah prehsyohn deh lohs nehoomahteekohs?*
Could you change the oil, please?	¿Podría cambiar el aceite? *pohdreeah kahmbyahr ehl atheheeteh?*
Could you clean the windows/the windscreen, please?	¿Podría limpiar los cristales/el parabrisas? *pohdreeah leempyahr lohs kreestahlehs/ehl pahrahbreesahs?*
Could you give the car a wash, please?	¿Podría lavar el coche? *pohdreeah lahbahr ehl kohcheh?*

On the road

5 .7 **B**reakdown and repairs

I'm having car trouble. Could you give me a hand?	Tengo una avería. ¿Podría ayudarme? *tehngoh oonah ahbehreeah. pohdreeah ahyoodahrmeh?*
I've run out of petrol	Me he quedado sin gasolina *meh eh kehdahdoh seen gahsohleenah*
I've locked the keys in the car	Me he dejado las llaves en el coche *meh eh dehhahdoh lahs lyabehs ehn ehl kohcheh*
The car/motorbike/ moped won't start	El coche/la moto/el ciclomotor no arranca *ehl kohcheh/lah mohtoh/ehl theeklohmohtohr noh ahrrahnkah*
Could you contact the recovery service for me, please?	¿Podría avisar al auxilio en carretera? *pohdreeah ahbeesar ahl ahooxeelyoh ehn kahrrehtehrah?*
Could you call a garage for me, please?	¿Podría llamar por teléfono a un taller mecánico? *pohdreeah lyahmahr pohr tehlehfohnoh ah oon tahlyehr mehkahneekoh?*
Could you give me a lift to...?	¿Me podría llevar a...? *meh pohdreeah lyehbahr ah...?*
– a garage/into town?	¿Me podría llevar a un taller mecánico/a la ciudad? *meh pohdreeah lyehbahr ah oon tahlyehr mehkahneekoh/ah lah thyoodahdh?*
– a phone booth?	¿Me podría llevar a una cabina de teléfonos? *meh pohdreeah lyehbahr ah oonah kahbeenah deh tehlehfohnohs?*
– an emergency phone?	¿Me podría llevar a un teléfono de emergencia? *meh pohdreeah lyehbahr ah oon tehlehfohnoh deh ehmehrhehnthyah?*
Can we take my bicycle/moped?	¿Podríamos llevar la bicicleta/el ciclomotor? *pohdreeahmohs lyehbahr lah beetheeklehtah/ehl theeklohmohtohr?*
Could you tow me to a garage?	¿Podría remolcarme hasta un taller mecánico? *pohdreeah rehmohlkahrmeh ahstah oon tahlyehr mehkahneekoh?*
There's probably something wrong with...(See 5.8).	Me parece que está fallando el/la... *meh pahrehtheh keh ehstah fahlyahndoh ehl/lah...*
Can you fix it?	¿Podría arreglarlo? *pohdreeah ahrrehglahrloh?*
Could you fix my tyre?	¿Podría arreglar el neumático? *pohdreeah ahrrehglahr ehl nehoomahteekoh?*
Could you change this wheel?	¿Podría cambiar esta rueda? *pohdreeah kahmbyahr ehstah rwehdah?*

The parts of a car
(the diagram shows the numbered parts)

1	battery	la batería	*lah bahtehreeah*
2	rear light	el faro piloto	*ehl fahroh peelohtoh*
3	rear-view mirror	el retrovisor	*ehl rehtrohbeesohr*
	reversing light	la luz de marcha atrás	*lah looth deh mahrchah ahtrahs*
4	aerial	la antena	*lah ahntehnah*
	car radio	la autorradio	*lah ahootohrrahdyoh*
5	petrol tank	el depósito de gasolina	*ehl dehpohseetoh deh gahsohleenah*
	inside mirror	el espejo interior	*ehl ehspeh<u>h</u>oh eentehreeohr*
6	sparking plugs	las bujías	*lahs boo<u>h</u>eeahs*
	fuel filter/pump	el separador de gasolina	*ehl sehpahrahdohr deh gahsohleenah*
7	wing mirror	el espejo exterior	*ehl ehspe<u>h</u>oh ehxtehryohr*
8	bumper	el parachoques	*ehl pahrahchohkehs*
	carburettor	el carburador	*ehl kahrboorahdohr*
	crankcase	el cárter	*ehl kahrtehr*
	cylinder	el cilindro	*ehl theeleendroh*
	ignition	los contactos del ruptor	*lohs kohntahktohs dehl rooptohr*
	warning light	la luz piloto	*lah looth peelohtoh*
	dynamo	la dinamo	*lah deenahmoh*
	accelerator	el pedal del acelerador	*ehl pehdahl dehl ahthehlehrahdohr*
	handbrake	el freno de mano	*ehl frehnoh deh mahnoh*
	valve	la válvula	*lah bahlboolah*
9	silencer	el silenciador	*ehl seelehnthyahdohr*
10	boot	el maletero	*ehl mahlehtehroh*
11	headlight	el faro	*ehl fahroh*
	crank shaft	el cigüeñal	*ehl theegwehnyahl*
12	air filter	el filtro de aire	*ehl feeltroh deh ayreh*
	fog lamp	la luz antiniebla trasera	*lah looth ahnteenyehblah trahsehrah*
13	engine block	el bloque motor	*ehl blohkeh mohtohr*
	camshaft	el árbol de levas	*ehl ahrbohl deh lehbahs*
	oil filter/pump	el filtro de aceite	*ehl feeltroh deh ahtheheetah*
	dipstick	la varilla indicadora de nivel de aceite	*lah bahreelyah eendeekahdohrah deh neebehl deh ahtheyteh*
	pedal	el pedal	*ehl pehdahl*
14	door	la portezuela	*lah pohrtehthwehlah*
15	radiator	el radiador	*ehl rahdyahdohr*
16	brake disc	el disco del freno	*ehl deeskoh dehl frehnoh*
	spare wheel	la rueda de reserva	*lah rwehdah deh rehsehrbah*
17	indicator	el intermitente	*ehl eentehrmeetehnteh*
	steering wheel	el volante	*ehl bohlahnteh*
18	windscreen wiper	el limpiaparabrisas	*ehl leempyahpahrahbreesahs*
19	shock absorbers	los amortiguadores	*lohs ahmohrteegwahdohrehs*
	sunroof	el techo corredizo	*ehl tehchoh kohrrehdeethoh*
	spoiler	el spoiler	*ehl spoheelehr*
	starter motor	el motor de arranque	*ehl mohtohr deh ahrrahnkeh*

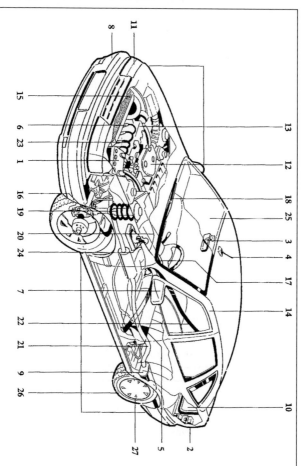

20	steering column	el cárter de la dirección	*ehl kahrtehr deh lah deerehkthyohn*
21	exhaust pipe	el tubo de escape	*ehl tooboh deh ehskahpeh*
22	seat belt	el cinturón de seguridad	*ehl theentoorohn deh sehgooreedahdh*
	fan	el ventilador	*ehl behnteelahdohr*
23	distributor cables	los cables del distribuidor	*lohs kahblehs dehl deestreebweedohr*
24	gear lever	la palanca de cambios	*lah pahlahnkah deh kahmbyohs*
25	windscreen	el parabrisas	*ehl pahrahbreesahs*
	water pump	la bomba de agua	*lah bohmbah deh ahgwah*
26	wheel	la rueda	*lah rwehdah*
27	hubcap	el tapacubos	*ehl tahpahkoobohs*
	piston	el émbolo	*ehl ehmbohloh*

Can you fix it so it'll _____ get me to...?	¿Podría arreglarlo de tal manera que pueda seguir hasta...?
	pohdreeah ahrrehglahrloh deh tahl mahnehrah keh pwehdah sehgheer ahstah...?
Which garage can _____ help me?	¿En qué taller me podrán ayudar entonces?
	ehn keh tahlyehr meh pohdrahn ahyoodahr ehntohnthehs?
When will my car/bicycle __ be ready?	¿Para cuándo estará mi coche/bicicleta?
	pahrah kwahndoh ehstahrah mee kohcheh/beetheeklehtah?
Can I wait for it here?_____	¿Puedo esperar aquí?
	pwehdoh ehspehrahr ahkee?
How much will it cost? ____	¿Por cuánto me va a salir?
	pohr kwahntoh meh bah ah sahleer?
Could you itemise _____ the bill?	¿Podría especificar la cuenta?
	pohdreeah ehspehtheefeekahr lah kwehntah?
Can I have a receipt for ____ the insurance?	¿Me podría dar un recibo para el seguro?
	meh pohdreeah dahr oon rehtheeboh pahrah ehl sehgooroh?

.8 The bicycle/moped

See the diagram on page 55.

● **Cycle paths** are rare in Spain. Not much consideration for bikes should be expected on the roads. The maximum speed for mopeds is 40km/h both inside and outside town centres. A helmet is compulsory.

No tengo piezas de recambio para su ___ coche/su bicicleta	I don't have parts for your car/bicycle
Las piezas de recambio me las tienen ___ que traer de otro sitio	I have to get the parts from somewhere else
Las piezas de recambio tengo que _____ encargarlas	I have to order the parts
Eso llevará medio día _____	That'll take half a day
Eso llevará un día _____	That'll take a day
Eso llevará unos días _____	That'll take a few days
Eso llevará una semana _____	That'll take a week
Su coche ha quedado totalmente _____ destruido	Your car is a write-off
Ya no se puede hacer nada para _____ arreglarlo	It can't be repaired
El coche/la moto/el ciclomotor/la_____ bicicleta estará para las...	The car/motor bike/moped/bicycle will be ready at... o'clock

52

I'd like to rent a..._____	Quisiera alquilar un...
	keesyehrah ahlkeelahr oon...
Do I need a (special)_____ licence for that?	¿Hace falta un permiso de conducir (especial)?
	ahteh fahltah oon pehrmeesoh deh kohndooteer (ehspehthyahl)?
I'd like to rent the...for... ___	Quisiera alquilar el/la...por...
	keesyehrah ahlkeelahr ehl/lah...pohr...
– one day _____	Quisiera alquilar el/la...por un día
	keesyehrah ahlkeelahr ehl/lah...pohr oon deeah
– two days _____	Quisiera alquilar el/la...por dos días
	keesyehrah ahlkeelahr ehl/lah...pohr dohs deeahs
How much is that per_____ day/week?	¿Cuánto sale por día/semana?
	kwahntoh sahleh pohr deeah/pohr sehmahnah?
How much is the _____ deposit?	¿Cuánto es la fianza?
	kwahntoh ehs lah fyahnthah?
Could I have a receipt _____ for the deposit?	¿Me podría dar un recibo por el pago de la fianza?
	meh pohdreeah dahr oon rehtheeboh pohr ehl pahgoh deh lah fyahnthah?
How much is the _____ surcharge per kilometre?	¿Cuánto hay que pagar extra por kilómetro?
	kwahntoh ay keh pahgahr ehxtrah pohr keelohmehtroh?
Does that include _____ petrol?	¿Está incluida la gasolina?
	ehstah eenklooeedah lah gahsohleenah?
Does that include _____ insurance?	¿Está incluido el seguro?
	ehstah eenklooeedoh ehl sehgooroh?
What time can I pick_____ the...up tomorrow?	¿A qué hora puedo pasar mañana a buscar el/la...?
	ah keh ohrah pwehdoh pahsahr mahnyahnah ah booskahr ehl/lah...?
When does the...have _____ to be back?	¿A qué hora tengo que devolver el/la...?
	ah keh ohrah tehngoh keh dehbohlbehr ehl/lah...?
Where's the petrol tank? ___	¿Dónde está el depósito de gasolina?
	dohndeh ehstah ehl dehpohseetoh deh gahsohleenah?
What sort of fuel does _____ it take?	¿Qué tipo de combustible hay que echarle?
	keh teepoh deh kohmboosteebleh ay keh ehchahrleh?

Where are you heading? ___	¿Adónde va?
	ahdohndeh bah?
Can I come along? _____	¿Me podría llevar?
	meh pohdreeah lyehbahr?
Can my boyfriend/ _____ girlfriend come too?	¿Podría llevar también a mi amigo/amiga?
	pohdreeah lyehbahr tahmbyehn ah mee ahmeegoh/ahmeegah?

The parts of a bicycle
(the diagram shows the numbered parts)

1 rear lamp	el piloto	*ehl peelohtoh*
2 rear wheel	la rueda trasera	*lah rwehdah trahsehrah*
3 (luggage) carrier	el portaequipajes	*ehl pohrtahehkeepah<u>h</u>ehs*
4 bicycle fork	la cabeza	*lah kahbehthah*
5 bell	el timbre	*ehl teembreh*
inner tube	la cámara	*lah kahmahrah*
tyre	el neumático/la cubierta	*ehl nehoomahteekoh/lah koobyehrtah*
6 crank	la biela	*lah byehlah*
7 gear change	el cambio de velocidades	*ehl kahmbyoh deh behlotheedahdehs*
wire	el hilo	*ehl eeloh*
dynamo	la dinamo	*lah deenahmoh*
bicycle trailer	el remolque de bicicleta	*ehl rehmohlkeh deh beetheeklehtah*
frame	el cuadro	*ehl kwahdroh*
8 dress guard	el guardafaldas	*ehl gwardahfahldahs*
9 chain	la cadena de rodillos	*lah kahdehnah deh rohdeelyohs*
chain guard	el cubrecadena/el cárter	*ehl koobrehkahdehnah/ehl kahrtehr*
chain lock	la cadena antirrobo	*lah kahdehnah ahnteerrohboh*
milometer	el contador kilométrico	*ehl kohntahdohr keelohmehtreekoh*
child's seat	el sillín para niños	*ehl seelyeen pahrah neenyohs*
10 headlamp	el faro	*ehl fahroh*
bulb	la bombilla	*lah bohmbeelyah*
11 pedal	el pedal	*ehl pehdahl*
12 pump	la bombilla	*lah bohmbeelyah*
13 reflector	el cristal reflectante	*ehl kreestahl rehflehktahnteh*
14 brake pad	la zapatilla del freno	*lah thahpahteelyah dehl frehnoh*
15 brake cable	el cable del freno	*ehl kahbleh dehl frehnoh*
16 ring lock	la cerradura	*lah thehrrahdoorah*
17 carrier straps	las bandas elásticas	*lahs bahndahs ehlahsteekahs*
18 spoke	el radio/el rayo	*ehl rahdyoh/ehl rahyoh*
19 mudguard	el guardabarros	*ehl gwahrdahbahrrohs*
20 handlebar	el manillar	*ehl mahneelyahr*
21 chain wheel	el piñón	*ehl peenyohn*
toe clip	el calapiés	*ehl kahlahpyehs*
22 crank axle	el eje del cigueñal	*ehl eh<u>h</u>eh dehl theegwehnyal*
drum brake	el freno de tambor	*ehl frehnoh deh tahmbohr*
23 tube	la llanta	*lah lyahntah*
24 valve	la válvula	*lah bahlboolah*
valve tube	el tubo de la válvula	*ehl tooboh deh lah bahlboolah*

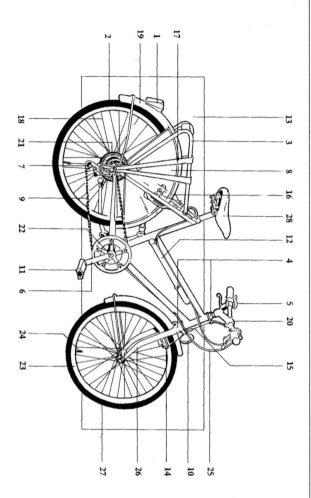

On the road

25	gear cable	el cable de velocidades	*ehl kahbleh deh behlohtheedahdehs*
26	fork	la horquilla	*lah ohrkeelyah*
27	front wheel	la rueda delantera	*lah rwehdah dehlahntehrah*
28	seat	el sillín	*el seelyeen*

I'm trying to get to...	Voy a...
	boy ah...
Is that on the way to...?	¿Eso está camino de...?
	ehsoh ehstah kahmeenoh deh...?
Could you drop me off...?	¿Me podría dejar...?
	meh pohdreeah dehhahr...?
– here?	¿Me podría dejar aquí mismo?
	meh pohdreeah dehhahr ahkee meesmoh?
– at the...exit?	¿Me podría dejar en la salida de...?
	meh pohdreeah dehhahr ehn lah sahleedah deh...?
– in the centre?	¿Me podría dejar en el centro?
	meh pohdreeah dehhahr ehn ehl thehntroh?
– at the next roundabout?	¿Me podría dejar en la próxima rotonda?
	meh pohdreeah dehhahr ehn lah prohxeemah rohtohndah?
Could you stop here, please?	¿Podría pararse aquí?
	pohdreeah pahrahrseh ahkee?
I'd like to get out here	Quisiera bajarme aquí
	keesyehrah bahhahrmeh ahkee
Thanks for the lift	Gracias por llevarme
	grahthyahs pohr lyehbahrmeh

Public transport

Public transport

6 .1 **I**n general

● **The rail network** has been substantially overhauled and expanded and there is now a good, fast service available with the Talgo and Ave in the south. These trains require payment of a supplement and it is advisable to reserve seats in advance, at the station or at travel agencies. Tickets for buses and the metro can be bought at an *estanco*, as well as metro stations.

Announcements

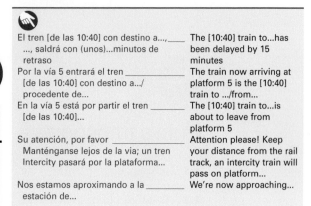

El tren [de las 10:40] con destino a...,____ ..., saldrá con (unos)...minutos de retraso	The [10:40] train to...has been delayed by 15 minutes
Por la vía 5 entrará el tren _____ [de las 10:40] con destino a.../ procedente de...	The train now arriving at platform 5 is the [10:40] train to .../from...
En la vía 5 está por partir el tren _____ [de las 10:40]...	The [10:40] train to...is about to leave from platform 5
Su atención, por favor _____ Manténganse lejos de la vía; un tren Intercity pasará por la plataforma...	Attention please! Keep your distance from the rail track, an intercity train will pass on platform...
Nos estamos aproximando a la _____ estación de...	We're now approaching...

Where does this train_____ go to?	¿Adónde va este tren? *ahdohndeh bah ehsteh trehn?*
Does this boat go to...? ____	¿Este barco va a...? *ehsteh bahrkoh bah ah...?*
Can I take this bus to...? ___	¿Puedo coger este autobús para ir a...? *pwehdoh koh<u>h</u>ehr ehsteh ahootohboos pahrah eer ah...?*
Does this train stop at...? __	¿Este tren para en...? *ehsteh trehn pahrah ehn...?*
Is this seat taken/free _____ /reserved?	¿Está ocupado/libre/reservado este asiento? *ehstah ohkoopahdoh/leebreh/rehsehrbahdoh ehsteh ahsyehntoh?*
I've booked... _____	He reservado... *eh rehsehrbahdoh...*
Could you tell me _____ where I have to get off for... ?	¿Me podría decir dónde me tengo que bajar para ir a...? *meh pohdreeah dehtheer dohndeh meh tehngoh keh bah<u>h</u>ar pahrah eer ah...?*
Could you let me_____ know when we get to...?	¿Me podría avisar cuando lleguemos a...? *meh pohdreeah ahbeesahr kwahndoh lyehghehmohs ah...?*
Could you stop at the_____ next stop, please?	La próxima parada, por favor *lah prohxeemah pahrahdah pohr fahbohr*

Where are we now? _____	¿Dónde estamos?
	dohndeh ehstahmohs?
Do I have to get off here? __	¿Tengo que bajarme aquí?
	tehngoh keh bah<u>h</u>ahrmeh ahkee?
Have we already _____ passed...?	¿Ya hemos pasado...?
	yah ehmohs pahsahdoh...?
How long have I been _____ asleep?	¿Cuánto tiempo he dormido?
	kwahntoh tyehmpoh eh dohrmeedoh?
How long does... _____ stop here?	¿Cuánto tiempo se queda aquí...?
	kwahntoh tyehmpoh seh kehdah ahkee?
Can I come back on the____ same ticket?	¿Este billete me sirve para volver?
	ehsteh beelyehteh meh seerbeh pahrah bohlbehr?
Can I change on this_____ ticket?	¿Se puede hacer trasbordo con este billete?
	seh pwehdeh ahtehhr trahsbohrdoh kohn ehsteh beelyehteh?
How long is this ticket _____ valid for?	¿Hasta cuándo es válido este billete?
	ahstah kwahndoh ehs bahleedoh ehsteh beelyehteh
How much is the _____ supplement for the Talgo/Ave (high speed train)?	¿Cuánto vale el suplemento para el Talgo/el Ave?
	kwahntoh bahleh ehl sooplehmehntoh pahrah ehl tahlgoh/ehl ahbeh?

6 .2 Questions to passengers

Ticket types

¿Primera o segunda clase? _____	First or second class?
¿Billete de ida o de ida y vuelta? _____	Single or return?
¿Fumadores o no fumadores? _____	Smoking or non-smoking?
¿Ventanilla o pasillo?_____	Window or aisle?
¿Adelante o atrás? _____	Front or back?
¿Asiento o litera? _____	Seat or couchette?
¿Arriba, en el medio o abajo?_____	Top, middle or bottom?
¿Clase turista o preferente?_____	Tourist class or business class?
¿Camarote o butaca? _____	Cabin or seat?
¿Individual o doble? _____	Single or double?
¿Cuántas personas viajan? _____	How many are travelling?

Public transport

6

Destination

¿Adónde quiere ir? _____	Where are you travelling?
¿Qué día sale? _____	When are you leaving?
Su...sale a las... _____	Your...leaves at...
Tiene que hacer trasbordo _____	You have to change trains
Tiene que bajarse en... _____	You have to get off at...
Tiene que pasar por... _____	You have to travel via...
El viaje de ida es el día... _____	The outward journey is on...
El viaje de vuelta es el día... _____	The return journey is on...
Tiene que embarcar a las...a _____ más tardar	You have to be on board by...

Inside the vehicle

Billetes, por favor _____	Your ticket, please
Su reserva, por favor _____	Your reservation, please
Su pasaporte, por favor _____	Your passport, please
Se ha equivocado de asiento _____	You're in the wrong seat
Se ha equivocado de... _____	You're on/in the wrong...
Este asiento está reservado _____	This seat is reserved
Tiene que pagar un suplemento _____	You'll have to pay a supplement
El...tiene un retraso de...minutos _____	The...has been delayed by...minutes

.3 Tickets

Where can I...? _____	¿Dónde...?
	dohndeh...?
– buy a ticket? _____	¿Dónde se compran los billetes?
	dohndeh seh kohmprahn lohs beelyehtehs?
– make a reservation? _____	¿Dónde se hacen las reservas?
	dohndeh seh ahtehn lahs rehsehrbahs?
– book a flight? _____	¿Dónde puedo hacer una reserva para un vuelo?
	dohndeh pwehdoh ahtehr oonah rehsehrbah pahrah oon bwehloh?
Could I have a...to..., _____ please?	Quiero un/una...a...
	kyehroh oon/oonah...ah...
– a single _____	Quiero un billete de ida a...
	kyehroh oon beelyehteh deh eedah ah...
– a return _____	Quiero un billete de ida y vuelta a...
	kyehroh oon beelyehteh deh eedah ee bwehltah ah...
first class _____	en primera clase
	ehn preemehrah klahseh
second class _____	en segunda clase
	ehn sehgoondah klahseh

Public transport

6

tourist class _____	en clase turista
	ehn klahseh tooreestah
business class _____	en clase preferente
	ehn klahseh prehfehrehnteh
I'd like to book a _____ seat/couchette/cabin	Quisiera reservar un asiento/una litera/un camarote
	keesyehrah rehsehrbahr oon ahsyehntoh/oonah leetehrah/oon kahmahrohteh
I'd like to book a berth _____ in the sleeping car	Quisiera reservar una plaza en un coche cama
	keesyehrah rehsehrbahr oonah plahthah ehn oon kohcheh kahmah
top/middle/bottom _____	arriba/en el medio/abajo
	ahrreebah/ehn ehl mehdyoh/ahbahhoh
smoking/no smoking _____	fumadores/no fumadores
	foomahdohrehs/noh foomahdohrehs
by the window _____	ventanilla
	behntahneelyah
single/double _____	individual/doble
	eendeebeedwahl/dohbleh
at the front/back_____	adelante/atrás
	ahdehlahnteh/ahtrahs
There are...of us_____	Somos...personas
	sohmohs...pehrsohnahs
a car _____	un coche
	oon kohcheh
a caravan _____	una caravana
	oonah kahrahbahnah
...bicycles_____	...bicicletas
	...beetheeklehtahs
Do you also have...? _____	¿Tienen...?
	tyehnehn...?
– season tickets? _____	¿Tienen billetes para varios viajes?
	tyehnen beelyehtehs pahrah bahryohs byahhehs?
– weekly tickets? _____	¿Tienen abonos semanales?
	tyehnehn ahbohnohs sehmahnahlehs?
– monthly season _____ tickets?	¿Tienen abonos mensuales?
	tyehnehn ahbohnohs mehnswahlehs?

6 .4 Information

Where's-? _____	¿Dónde hay...?
	dohndeh ay...?
Where's the information ___ desk?	¿Dónde está la oficina de información?
	dohndeh ehstah lah ohfeetheenah deh eenfohrmahthyohn?
Where can I find a_____ timetable?	¿Dónde hay un horario?
	dohndeh ay oon ohrahryoh?
Where's the...desk? _____	¿Dónde está el mostrador de...?
	dohndeh ehstah ehl mohstrahdohr deh...?
Do you have a city map____ with the bus/the underground routes on it?	¿Tendría un plano de la ciudad con la red de autobuses/metro?
	tehndreeah oon plahnoh deh lah thyoodahdh kohn lah rehth deh ahootohboosehs/mehtroh?

6

Do you have a _____ timetable?	¿Tendría un horario?
	tehndreeah oon ohrahryoh?
I'd like to confirm/ _____ cancel/change my booking for/trip to...	Quisiera confirmar/cancelar/cambiar mi reserva/mi viaje a...
	keesyehrah kohnfeermahr/kahnthehlahr/kahmbyahr mee rehsehrbah/mee byahheh ah...
Will I get my money _____ back?	¿Me devuelven el dinero?
	meh dehbwehlbehn ehl deenehroh?
I want to go to... _____ How do I get there? (What's the quickest way there?)	Tengo que ir a...¿Cómo hago para llegar (lo más rápido posible)?
	tehngoh keh eer ah...kohmoh ahgoh pahrah lyehgahr(loh mahs rahpeedoh pohseebleh)?
How much is a _____ single/return to...?	¿Cuánto vale un billete de ida/de ida y vuelta a...?
	kwahntoh bahleh oon beelyehteh deh eedah ee bwehltah ah...?
Do I have to pay a _____ supplement?	¿Tengo que pagar algún suplemento?
	tehngoh keh pahgahr ahlgoon sooplehmehntoh?
Can I interrupt my _____ journey with this ticket?	¿Con este billete puedo hacer una parada intermedia?
	kohn ehsteh beelyehteh pwehdoh ahtehehr oonah pahrahdah eentehrmehdyah?
How much luggage _____ am I allowed?	¿Cuánto equipaje puedo llevar?
	kwahntoh ehkeepahheh pwehdoh lyebahr?
Can I send my luggage _____ in advance?	¿Puedo enviar mi equipaje por anticipado?
	pwehdoh ehnbeeahr mee ehkeepahheh pohr ahnteetheepahdoh?
Does this...travel direct? _____	¿Este...va directo?
	ehsteh...bah deerehktoh?
Do I have to change? _____ Where?	¿Tengo que hacer trasbordo? ¿Dónde?
	tehngoh keh ahtehehr trahsbohrdoh? dohndeh?
Will there be any _____ stopovers?	¿Habrá escalas?
	ahbrah ehskahlahs?
Does the boat call in at _____ any ports on the way?	¿El barco hace alguna escala?
	ehl bahrkoh ahteh ahlgoonah ehskahlah?
Does the train/ _____ bus stop at...?	¿Este tren/este autobús para en...?
	ehsteh trehn/ehsteh ahootohboos pahrah ehn...?
Where should I get off? _____	¿Dónde me tengo que bajar?
	dohndeh meh tehngoh keh bahhahr?
Is there a connection _____ to...?	¿Hay enlace para...?
	ay ehnlahtheh pahrah...?
How long do I have to _____ wait?	¿Cuánto tengo que esperar?
	kwahntoh tehngoh keh ehspehrahr?
When does...leave? _____	¿Cuándo sale...?
	kwahndoh sahleh...?
What time does the _____ first/next/last...leave?	¿A qué hora sale el primer/próximo/último...?
	ah keh ohrah sahleh ehl preemehr/prohxeemoh/oolteemoh...?
How long does...take? _____	¿Cuánto tarda...en llegar?
	kwahntoh tahrdah...ehn lyehgahr?

What time does...arrive in...? _____	¿A qué hora llega...a...?
	ah keh ohrah lyegah...ah...?
Where does the...to... leave from? _____	¿De dónde sale el...a...?
	deh dohndeh sahleh ehl...ah...?
Is this...to...? _____	¿Este es...a...?
	ehsteh ehs...ah...?

.5 Aeroplanes

● **On arrival** at a Spanish airport, you will find the following signs:

llegadas	salidas
arrivals	departures

.6 Trains

● **The rail network** is very extensive, run by the RENFE (Red Nacional de Ferrocarriles Españoles). Some local trains are still rather slow so it is preferable to stipulate Talgo or Rápido when buying tickets. During the summer and before public holidays it is advisable to buy train tickets well in advance. Porters are few and far between.

.7 Taxis

● **There are plenty of taxis** in most cities. Supplements are payable for luggage and travel to stations or airports. It is advisable to inquire about the price in advance and make sure that you are hiring a city taxi.

libre	ocupado	parada de taxis
for hire	booked	taxi rank

Taxi! _____	¡Taxi!
	tahxee!
Could you get me a taxi, please? _____	¿Me podría llamar un taxi?
	meh pohdreeah lyahmahr oon tahksee?
Where can I find a taxi around here? _____	¿Dónde se puede coger un taxi por aquí?
	dohndeh seh pwehdeh kohhehr oon tahxee pohr ahkee?
Could you take me to..., please? _____	A..., por favor
	ah..., pohr fahbohr
– this address _____	A esta dirección, por favor
	ah ehstah deerehkthyohn, pohr fahbohr
– the...hotel _____	Al hotel..., por favor
	ahl ohtehl..., pohr fahbohr
– the town/city centre _____	Al centro, por favor
	ahl thehntroh, pohr fahbohr
– the station _____	A la estación, por favor
	ah lah ehstahthyohn, pohr fahbohr
– the airport _____	Al aeropuerto, por favor
	ahl ahehrohpwehrtoh, pohr fahbohr

Public transport

How much is the _____ ¿Cuánto sale el recorrido hasta...?
  trip to...? *kwahntoh sahleh ehl rehkohrreedoh*
  ahstah...?

How far is it to...? _____ ¿Cuánto es hasta...?
  kwahntoh ehs ahstah...?

Could you turn on the _____ ¿Podría poner en marcha el taxímetro?
  meter, please? *pohdreeah pohnehr ehn mahrchah ehl*
  tahxeemehtroh?

I'm in a hurry _____ Llevo prisa
  lyehboh preesah

Could you speed up/slow __ ¿Podría ir más rápido/más despacio?
  down a little? *pohdreeah eer mahs rahpeedoh/mahs*
  dehspathyoh?

Could you take a _____ ¿Podría ir por otro camino?
  different route? *pohdreeah eer pohr ohtroh kahmeenoh?*

I'd like to get out here,_____ Déjeme aquí
  please *dehhehmeh ahkee*

You have to go...here _____ Siga...aquí
  seegah...ahkee

You have to go straight ____ Siga todo recto aquí
  on here *seegah tohdoh rehktoh akee*

You have to turn left_____ Doble a la izquierda aquí
  here *dohbleh ah lah eethkyehrdah ahkee*

You have to turn right _____ Doble a la derecha aquí
  here *dohbleh ah lah dehrehchah ahkee*

This is it _____ Es aquí
  ehs ahkee

Could you wait a minute ___ Espéreme un momentito, por favor
  for me, please? *ehspehrehmeh oon mohmehnteetoh, pohr*
  fahbohr

Overnight accommodation

7 Overnight accommodation

7 .1 General

● **There is great variety** in overnight accommodation in Spain. It is advisable to book (and send confirmation) in advance.
Hotel: stars indicate the degree of comfort; from five stars, the most luxurious, to one star, very basic. Most hotels offer *pensión completa* (full board) or *media pensión* (half board).
Parador: Mainly, but not always, luxurious hotels in converted castles or palaces in exceptional areas. These are very popular and have to be booked very well in advance, but are well worth the visit. They are under government supervision.
Hostal: Family run businesses for the most part, with one to three stars. They do not always provide breakfast, but are clean and can be very well situated.
Albergue: usually country inns.
Albergue de juventud: restricted to members of the international Youth Hostels Association.
Camping: a list of sites can be found at any Tourist Office.

¿Cuánto tiempo piensa quedarse? _____	How long will you be staying?
Rellene este formulario, por favor _____	Fill in this form, please
¿Me permite su pasaporte? _____	Could I see your passport?
Tiene que pagar una fianza _____	I'll need a deposit
Tiene que pagar por adelantado_____	You'll have to pay in advance

My name's...I've made_____ a reservation over the phone/by mail	Me llamo...He reservado una habitación por teléfono/por carta *meh lyahmoh...eh rehsehrbahdoh oonah ahbeetahthyohn pohr tehlehfohnoh/pohr kahrtah*
How much is it per _____ night/week/ month?	¿Cuánto sale por noche/semana/mes? *kwahntoh sahleh pohr nohcheh/sehmahnah/mehs?*
We'll be staying at _____ least...nights/weeks	Pensamos quedarnos al menos...noches/semanas *pehnsahmohs kehdahrnohs ahl mehnohs...nohchehs/sehmahnahs*
We don't know yet _____	Todavía no lo sabemos exactamente *tohdahbeeah noh loh sahbehmohs ehxahktahmehnteh*
Do you allow pets _____ (cats/dogs)?	¿Están permitidos los animales domésticos (perros/gatos)? *ehstahn pehrmeeteedohs lohs ahneemahlehs dohmehsteekohs(pehrrohs/gahtohs)?*
What time does the _____ gate/door open/close?	¿A qué hora cierran/abren la verja/la puerta de entrada? *ah keh ohrah thyehrrahn/ahbrehn lah behrhah/lah pwehrtah deh ehntrahdah?*

Could you get me _____ a taxi, please?	¿Podría llamar un taxi? *pohdreeah lyahmahr oon tahxee?*
Is there any mail _____ for me?	¿Hay carta para mí? *ay kahrtah pahrah mee?*

.2 Camping

See the diagram on page 69.

Puede elegir el sitio usted mismo _____	You can pick your own site
El sitio se lo asignamos nosotros _____	You'll be allocated a site
Este es el número de su _____ emplazamiento	This is your site number
Por favor pegue esto en el parabrisas ___ del coche	Stick this on your car, please
No pierda esta tarjeta _____	Please don't lose this card

Where's the manager? _____	¿Dónde está el encargado? *dohndeh ehstah ehl ehnkahrgahdoh?*
Are we allowed to _____ camp here?	¿Podemos acampar aquí? *pohdehmohs ahkahmpahr ahkee?*
There are...of us and _____ ...tents	Somos...personas y...tiendas *sohmohs...pehrsohnahs ee...tyehndahs*
Can we pick our _____ own site?	¿Podemos elegir el sitio nosotros mismos? *pohdehmohs ehleh<u>h</u>eer ehl seetyoh nohsohtrohs meesmohs?*
Do you have a quiet _____ spot for us?	¿Nos podría dar un sitio tranquilo? *nohs pohdreeah dahr oon seetyoh trahnkeeloh?*
Do you have any other ____ sites available?	¿No tiene otro sitio libre? *noh tyehneh ohtroh seetyoh leebreh?*
It's too windy/sunny/ _____ shady here.	Hay mucho viento/mucho sol/mucha sombra *ay moochoh byehntoh/moochoh sohl/moochah sohmbrah*
It's too crowded here _____	Hay mucha gente *ay moochah <u>h</u>ehnteh*
The ground's too _____ hard/uneven	El suelo es muy duro/muy desigual *ehl swehloh ehs mwee dooroh/mwee dehseegwahl*
Do you have a level _____ spot for the camper/caravan/folding caravan?	¿Tiene un sitio plano para el autocaravana/la caravana/el remolque tienda? *tyehneh oon seetyoh plahnoh pahrah ehl ahootohkahrahbahnah/lah kahrahbahnah/ehl rehmohlkeh-tyehndah?*
Could we have _____ adjoining sites?	¿Tiene dos plazas juntas? *tyehneh dohs plahthahs <u>h</u>oontahs?*
Can we park the car _____ next to the tent?	¿Podemos aparcar el coche junto a la tienda? *pohdehmohs ahpahrkahr ehl kohcheh <u>h</u>oontoh ah lah tyehndah?*

Camping equipment
(the diagram shows the numbered parts)

	luggage space	el compartimiento de equipaje	*ehl kohmpahrteemyehntoh de ehkeepah<u>h</u>eh*
	can opener	el abrelatas	*ehl ahbrehlahtahs*
	butane gas bottle	la bombona (de gas butano)	*lah bohmbohnah (deh gahs bootahnoh)*
1	pannier	la ciclobolsa	*lah theeklohbohlsah*
2	gas cooker	el hornillo de gas	*ehl ohrneelyoh deh gahs*
3	groundsheet	la lona del suelo	*lah lohnah dehl swehloh*
	mallet	el martillo	*ehl mahrteelyoh*
	hammock	la hamaca	*lah ahmahkah*
4	jerry can	el bidón	*ehl beedohn*
	campfire	la fogata	*lah fohgahtah*
5	folding chair	la silla plegable	*lah seelyah plehgahbleh*
6	insulated picnic box	la nevera portátil/la bolsa nevera	*lah nehbehrah pohrtahteel/lah bohlsah nehbehrah*
	ice pack	el acumulador	*ehl akoomoolahdohr*
	compass	la brújula	*lah broo<u>h</u>oolah*
	wick	la mecha	*lah mehchah*
	corkscrew	el sacacorchos	*ehl sahkahkohrchohs*
7	airbed	el colchón neumático	*ehl kohlchohn nehoomahteekoh*
8	airbed plug	el taponcito de la válvula del colchón	*ehl tahpohntheetoh deh lah bahlboolah dehl kohlchohn*
	pump	la bomba neumática	*lah bohmbah nehoomahteekah*
9	awning	el tejadillo	*ehl teh<u>h</u>ahdeelyoh*
10	karimat	la esterilla	*lah ehstehreelyah*
11	pan	la olla	*lah ohlyah*
12	pan handle	el mango de la olla	*ehl mahngoh deh lah ohlyah*
	primus stove	el hornillo de querosén	*ehl ohrneelyoh deh kehrohsehn*
	zip	la cremallera	*lah krehmalyehrah*
13	backpack	la mochila	*lah mohcheelah*
14	guy rope	el viento	*ehl byehntoh*
	sleeping bag	el saco de dormir	*ehl sahkoh deh dohrmeer*
15	storm lantern	el farol de tormentas	*ehl fahrohl deh tohrmehntahs*
	camp bed	el catre (de tijera)	*ehl kahtreh (deh tee<u>h</u>ehrah)*
	table	la mesa	*lah mehsah*
16	tent	la tienda	*lah tyehndah*
17	tent peg	la estaca	*lah ehstakah*
18	tent pole	el palo de tienda	*ehl pahloh deh tyehndah*
	vacuum flask	el termo	*ehl tehrmoh*
19	water bottle	la cantimplora	*lah kahnteemplohrah*
	clothes peg	la pinza	*lah peenthah*
	clothes line	la cuerda de tender ropa	*lah kwehrdah deh tehndehr rohpah*
	windbreak	el paravientos/el paraván	*ehl pahrahbyehntohs/ehl pahrahbahn*
20	torch	la linterna de bolsillo	*lah leentehrnah deh bohlseelyoh*
	pocket knife	la navaja	*lah nahbah<u>h</u>ah*

7

Overnight accommodation

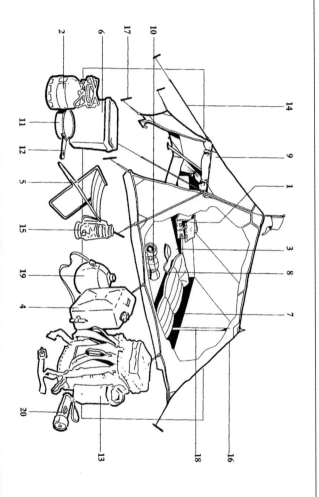

How much is it per _____ person/tent/caravan/car?	¿Cuánto sale por persona/tienda/caravana/coche? *kwahntoh sahleh pohr pehrsohnah/tyehndah/ kahrahbahnah/kohcheh?*
Are there any...?_____	¿Hay...? *ay...?*
– any hot showers?_____	¿Hay duchas con agua caliente? *ay doochahs kohn ahgwah kahlyehnteh?*
– washing machines?_____	¿Hay lavadoras? *ay lahbahdohrahs?*
Is there a...on the site?_____	¿En este camping hay...? *ehn ehsteh kahmpeen ay...?*
Is there a children's _____ play area on the site?	¿En este camping hay un sitio para que jueguen los niños? *ehn ehsteh kahmpeen ay oon seetyoh pahrah keh hwehghehn lohs neenyohs?*
Are there covered _____ cooking facilities on the site?	¿En este camping hay un sitio cubierto para cocinar? *ehn ehsteh kahmpeen ay oon seetyoh koobyehrtoh pahrah kohtheenahr?*
Can I rent a safe here?_____	¿Tienen caja fuerte para alquilar? *tyehnehn kahhah fwehrteh pahrah ahlkeelahr?*
Are we allowed to _____ barbecue here?	¿Se pueden hacer barbacoas? *seh pwehdehn ahtehr bahrbahkohahs?*
Are there any power _____ points?	¿Hay tomas de corriente eléctrica? *ay tohmahs deh kohrryehnteh ehlehktreekah?*
Is there drinking water?_____	¿Hay agua potable? *ay ahgwah pohtahbleh?*
When's the rubbish _____ collected?	¿Cuándo pasan a recoger la basura? *kwahndoh pahsahn ah rehkohhehr lah bahsoorah?*
Do you sell gas bottles _____ (butane gas/propane gas)?	¿Venden bombonas de gas (butano/propano)? *behndehn bohmbohnahs deh gahs(bootahnoh/prohpahnoh)?*

7 .3 Hotel/B&B/apartment/holiday house

Do you have a _____ single/double room available?	¿Le queda alguna habitación individual/doble? *leh kehdah ahlgoonah ahbeetahthyohn eendeebeedwahl/dohbleh?*
per person/per room _____	por persona/por habitación *pohr pehrsohnah/pohr ahbeetahthyohn*
Does that include _____ breakfast/lunch/dinner?	¿Incluye desayuno/comida/cena? *eenklooyeh dehsahyoonoh/kohmeedah/thehnah?*
Could we have two _____ adjoining rooms?	¿Nos puede dar dos habitaciones una al lado de la otra? *nohs pwehdeh dahr dohs ahbeetahthyohnehs oonah ahl lahdoh deh lah ohtrah?*
with/without _____ toilet/bath/shower	con/sin lavabo propio/baño propio/ducha propia *kohn/seen lahbahboh prohpyoh/bahnyoh prohpyo/doochah prohpyah?*

(not) facing the street_____	que (no) dé a la calle
	keh (noh) deh ah lah kahlyeh
with/without a view _____	con/sin vista al mar
of the sea	*kohn/seen beestah ahl mahr*
Is there...in the hotel?_____	¿El hotel tiene...?
	ehl ohtehl tyehneh...?
Is there a lift in the _____	¿El hotel tiene ascensor?
hotel?	*ehl ohtehl tyehneh ahsthehnsohr?*
Do you have room _____	¿El hotel tiene servicio de habitación?
service?	*ehl ohtehl tyehneh sehrbeethyoh deh*
	ahbeetahthyohn?

Tiene lavabo y ducha en el mismo _____	You can find the toilet and
piso/en su habitación	shower on the same
	floor/en suite
Por aquí, por favor _____	This way, please
Su habitación está en el...piso; es la_____	Your room is on the...floor,
número...	number...

Could I see the room? _____	¿Puedo ver la habitación?
	pwehdoh behr lah ahbeetahthyohn?
I'll take this room_____	Me quedo con esta habitación
	meh kehdoh kohn ehstah abeetathyohn
We don't like this one _____	Esta no nos gusta
	ehstah noh nohs goostah
Do you have a larger/_____	¿Tiene una habitación más grande/más
less expensive room?	barata?
	tyehneh oonah ahbeetathyohn mahs
	grahnde/mahs bahrahtah?
Could you put in a cot? ____	¿Puede agregar una cuna?
	pwehde ahgrehgahr oonah koonah?
What time's breakfast? ____	¿A qué hora es el desayuno?
	ah keh ohrah ehs ehl dehsahyoonoh?
Where's the dining _____	¿Dónde está el comedor?
room?	*dohndeh ehstah ehl kohmehdohr?*
Can I have breakfast_____	¿Me pueden traer el desayuno a la
in my room?	habitación?
	meh pwehdehn trahehr ehl dehsahyoonoh
	ah lah ahbeetahthyohn?
Where's the emergency____	¿Dónde está la salida de emergencia/la
exit/fire escape?	escalera de incendios?
	dohndeh ehstah lah sahleedah deh
	ehmehrhehnthyah/lah ehskahlehrah de
	eenthehndyohs?
Where can I park my _____	¿Dónde hay un sitio (seguro) para aparcar
car (safely)?	el coche?
	dohndeh ay oon seetyoh sehgooroh pahrah
	ahpahrkahr ehl kohcheh?
The key to room..., _____	La llave de la habitación..., por favor
please	*lah lyahbeh deh lah ahbeetahthyohn..., pohr*
	fahbohr
Could you put this in _____	¿Podría dejar esto en la caja fuerte?
the safe, please?	*pohdreeah dehhahr ehstoh ehn lah cahhah*
	fwehrteh?

Could you wake me _____ at...tomorrow?	¿Me podría despertar mañana a las...?
	meh pohdhreeah dehspehrtahr mahnyahnah ah lahs...?
Could you find a _____ babysitter for me?	¿Me podría conseguir una niñera para el bebé?
	meh pohdreeah kohnsehgeer oonah neenyehrah pahrah ehl behbeh?
Could I have an extra_____ blanket?	¿Tendría una manta extra?
	tehndreeah oonah mahntah ehxtrah?
What days do the _____ cleaners come in?	¿Qué días limpian la habitación?
	keh deeahs leempyahn lah ahbeetahthyohn?
When are the sheets/ _____ towels/tea towels changed?	¿Cuándo cambian las sábanas/las toallas/los paños de cocina?
	kwahndoh kahmbyahn lahs sahbahnahs/lahs tohahlyahs/lohs pahnyohs deh kohtheenah?

 .4 Complaints

We can't sleep for _____ the noise	No podemos dormir por el ruido
	noh pohdehmohs dohrmeer pohr ehl rweedoh
Could you turn the _____ radio down, please?	¿Podría bajar el volumen de la radio?
	pohdreeah bahhahr ehl vohloomehn deh lah rahdyoh?
We're out of toilet paper ___	Se ha acabado el papel higiénico.
	seh ah ahkahbahdoh ehl pahpehl eehyehneekoh
There aren't any.../ _____ there's not enough...	No hay.../no hay suficientes...
	noh ay.../noh ay soofeethyehntehs...
The bed linen's dirty_____	La ropa de cama está sucia
	lah rohpah deh kahmah ehstah soothyah
The room hasn't been _____ cleaned.	No han limpiado la habitación
	noh ahn leempyahdoh lah ahbeetahthyohn
The kitchen is not clean____	La cocina no está limpia
	lah kohtheenah noh ehstah leempyah
The kitchen utensils are____ dirty	Los utensilios de cocina están sucios
	lohs ootehnseelyohs deh kohtheenah ehstahn soothyohs
The heater's not_____ working	La calefacción no funciona
	lah kahlehfahkthyohn noh foonthyohnah
There's no (hot) _____ water/electricity	No hay agua (caliente)/electricidad
	noh ay ahgwah(kahlyehnteh)/ehlehktreetheedahdh
...is broken_____	...está estropeado
	...ehstah ehstrohpehahdoh
Could you have that _____ seen to?	¿Podrían hacerlo ver?
	pohdreeahn ahtehrloh behr?
Could I have another _____ room/site?	¿Tendría otra habitación/sitio para la tienda?
	tehndreeah ohtrah abeetahthyohn/seetyoh pahrah lah tyehndah?
The bed creaks terribly ____	La cama hace mucho ruido
	lah kahmah ahtheh moochoh rweedoh
The bed sags _____	La cama es demasiado blanda
	lah kahmah ehs dehmahsyahdoh blahndah

There are bugs/insects_____ in our room	Hay muchos bichos/insectos en nuestra habitación
	ay moochohs beechohs/eensehktohs ehn nwehstrah ahbeetahthyohn
This place is full_____ of mosquitos	Está lleno de mosquitos
	ehstah lyehnoh deh mohskeetohs
– cockroaches_____	Está lleno de cucarachas
	ehstah lyehnoh deh kookahrahchahs

7 .5 Departure

See also 8.2 Settling the bill

I'm leaving tomorrow. _____ Could I settle my bill, please?	Mañana me voy. ¿Podría pagar la cuenta ahora?
	mahnyahnah meh boy. pohdreeah pahgahr lah kwehntah ahohrah?
What time should we_____ vacate?	¿A qué hora tenemos que dejar...?
	ah keh ohrah tehnehmohs keh dehhahr...?
Could I have my_____ deposit/passport back, please?	¿Me devuelve la fianza/el pasaporte?
	meh dehbwehlbeh lah fyahnthah/ehl pahsahpohrteh?
We're in a terrible hurry ___	Llevamos mucha prisa
	lyehbahmohs moochah preesah
Could you forward _____ my mail to this address?	¿Podría enviarme la correspondencia a esta dirección?
	pohdreeah ehnbyahrmeh lah kohrrehspohndehnthyah ah ehstah deerehkthyohn?
Could we leave our_____ luggage here until we leave?	¿Podríamos dejar las maletas aquí hasta que nos marchemos?
	pohdreeahmohs dehhahr lahs mahlehtahs ahkee ahstah keh nohs mahrchehmohs?
Thanks for your _____ hospitality	Muchas gracias por la hospitalidad
	moochahs grahthyahs pohr lah ohspeetahleedahd

Money matters

● **In general,** banks are open to the public between 9am and 2pm; they are closed on Saturdays. In large cities it is possible to find main branches open until 4.30. To exchange currency a passport is required. Some travel agencies also provide facilities. The sign *cambio* indicates that money can be exchanged. Hotels may also offer this service, but at a less favourable rate.

8 .1 **B**anks

Where can I find a _____ bank/an exchange office around here?

¿Dónde hay un banco/una oficina de cambios por aquí?
dohndeh ay oon bahnkoh/oonah ohfeetheenah deh kahmbyohs pohr ahkee?

Where can I cash this _____ traveller's cheque/giro cheque?

¿Dónde puedo cambiar este cheque de viajero/este cheque postal?
dohndeh pwehdoh kahmbyahr ehsteh chehkeh deh byahhehroh/ehsteh chehkeh pohstahl?

Can I cash this...here? _____

¿Puedo cambiar aquí este...?
pwehdoh kahmbyahr ahkee ehsteh...?

Can I withdraw money _____ on my credit card here?

¿Se puede sacar dinero con una tarjeta de crédito?
seh pwehdeh sahkahr deenehroh kohn oonah tahrhehtah deh krehdeetoh?

What's the minimum/ _____ maximum amount?

¿Cuál es el mínimo/el máximo?
kwahl ehs ehl meeneemoh/ehl mahxeemoh?

Can I take out less _____ than that?

¿También puedo sacar menos?
tahmbyehn pwehdoh sahkahr mehnohs?

I've had some money _____ transferred here. Has it arrived yet?

He pedido un giro telegráfico. ¿Me ha llegado ya?
eh pehdeedoh oon heeroh tehlehgrahfeekoh. meh ah lyehgahdoh yah?

These are the details _____ of my bank in the UK

Estos son los datos de mi banco en el Reino Unido
ehstohs sohn lohs dahtohs deh mee bahnkoh ehn ehl reynoh ooneedoh

This is my bank/giro _____ number

Este es mi número de cuenta bancaria/de la caja postal
ehsteh ehs mee noomehroh deh kwehntah bahnkahryah/deh lah kahhah pohstahl

I'd like to change _____ some money

Quisiera cambiar dinero
keesyehrah kahmbyahr deenehroh

– pounds into... _____

Libras esterlinas por...
leebrahs ehstehrleenahs pohr...

– dollars into... _____

Dólares estadounidenses por...
dohlahrehs ehstahdohooneedehnsehs pohr...

What's the exchange _____ rate?

¿A cuánto está el cambio?
ah kwahntoh ehstah ehl kahmbyoh?

Could you give me _____ some small change with it?

¿Me podría dar sencillo/cambio?
meh pohdreeah dahr sehntheelyoh/kahmbyoh?

This is not right _____

Esto está mal
ehstoh ehstah mahl

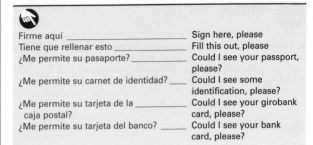

Firme aquí _____	Sign here, please
Tiene que rellenar esto _____	Fill this out, please
¿Me permite su pasaporte? _____	Could I see your passport, please?
¿Me permite su carnet de identidad? ____	Could I see some identification, please?
¿Me permite su tarjeta de la _____ caja postal?	Could I see your girobank card, please?
¿Me permite su tarjeta del banco? _____	Could I see your bank card, please?

🔘 .2 Settling the bill

Could you put it on_____ my bill?	¿Podría cargarlo a mi cuenta? *pohdreeah kahrgahrloh ah mee kwehntah?*
Does this amount _____ include service?	¿Está incluido el servicio en esta cifra? *ehstah eenklooeedoh ehl sehrbeethyoh ehn ehstah theefrah?*
Can I pay by...?_____	¿Puedo pagar con...? *pwehdoh pahgahr kohn...?*
Can I pay by credit card?___	¿Puedo pagar con tarjeta de crédito? *pwehdoh pahgahr kohn tahrhehtah deh krehdeetoh?*
Can I pay by traveller's _____ cheque?	¿Puedo pagar con un cheque de viajero? *pwehdoh pahgahr kohn oon chehkeh de byahhehroh?*
Can I pay with foreign _____ currency?	¿Puedo pagar con moneda extranjera? *pwehdoh pahgahr kohn mohnehdah ehxtrahnhehrah?*
You've given me too _____ much/you haven't given me enough change	Me ha devuelto de más/de menos *meh ah dehbwehltoh deh mahs/deh mehnohs*
Could you check the_____ bill again, please?	¿Puede volver a hacer la cuenta? *pwehdeh bohlbehr ah ahthehr lah kwehntah?*
Could I have a receipt, _____ please?	¿Podría darme un recibo? *pohdreeah dahrmeh oon rehtheeboh?*
I don't have enough _____ money on me	No me alcanza el dinero *noh meh ahlkahnthah ehl deenehroh*

No aceptamos tarjetas de _____ crédito/cheques de viajero/moneda extranjera	We don't accept credit cards/traveller's cheques/foreign currency

This is for you _____	Tenga, esto es para usted *tehngah, ehstoh ehs pahrah oostehdh*
Keep the change _____	Quédese con la vuelta *kehdehseh kohn lah bwehltah*

Post and telephone

Post and telephone

9 .1 Post

For giros, see 8 Money matters

● **Post offices** are open from Monday to Saturday from 9am to 1 or 1.30pm. However stamps (*sellos*) can be bought at any *estanco* and many hotels also provide stamps. It is advisable to post letters at a post office, rather than the yellow mail boxes (*buzón*).

Post and telephone

giros postales money orders	telegramas telegrams	sellos stamps
paquetes parcels		

Where's...?	¿Dónde está...? *dohndeh ehstah...?*
Where's the post office?	¿Dónde hay una oficina de Correos por aquí? *dohndeh ay oonah ohfeetheenah deh kohrrehohs pohr ahkee?*
Where's the main post office?	¿Dónde está la oficina central de Correos? *dohndeh ehstah lah ohfeetheenah thehntrahl deh kohrrehohs?*
Where's the postbox?	¿Dónde hay un buzón por aquí? *dohndeh ahee oon boothohn pohr ahkee?*
Which counter should I go to...?	¿Cuál es la ventanilla para...? *kwahl ehs lah behntahneelyah pahrah...?*
– to send a fax	¿Cuál es la ventanilla para enviar un fax? *kwahl ehs lah behntahneelyah pahrah ehnbyahr oon fahx?*
– to change money	¿Cuál es la ventanilla para cambiar dinero? *kwahl ehs lah behntahneelyah pahrah kahmbyahr deenehroh?*
– to change giro cheques	¿Cuál es la ventanilla para los cheques postales? *kwahl ehs lah behntahneelyah pahrah lohs chehkehs pohstahlehs?*
– for a Telegraph Money Order?	¿Cuál es la ventanilla para los giros telegráficos? *kwahl ehs lah behntahneelyah pahrah lohs heerohs tehlehgrahfeekohs?*
Poste restante	Lista de correos *leestah deh kohrrehohs*
Is there any mail for me? My name's...	¿Hay carta para mí? Me llamo... *ay kahrtah pahrah mee? meh lyahmoh...*

Stamps

What's the postage _____ for a...to...?	¿Cuánto se le pone a un(a)...para...? *kwahntoh seh leh pohneh ah oon(ah)...pahrah...?*
Are there enough _____ stamps on it?	¿Lleva suficiente franqueo? *lyehbah soofeethyehnteh frahnkehoh?*
I'd like... ...peseta stamps __	Déme...sellos de... *dehmeh...sehlyohs deh...*
I'd like to send this... _____	Quisiera enviar esto... *keesyehrah ehnbyahr ehstoh...*
– express _____	Quisiera enviar esto por correo urgente *keesyehrah ehnbyahr ehstoh pohr kohrrehoh oorhehnteh*
– by air mail _____	Quisiera enviar esto por avión *keesyehrah ehnbyahr ehstoh pohr ahbyohn*
– by registered mail _____	Quisiera enviar esto certificado *keesyehrah ehnbyahr ehstoh thehrteefeekahdoh*

Telegram / fax

I'd like to send a _____ telegram to...	Quisiera mandar un telegrama a... *keesyehrah mahndahr oon tehlehgrahmah ah...*
How much is that _____ per word?	¿Cuánto cuesta por palabra? *kwahntoh kwehstah pohr pahlahbrah?*
This is the text I want_____ to send	Este es el texto que quiero enviar *ehsteh ehs ehl tehxtoh keh kyehroh ehnbyahr*
Shall I fill in the form _____ myself?	¿Relleno yo mismo el formulario? *rehlyehnoh yoh meesmoh ehl fohrmoolahryoh?*
Can I make photocopies/___ send a fax here?	¿Se pueden hacer fotocopias/se puede enviar un fax aquí? *seh pwehdehn ahthehr fohtohkohpyahs/seh pwehdeh ehnbyahr oon fahx ahkee?*
How much is it_____ per page?	¿Cuánto cuesta por página? *kwahntoh kwehstah pohr pahheenah?*

9 .2 Telephone

See also 1.8 Telephone alphabet

● **All phone booths** offer a direct international service to the UK or US (07 - country code 44 (UK) or 1 (US) – trunk code minus 0 – number). Area codes are displayed. It is easier, and may even be cheaper to place your call from the *Telefónica* or telephone office. When phoning someone in Spain, you will not be greeted with the subscriber's name but *diga* or *dígame*.

Is there a phone box _____ around here?	¿Hay alguna cabina telefónica por aquí? *ay ahlgoonah kahbeenah tehlehfohneekah pohr ahkee?*
Could I use your _____ phone, please?	¿Podría usar su teléfono? *pohdreeah oosahr soo tehlehfohnoh?*

Do you have a _____ (city/region)...phone directory?	¿Tiene una guía de teléfonos de la ciudad/la provincia de...? *tyehneh oonah gheeah deh tehlehfohnohs deh lah thyoodahdh/lah prohbeenthyah deh...?*
Where can I get a _____ phone card?	¿Dónde puedo conseguir una tarjeta de teléfonos? *dohndeh pwehdoh kohnsehgheer oonah tahrhehtah deh tehlehfohnohs?*
Could you give me...? ____	¿Me podría dar...? *meh pohdreeah dahr...?*
– the number for _____ international directory enquiries	¿Me podría dar el número de información internacional? *meh pohdreeah dahr ehl noomehroh deh eenfohrmahthyohn eentehrnahthyohnahl?*
– the number of room... ___	¿Me podría dar el número de la habitación...? *meh pohdreeah dahr ehl noomehroh deh lah ahbeetahthyohn...?*
– the international _____ access code	¿Me podría dar el indicativo internacional? *meh pohdreeah dahr ehl eendeekahteeboh eentehrnahthyonahl...?*
– the country code for... ___	¿Me podría dar el indicativo de...? *meh pohdreeah dahr ehl eendeekahteeboh deh...?*
– the trunk code for... _____	¿Me podría dar el prefijo de...? *meh pohdreeah dahr ehl prehfeehoh deh...?*
– the number of... _____	¿Me podría dar el número de abonado de...? *meh pohdreeah dahr ehl noomehroh deh ahbohnahdoh deh...?*
Could you check if this ____ number's correct?	¿Podría controlar si está bien este número? *pohdreeah kohntrohlahr see ehstah byehn ehsteh noomehroh?*
Can I dial international _____ direct?	¿Se puede llamar directamente al extranjero? *seh pwehdeh lyahmahr deerehktahmehnteh ahl ehxtrahnhehroh?*
Do I have to go through ___ the switchboard?	¿Hay que llamar por operadora? *ay keh lyahmahr pohr ohpehrahdohrah?*
Do I have to dial '0' _____ first?	¿Hay que marcar primero el cero? *ay keh mahrkahr preemehroh ehl thehroh?*
Do I have to book _____ my calls?	¿Hay que pedir línea? *ay keh pehdeer leenehah?*
Could you dial this _____ number for me, please?	¿Podría usted llamar a este número? *pohdreeah oostehdh lyahmahr ah ehsteh noomehroh?*
Could you put me _____ through to.../extension..., please?	¿Me podría poner con.../con la extensión...? *meh pohdreeah pohnehr kohn.../kohn lah ehxtehnsyohn...?*
I'd like to place a _____ reverse-charge call to...	Quisiera una llamada de cobro revertido a... *keesyehrah oonah lyahmahdah deh kohbroh rehbehrteedoh ah...*

What's the charge per _____ minute?	¿Cuánto cuesta por minuto?
	kwahntoh kwehstah pohr meenootoh?
Have there been any _____ calls for me?	¿Ha habido alguna llamada para mí?
	ah ahbeedoh ahlgoonah lyahmahdah pahrah mee?

The conversation

Hello, this is... _____	Buenos días, soy...
	bwehnohs deeahs, soy...
Who is this, please? _____	¿Con quién hablo?
	kohn kyehn ahbloh?
Is this...? _____	¿Hablo con...?
	ahbloh kohn...?
I'm sorry, I've dialled _____ the wrong number	Perdone, me he equivocado de número
	pehrdohneh, meh eh ehkeebohkahdoh deh noomehroh
I can't hear you _____	No le oigo bien
	noh leh oygoh byehn
I'd like to speak to... _____	Quisiera hablar con...
	keesyehrah ahblahr kohn...
Is there anybody _____ who speaks English?	¿Hay alguien que hable inglés?
	ay ahlghyehn keh ahbleh eenglehs?
Extension..., please _____	¿Me pone con la extensión...?
	meh pohneh kohn lah ehxtehnsyohn...?
Could you ask him/her _____ to call me back?	¿Podría decirle que me llame?
	pohdreeah dehtheerleh keh meh lyahmeh?
My name's... _____ My number's...	Me llamo...Mi número es...
	meh lyahmoh...mee noomehroh ehs...
Could you tell him/her _____ I called?	¿Puede decirle que he llamado?
	pwehdeh dehtheerleh keh eh lyahmahdoh?
I'll call back tomorrow _____	Lo/la volveré a llamar mañana
	loh/lah bohlbehreh ah lyahmahr mahnyahnah

Lo llaman por teléfono _____	There's a phone call for you
Primero tiene que marcar el cero _____	You have to dial '0' first
Un momento, por favor _____	One moment, please
No contestan _____	There's no answer
Está comunicando _____	The line's engaged
¿Quiere esperar? _____	Do you want to hold?
Ahora le paso _____	Putting you through
Se ha equivocado de número _____	You've got a wrong number
El señor/la señora...no está en estos ____ momentos.	He's/she's not here right now
El señor/la señora...no estará hasta... ____	He'll/she'll be back...
Este es el contestador _____ automático de...	This is the answering machine of...

81

Shopping

10

10 **S**hopping

● **Opening times:** Monday to Friday, 9.30am-1.30pm and 5pm-8pm.
Department stores are open in the afternoons from 4pm and remain
open on Saturdays. Other shops generally close on Saturdays at 1pm.
In tourist areas shops open for longer periods.
Chemists display the list of *farmacias de guardia* (those open on
Sundays and after hours).

almacén	droguería	panadería
department store	household products	bakery
antigüedades	and cosmetics	pastelería
antiques	electrodomésticos	cake shop
artículos de deporte	electrical appliances	peluquería (señoras,
sports shop	estanco	caballeros)
artículos del hogar	tobacconist	hairdresser
household goods	farmacia	perfumería
artículos dietéticos	chemist	cosmetics
health food shop	ferretería	pescadería
artículos fotográficos	hardware shop	fishmonger
camera shop	floristería	quiosco
artículos usados	florist	news stand
second hand goods	frutas y verduras	recuerdos de viaje
autoservicio	greengrocer	souvenir shop
self service	galería comercial	reparación de
bicicletas	shopping arcade	bicicletas
bicycle shop	heladería	bicycle repair shop
bodega	ice cream parlour	revistas y prensa
off licence	joyería	newsagent
bricolaje	jeweller	salón de belleza
DIY-store	juguetería	beauty parlour
carnicería	toy shop	supermercado
butcher's shop	lavandería	supermarket
casa de música	laundry	tienda
music shop	lechería	shop
centro comercial	dairy	tienda de modas
shopping centre	librería	clothes shop
comestibles	book shop	tintorería
grocery store	mercado	drycleaner
decoración	market	zapatería
(de interiores)	mercería	shoe shop
interior design shop	draper	zapatero
	óptica	cobbler
	optician	

10.1 Shopping conversations

Where can I get...?	¿Dónde puedo conseguir...? *dohndeh pwehdoh kohnsehgheer...?*
When does this shop open?	¿De qué hora a qué hora abren? *deh keh ohrah ah keh ohrah ahbrehn?*
Could you tell me where the...department is?	¿Me podría indicar la sección de...? *meh pohdreeah eendeekahr lah sehkthyohn deh...?*
Could you help me, please? I'm looking for...	¿Podría ayudarme? Busco... *pohdreeah ahyoodahrmeh? booskoh...*
Do you sell British/ American newspapers?	¿Venden periódicos británicos/americanos? *behndehn pehryohdeekohs breetahneekohs/ahmehreekahnohs?*

¿Lo/la atienden? — Are you being served?

No, I'd like...	No. Quisiera... *noh. keesyehrah...*
I'm just looking, if that's all right	Sólo estoy mirando, gracias *sohloh ehstoy meerahndoh, grahthyahs*

¿Algo más? — Anything else?

Yes, I'd also like...	Sí, también déme... *see, tahmbyehn dehmeh...*
No, thank you. That's all	No, gracias. Es todo *noh, grahthyahs, ehs tohdoh*
Could you show me...?	¿Me podría mostrar...? *meh pohdreeah mohstrahr...?*
I'd prefer...	Prefiero... *prehfyehroh...*
This is not what I'm looking for	No es lo que busco *noh ehs loh keh booskoh*
Thank you. I'll keep looking	Gracias. Voy a seguir mirando *grahthyahs. boy ah sehgheer meerahndoh*
Do you have something...?	¿No tendría algo ...? *noh tehndreeah ahlgoh ...?*
– less expensive?	¿No tendría algo más barato? *noh tehndreeah ahlgoh mahs bahrahtoh?*
– smaller?	¿No tendría algo más pequeño? *noh tehndreeah ahlgoh mahs pehkehnyoh?*
– larger?	¿No tendría algo más grande? *noh tehndreeah ahlgoh mahs grahndeh?*
I'll take this one	Me llevo éste/ésta *meh lyehboh ehsteh/ehstah*
Does it come with instructions?	¿Viene con instrucciones? *byehneh kohn eenstrookthyohnehs?*
It's too expensive	Me parece muy caro *meh pahrehtheh mwee kahroh*

I'll give you...	Le doy...
	leh doy...
Could you keep this for ____ me? I'll come back for it later	¿Me lo/la podría guardar? Volveré más tarde a buscarlo
	meh loh/lah pohdreeah gwahrdahr? bohlbehreh mahs tahrdeh ah booskahrloh
Have you got a bag _____ for me, please?	¿Tendría una bolsita?
	tehndreeah oonah bohlseetah?
Could you giftwrap_____ it, please?	¿Me lo podría envolver para regalo?
	meh loh pohdreeah ehnbohlbehr pahrah rehgahloh?

Lo siento; no lo tenemos _____	I'm sorry, we don't have that
Lo siento; ya no queda _____	I'm sorry, we're sold out
Lo siento, hasta el...no lo _____ tendremos	I'm sorry, that won't be in until...
Pague en la caja, por favor _____	You can pay at the cash desk
No aceptamos tarjetas de crédito _____	We don't accept credit cards
No aceptamos cheques de viajero _____	We don't accept traveller's cheques
No aceptamos moneda extranjera _____	We don't accept foreign currency

10 .2 **F**ood

I'd like a hundred_____ grams of..., please	Quisiera cien gramos de...
	keesyehrah thyehn grahmohs deh...
– half a kilo of... _____	Quisiera medio kilo de...
	keesyehrah mehdyoh keeloh deh...
– a kilo of... _____	Quisiera un kilo de...
	keesyehrah oon keeloh deh...
Could you...it for me, _____ please?	¿Me lo podría...?
	meh loh pohdreeah...?
Could you slice it/_____ dice it for me, please?	¿Me lo podría cortar en lonchas/en trozos?
	meh loh pohdreeah kohrtahr ehn lohnchahs/ehn trohthohs?
Could you grate it _____ for me, please?	¿Me lo podría rallar?
	meh loh pohdreeah rahlyahr?
Can I order it?_____	¿Se lo podría encargar?
	seh loh pohdreeah ehnkahrgahr?
I'll pick it up tomorrow/ ____ at...	Pasaré a buscarlo mañana/a las...
	pahsahreh ah booskahrloh mahnyahnah/ah lahs...
Can you eat/drink this? ____	¿Es para comer/beber?
	ehs pahrah kohmehr/behbehr?
What's in it? _____	¿Qué lleva dentro?
	keh lyehbah dehntroh?

Shopping

10

I saw something in the ____ window. Shall I point it out?	He visto algo en el escaparate. ¿Se lo enseño? *eh beestoh ahlgoh ehn ehl ehskahpahrahteh, seh loh ehnsehnyoh?*
I'd like something to____ go with this	Busco algo que haga juego con esto *booskoh ahlgoh keh ahgah hwehgoh kohn ehstoh*
Do you have shoes ____ in this colour?	¿Tiene zapatos de este color? *tyehneh thahpahtohs deh ehsteh kohlohr?*
I'm a size...in the UK____	En el Reino Unido tengo el número... *ehn ehl reheenoh ooneedoh tehngoh ehl noomehroh...*
Can I try this on? ____	¿Me lo podría probar? *meh loh pohdreeah prohbahr?*
Where's the fitting____ room?	¿Dónde está el probador? *dohndeh ehstah ehl prohbahdohr?*
It doesn't fit____	No me vale *noh meh bahleh*
This is the right size ____	Este es mi número *ehsteh ehs mee noomehroh*
It doesn't suit me____	No me está bien *noh meh ehstah byehn*
Do you have this/ ____ these in...?	¿Tiene éste/ésta, pero en...? *tyehneh ehsteh/ehstah pehroh ehn...?*
The heel's too high/low ____	El tacón me parece muy alto/bajo *ehl tahkohn meh pahrehtheh mwee ahltoh/bahhoh*
Is this/are these ____ genuine leather?	¿Es/son de piel auténtica? *ehs/sohn deh pyehl ah-ootehnteekah?*
I'm looking for a...____ for a...-year-old baby/child	Busco un/una...para un bebé/niño de...años *booskoh oon/oonah...pahrah oon behbeh/neenyoh deh...ahnyohs*
I'd like a... ...____	Quisiera un/una...de... *keesyehrah oon/oonah...deh...*
– silk ____	Quisiera un/una...de seda *keesyehrah oon/oonah...deh sehdah*
– cotton ____	Quisiera un/una...de algodón *keesyehrah oon/oonah...deh ahlgohdohn*
– woollen ____	Quisiera un/una...de lana *keesyehrah oon/oonah...deh lahnah*
– linen ____	Quisiera un/una...de hilo *keesyehrah oon/oonah...deh eeloh*
What temperature____ can I wash it at?	¿A qué temperatura lo puedo lavar? *ah keh tehmpehrahtoorah loh pwehdoh lahbahr?*
Will it shrink in the ____ wash?	¿Encoge al lavarlo? *enkohheh ahl lahbahrloh?*

No planchar	Colgar mojado	Lavado a mano
Do not iron	Drip dry	Hand wash
No centrifugar	Lavado en seco	Lavado a máquina
Do not spin dry	Dry clean	Machine wash

At the cobbler

Could you mend _____ these shoes?	¿Podría arreglar estos zapatos?
	pohdreeah ahrrehglahr ehstohs thahpahtohs?
Could you put new _____ soles/heels on these?	¿Podría ponerle nuevas suelas/nuevos tacones?
	pohdreeah pohnehrleh nwehbahs swehlahs/nwehbohs tahkohnehs?
When will they be _____ ready?	¿Para cuándo van a estar?
	pahrah kwahndoh bahn ah ehstahr?
I'd like..., please _____	Quisiera..., por favor
	keesyehrah..., pohr fahbohr
– a tin of shoe polish _____	Quisiera una crema para zapatos
	keesyehrah oonah krehmah pahrah thahpahtohs
– a pair of shoelaces_____	Quisiera un par de cordones
	keesyehrah oon pahr deh kohrdohnehs

🔟 .4 Photographs and video

I'd like a film for this_____ camera, please	Quisiera un rollo/carrete para esta cámara
	keesyehrah oon rohlyoh/kahrrehteh pahrah ehstah kahmahrah
– a 126 cartridge _____	Quisiera una película en cassette de 126
	keesyehrah oonah pehleekoolah ehn kahseht deh thyehntoh beheenteesehees
– a 35mm colour slide _____	Un carrete de 35mm para diapositivas en color
	oon kahrrehteh deh treyntah ee theenkoh meeleemehtrohs pahrah deeapohseeteebahs ehn kohlohr
– a 35mm colour _____ print	Un carrete de 35mm en color
	oon kahrrehteh deh treyntah ee theenkoh meeleemehtrohs ehn kohlohr
– a 35mm black _____ and white	Un carrete de 35mm en blanco y negro
	oon kahrrehteh deh treyntah ee theenkoh meeleemehtrohs ehn blahnkoh ee nehgroh
– a videotape _____	Quisiera una cinta de vídeo
	keesyehrah oonah theentah deh veedehoh
colour/black and white_____	color/blanco y negro
	kohlohr/blahnkoh ee nehgroh
super eight _____	superocho
	soopehrohchoh
12/24/36 exposures _____	doce/veinticuatro/treinta y seis fotos
	dohtheh/beheenteekwahtroh/treheentah ee sehees fohtohs
ASA/DIN number_____	valor ISO
	bahlohr eesoh
daylight film _____	película para luz natural
	pehleekoolah pahrah looth nahtoorahl
film for artificial light _____	película para luz artificial
	pehleekoolah pahrah looth ahrteefeethyahl

Problems

Could you load the _____ film for me, please?	¿Me podría poner el rollo/carrete en la cámara? *meh pohdreeah pohnehr ehl rohlyoh/kahrrehteh ehn lah kahmahrah?*
Could you take the film _____ out for me, please?	¿Me podría sacar el rollo/carrete de la cámara? *meh pohdreeah sahkahr ehl rohlyoh/kahrrehteh deh lah kahmahrah?*
Should I replace _____ the batteries?	¿Tengo que cambiar las pilas? *tehngoh keh kahmbyahr lahs peelahs?*
Could you have a look _____ at my camera, please? It's not working	¿Me podría revisar la cámara? Ya no funciona. *meh pohdreeah rehbeesahr lah kahmahrah? yah noh foonthyohnah*
The...is broken _____	Está estropeado el... *ehstah ehstrohpehahdoh ehl...*
The film's jammed _____	Se ha atascado el rollo/carrete *seh ah ahtahskahdoh ehl rohlyoh /kahrrehteh*
The film's broken _____	Se ha roto el rollo/carrete *seh ah rohtoh ehl rohlyoh/kahrrehteh*
The flash isn't working ____	No funciona el flash *noh foonthyohnah ehl flahsh*

Processing and prints

I'd like to have this film _____ developed/printed, please	Quisiera mandar a revelar/copiar este rollo/carrete *keesyehrah mahndahr ah rehbehlahr/kohpyahr ehsteh rohlyoh/kahrrehteh*
I'd like...prints from _____ each negative	Quisiera...copias de cada negativo *keesyehrah...kohpyahs deh kahdah nehgahteeboh*
glossy/mat _____	brillante/mate *breelyahnte/mahteh*
I'd like to reorder _____ these photos	Quisiera encargar más copias de estas fotos *keesyehrah ehnkahrgahr mahs kohpyahs deh ehstahs fohtohs*
I'd like to have this _____ photo enlarged	Quisiera una ampliación de esta foto *keesyehrah oonah ahmplyahthyohn deh ehstah fohtoh*
How much is _____ processing?	¿Cuánto sale el revelado? *kwahntoh sahleh ehl rehbehlahdoh?*
– printing? _____	¿Cuánto sale el copiado? *kwahntoh sahleh ehl kohpyahdoh?*
– extra copies? _____	¿Cuánto salen las copias adicionales? *kwahntoh sahlehn lahs kohpyahs ahdeethyohnahlehs?*
– the enlargement? _____	¿Cuánto sale la ampliación? *kwahntoh sahleh lah ahmplyahthyohn?*
When will they _____ be ready?	¿Para cuándo van a estar? *pahrah kwahndoh bahn ah ehstahr?*

10 Shopping

Do I have to make an _____ appointment?	¿Tengo que pedir hora? *tehngoh keh pehdeer ohrah?*
Can I come in straight _____ away?	¿Podría atenderme en seguida? *pohdreeah ahtehndehrmeh ehn sehgheedah?*
How long will I have_____ to wait?	¿Cuánto tengo que esperar? *kwahntoh tehngoh keh ehspehrahr?*
I'd like a shampoo/ _____ haircut	Quisiera lavarme/cortarme el pelo *keesyehrah lahbahrmeh/kohrtahrmeh ehl pehloh*
I'd like a shampoo for _____ oily/dry hair, please	Quisiera un champú para cabello graso/seco *keesyehrah oon chahmpoo pahrah kahbehlyoh grahsoh/sehkoh*
an anti-dandruff_____ shampoo	Quisiera un champú anticaspa *keesyehrah oon chahmpoo ahnteekahspah*
– a shampoo for_____ permed/coloured hair	Quisiera un champú para cabello con permanente/teñido. *keesyehrah oon chahmpoo pahrah kahbehlyoh kohn pehrmahnehnteh/tehnyeedoh*
– a colour rinse shampoo __	Quisiera un champú color *keesyehrah oon chahmpoo kohlohr*
– a shampoo with _____ conditioner	Quisiera un champú con acondicionador *keesyehrah oon chahmpoo kohn ahkohndeethyohnahdohr*
– highlights _____	Quisiera que me hagan claritos *keesyehrah keh meh ahgahn klahreetohs*
Do you have a colour_____ chart, please?	¿Tendría una carta de colores? *tehndreeah oonah kahrtah deh kohlohrehs?*
I want to keep it the _____ same colour	Quiero conservar el mismo color *kyehroh kohnsehrbahr ehl meesmoh kohlohr*
I'd like it darker/lighter_____	Quisiera un color más oscuro/más claro *keesyehrah oon kohlohr mahs ohskooroh/mahs klahroh*
I'd like/I don't want _____ hairspray	(No) quiero fijador *(noh) kyehroh feehahdohr*
– gel_____	(No) quiero gel *(noh) kyehroh hehl*
– lotion _____	(No) quiero loción *(noh) kyehroh lohthyohn*
I'd like a short fringe _____	Quisiera el flequillo corto *keesyehrah ehl flehkeelyoh kohrtoh*
Not too short at _____ the back	No lo quisiera demasiado corto por detrás *noh loh keesyehrah dehmahsyahdoh kohrtoh pohr dehtrahs*
Not too long here _____	No lo quisiera demasiado largo aquí *noh loh keesyehrah dehmahsyahdoh lahrgoh ahkee*
I'd like/I don't want _____ (many) curls	(No) quisiera (demasiados) rizos *(noh) keesyehrah (dehmahsyadohs) reethohs*

Shopping

10

It needs a little/_____ a lot taken off	Hay que cortar sólo un trocito/un buen trozo
	ay keh kohrtahr sohloh oon trohtheetoh/oon bwehn trohthoh
I want a completely _____ different style	Quisiera un modelo totalmente diferente
	keesyehrah oon mohdehloh tohtahlmehnteh deefehrehnteh
I'd like it the same as... _____	Quisiera el pelo como...
	keesyehrah ehl pehloh kohmoh...
– as that lady's _____	Quisiera el pelo como esa señora
	keesyehrah ehl pehloh kohmoh ehsah sehnyohrah
– as in this photo_____	Quisiera el pelo como en esta foto
	keesyehrah ehl pehloh kohmoh ehn ehstah fohtoh
Could you put the _____ drier up/down a bit?	¿Podría poner el casco más alto/bajo?
	pohdreeah pohnehr ehl kahskoh mahs ahltoh/ bahhoh?
I'd like a facial_____	Quisiera una máscara facial
	keesyehrah oonah mahskahrah fahthyahl
– a manicure_____	Quisiera que me hagan manicura
	keesyehrah keh meh ahgahn mahneekoorah
– a massage _____	Quisiera que me hagan masaje
	keesyehrah keh meh ahgahn mahsahheh
Could you trim_____ my fringe?	¿Me podría recortar el flequillo?
	meh pohdreeah rehkohrtahr ehl flehkeelyoh?
– my beard? _____	¿Me podría recortar la barba?
	meh pohdreeah rehkohrtahr lah bahrbah?
– my moustache? _____	¿Me podría recortar el bigote?
	meh pohdreeah rehkohrtahr ehl beegohteh?
I'd like a shave, please_____	Aféiteme, por favor
	ahfeheetehmeh, pohr fahbohr
I'd like a wet shave, _____ please	Aféiteme a navaja, por favor
	ahfeheetehmeh ah nahbahhah, pohr fahbohr

Shopping

10

¿Cómo quiere el corte de pelo? _____	How do you want it cut?
¿Qué modelo deseaba? _____	What style did you have in mind?
¿Qué color quiere?_____	What colour do you want it?
¿Esta temperatura le va bien?_____	Is the temperature all right for you?
¿Quiere algo para leer?_____	Would you like something to read?
¿Quiere algo para beber?_____	Would you like a drink?
¿Así está bien? _____	Is this what you had in mind?

At the Tourist Information Centre

11 At the Tourist Information Centre

11 .1 Places of interest

At the Tourist Information Centre

Where's the Tourist _____ Information, please?	¿Dónde está la oficina de turismo? *dohndeh ehstah lah ohfeeteenahn deh tooreesmoh?*
Do you have a city map?___	¿Tendría un plano de la ciudad? *tehndreeah oon plahnoh deh lah thyoodahdh?*
Where is the museum? ____	¿Dónde está el museo? *dohndeh ehstah ehl moosehoh?*
Where can I find _____ a church?	¿Dónde podría encontrar una iglesia? *dohndeh pohdreeah ehnkohntrahr oonah eeglehsyah?*
Could you give me _____ some information about...?	¿Me podría dar información sobre...? *meh pohdreeah dahr eenfohrmahthyohn sohbreh...?*
How much is that? _____	¿Cuánto le debemos por esto? *kwahntoh leh dehbehmohs pohr ehstoh?*
What are the main _____ places of interest?	¿Cuáles son los sitios más interesantes para visitar? *kwahlehs sohn lohs seetyohs mahs eentehrehsahntehs pahrah veeseetahr?*
Could you point them ____ out on the map?	¿Me los podría señalar en el plano? *meh lohs pohdreeah sehnyahlahr ehn ehl plahnoh?*
What do you_____ recommend?	¿Qué nos recomienda? *keh nohs rehkohmyehndah?*
We'll be here for a_____ few hours	Pensamos quedarnos unas horas *pehnsahmohs kehdahrnohs oonahs ohrahs*
– a day _____	Pensamos quedarnos un día *pehnsahmohs kehdahrnohs oon deeah*
– a week_____	Pensamos quedarnos una semana *pehnsahmohs kehdahrnohs oonah sehmahnah*
We're interested in... _____	Nos interesa... *nohs eentehrehsah...*
Is there a scenic walk_____ around the city?	¿Hay algún circuito turístico para visitar la ciudad a pie? *ay ahlgoon theerkweetoh tooreesteekoh pahrah veeseetar lah thyoodahdh ah pyeh?*
How long does it take? ____	¿Cuánto dura? *kwahntoh doorah?*
Where does it start/end? ___	¿De dónde sale?/¿Dónde termina? *deh dohndeh sahleh?/dohndeh tehrmeenah?*
Are there any boat _____ cruises here?	¿Hay excursiones en barco? *ay ehxkoorsyohnehs ehn bahrkoh?*
Where can we board? _____	¿Dónde se puede embarcar? *dohndeh seh pwehdeh ehmbahrkahr?*
Are there any bus tours?___	¿Hay excursiones en autocar? *ay ehxkoorsyohnehs ehn ahootohkahr?*
Where do we get on?_____	¿De dónde salen? *deh dohndeh sahlehn?*
Is there a guide who_____ speaks English?	¿Hay algún guía que hable inglés? *ay ahlgoon gheeah keh ahbleh eenglehs?*

What trips can we take around the area?	¿Qué excursiones se pueden hacer en los alrededores?
	keh ehxkoorsyohnehs seh pwehdehn ahthehr ehn lohs ahlrehdehdohrehs?
Are there any _____ excursions?	¿Hay excursiones organizadas?
	ay ehxkoorsyohnehs ohrgahneethahdahs?
Where do they go to? ____	¿Hacia dónde van?
	ahthyah dohndeh bahn?
We'd like to go to... _____	Quisiéramos ir a...
	keesyehrahmohs eer ah...
How long is the trip? _____	¿Cuánto se tarda en llegar?
	kwahntoh seh tahrdah ehn lyehgahr?
How long do we _____ stay in...?	¿Cuánto dura la visita a...?
	kwahntoh doorah lah beeseetah ah...
Are there any guided _____ tours?	¿Hay visitas guiadas?
	ay beeseetahs gheeahdahs?
How much free time_____ will we have there?	¿Cuánto tiempo libre tenemos allí?
	kwahntoh tyehmpoh leebreh tehnehmohs alyee?
We want to go hiking_____	Nos gustaría hacer una excursión a pie
	nohs goostahreeah ahthehr oonah ehxkoorsyohn ah pyeh
Can we hire a guide? _____	¿Es posible contratar un guía?
	ehs pohseebleh kohntrahtahr oon gheeah?
Can I book mountain _____ huts?	¿Se puede hacer una reserva para un refugio (en la montaña)?
	seh pwehdeh ahthehr oonah rehsehrbah pahrah oon rehfoohyoh (ehn lah mohntahnyah)?
What time does... _____ open/close?	¿A qué hora abre/cierra...?
	ah keh ohrah ahbreh/thyehrrah...?
What days is...open/_____ closed?	¿Qué días tiene abierto/cerrado...?
	keh deeahs tyehneh ahbyehrtoh/thehrrahdoh...?
What's the admission_____ price?	¿Cuánto sale la entrada?
	kwahntoh sahleh lah ehntrahdah?
Is there a group _____ discount?	¿Hay descuento para grupos?
	ay dehskwehntoh pahrah groopohs?
Is there a child _____ discount?	¿Hay descuento para niños?
	ay dehskwehntoh pahrah neenyohs?
Is there a discount_____ for pensioners?	¿Hay descuento para jubilados?
	ay dehskwehntoh pahrah hoobeelahdohs?
Can I take (flash) _____ photos/can I film here?	¿Se pueden sacar fotos (con flash)/filmar aquí?
	seh pwehdehn sahkahr fohtohs(kohn flahsh)/feelmahr ahkee?
Do you have any _____ postcards of...?	¿Venden postales de...?
	behndehn pohstahlehs deh...?
Do you have an _____ English...?	¿Tiene un...en inglés?
	tyehneh oon...ehn eenglehs?
– an English catalogue?____	¿Tiene un catálogo en inglés?
	tyehneh oon kahtahlohgoh ehn eenglehs?
– an English programme?__	¿Tiene un programa en inglés?
	tyehneh oon prohgrahmah ehn eenglehs?
– an English brochure? ____	¿Tiene un folleto en inglés?
	tyehneh oon fohlyehtoh ehn eenglehs?

● **At the cinema** most films are dubbed in Spanish. Sometimes there are only two showings, in the evening, at 7 and 11pm. In this case advance booking is advisable.

Do you have this _____ week's/month's entertainment guide?
¿Tiene la guía de los espectáculos de esta semana/este mes?
tyehneh lah gheeah deh lohs ehspehktahkoolohs deh ehstah sehmahnah/ehsteh mehs?

What's on tonight? _____
¿Adónde podríamos ir esta noche?
ahdohndeh pohdreeahmohs eer ehstah nohcheh?

We want to go to... _____
Nos gustaría ir a...
nohs goostahreeah eer ah...

Which films are _____ showing?
¿Qué películas dan?
keh pehleekoolahs dahn?

What sort of film is that?___
¿Qué clase de película es?
keh klahseh deh pehleekoolah ehs?

suitable for everyone _____
para todos los públicos
pahrah tohdohs lohs poobleekohs

not suitable for_____ children
prohibido para menores de 12/16 años
proheebeedoh pahrah mehnohrehs deh dohtheh/dyehtheesehees ahnyohs

original version _____
versión original
behrsyohn ohreeheenahl

subtitled_____
subtitulada
soobteetoolahdah

dubbed_____
doblada
dohblahdah

Is it a continuous_____ showing?
¿Es sesión continua?
ehs sehsyohn kohnteenooah?

What's on at...? _____
¿Qué dan en...?
keh dahn ehn...?

– the theatre? _____
¿Qué dan en el teatro?
keh dahn ehn ehl tehahtroh?

– the concert hall?_____
¿Qué dan en la sala de conciertos?
keh dahn ehn lah sahlah deh kohnthyehrtohs?

– the opera? _____
¿Qué dan en la ópera?
keh dahn ehn lah ohpehrah?

Where can I find a good ___ disco around here?
¿Dónde hay una buena discoteca por aquí?
dohndeh ay oonah bwehnah deeskohtehkah pohr ahkee?

Is it for members only? ____
¿Hay que ser socio?
ay keh sehr sohthyoh?

Where can I find a good ___ cabaret club around here?
¿Dónde hay un buen cabaret por aquí?
dohndeh ay oon bwehn kahbahreh pohr ahkee?

Is it evening wear only? ___
¿Hay que ir en traje de etiqueta?
ay keh eer ehn trahheh deh ehteekehtah?

Should I/we dress up? _____	¿Es recomendable ir en traje de etiqueta? *ehs rehkohmehndahbleh eer ehn trahhheh* *deh ehteekehtah?*
What time does the _____ show start?	¿A qué hora empieza el espectáculo? *ah keh ohrah ehmpyehthah ehl* *ehspehktahkooloh?*
When's the next soccer ____ match?	¿Cuándo es el próximo partido de fútbol? *kwahlndoh ehs ehl prohxeemoh pahrteedoh* *deh footbohl?*
Who's playing?_____	¿Quiénes juegan? *kyehnehs hwehgahn?*
I'd like an escort for _____ tonight. Could you arrange that for me?	Quisiera contratar un/una acompañante para esta noche. ¿Podría hacerme una reserva? *keesyehrah kohntrahtahr oon/oonah* *ahkohmpahnyahnteh pahrah ehstah* *nohcheh. podreeah ahthehrmeh oonah* *rehsehrbah?*

⑪ .3 Booking tickets

Could you book some _____ tickets for us?	¿Podría hacernos una reserva? *pohdreeah ahthehrnohs oonah rehsehrbah?*
We'd like to book... _____ tickets/a table...	Quisiéramos...entradas/una mesa... *keesyehrahmohs...ehntrahdahs/oonah* *mehsah...*
– tickets/seats in the _____ stalls	Quisiéramos...entradas en la platea *keesyehrahmohs...ehntrahdahs ehn lah* *plahtehah*
– tickets/seats on the _____ balcony	Quisiéramos...entradas en el palco *keesyehrahmohs...ehntrahdahs ehn ehl* *pahlkoh*
– box seats _____	Quisiéramos...entradas en el palco privado *keesyehrahmohs...ehntrahdahs ehn ehl* *pahlkoh preebahdoh*
– a table at the front_____	Quisiéramos una mesa adelante *keesyehrahmohs oonah mehsah* *ahdehlahnteh*
– in the middle _____	Quisiéramos una mesa al centro *keesyehrahmohs oonah mehsah ahl* *thehntroh*
– at the back _____	Quisiéramos una mesa atrás *keesyehrahmohs oonah mehsah ahtrahs*
Could I book...seats for ____ the...o'clock performance?	¿Podría reservar...entradas para la función de las...? *pohdreeah rehsehrbahr...ehntrahdahs pahrah* *lah foonthyohn deh lahs...?*
Are there any seats left ____ for tonight?	¿Quedan entradas para esta noche? *kehdahn ehntrahdahs pahrah ehstah* *nohcheh?*
How much is a ticket? _____	¿Cuánto sale la entrada? *kwahntoh sahleh lah ehntrahdah?*

11

When can I pick the _____ tickets up?	¿Cuándo puedo pasar a retirar las entradas?
	kwahndoh pwehdoh pahsahr ah rehteerahr lahs ehntrahdahs?
I've got a reservation _____	Tengo una reserva
	tehngoh oonah rehsehrbah
My name's... _____	Me llamo...
	meh lyahmoh...

¿Para qué función desea reservar? _____	Which performance do you want to book for?
¿Qué sector prefiere? _____	Where would you like to sit?
No hay billetes. _____	Everything's sold out
Sólo quedan entradas de pie _____	It's standing room only
Sólo quedan entradas en el palco _____	We've only got balcony seats left
Sólo quedan entradas en la galería _____	We've only got seats left in the gallery
Sólo quedan entradas en la platea _____	We've only got stalls seats left
Sólo quedan entradas adelante _____	We've only got seats left at the front
Sólo quedan entradas atrás _____	We've only got seats left at the back
¿Cuántas entradas quiere? _____	How many seats would you like?
Tiene que retirar las entradas antes de las... _____	You'll have to pick up the tickets before...o'clock
¿Me permite las entradas? _____	Tickets, please
Este es su asiento _____	This is your seat

11

Sports

12.1 **S**porting questions

Where can we... _____ around here?	¿Dónde se puede...? *dohndeh seh pwehdeh...?*
Is there a... _____ around here?	¿Hay algún...por aquí cerca? *ay ahlgoon...pohr ahkee thehrkah?*
Can I hire a...here? _____	¿Alquilan...? *ahlkeelahn...?*
Can I take...lessons? _____	¿Dan clases de...? *dahn klahsehs deh...?*
How much is that per_____ hour/per day/class?	¿Cuánto sale por hora/día/clase? *kwahntoh sahleh pohr ohrah/deeah/klahseh?*
Do I need a permit _____ for that?	¿Se necesita un permiso? *seh nehthehseetah oon pehrmeesoh?*
Where can I get _____ the permit?	¿Dónde se consiguen los permisos? *dohndeh seh kohnseeghehn lohs pehrmeesohs?*

12.2 **B**y the waterfront

Is it a long way to _____ the sea still?	¿Falta mucho para llegar al mar? *fahltah moochoh pahrah lyehgahr ahl mahr?*
Is there a...around here? ___	¿Hay algún...por aquí? *ay ahlgoon...pohr ahkee?*
– an outdoor/indoor/_____ public swimming pool	¿Hay alguna piscina por aquí? *ay ahlgoonah peestheenah pohr ahkee?*
– a sandy beach _____	¿Hay alguna playa con arena por aquí? *ay ahlgoonah plahyah kohn ahrehnah pohr ahkee?*
– a nudist beach _____	¿Hay alguna playa nudista por aquí? *ay ahlgoonah plahyah noodeestah pohr ahkee?*
– mooring _____	¿Hay algún atracadero por aquí? *ay ahlgoon ahtrahkahdehroh pohr ahkee?*
Are there any rocks_____ here?	¿Hay rocas? *ay rohkahs?*
When's high/low tide? _____	¿Cuándo sube/baja la marea? *kwahndoh soobeh/bahhah lah mahrehah?*
What's the water _____ temperature?	¿Qué temperatura tiene el agua? *keh tehmpehrahtoorah tyehneh ehl ahgwah?*
Is it (very) deep here? _____	¿Es (muy) profundo? *ehs mwee prohfoondoh?*
Can you stand here?_____	¿Se puede hacer pie? *seh pwehdeh ahtehr pyeh?*
Is it safe to swim here? ____	¿Es seguro para nadar? *ehs sehgooroh pahrah nahdahr?*
Are there any currents?____	¿Hay corriente? *ay kohrryehnteh?*
Are there any rapids/ _____ waterfalls in this river?	¿Este río tiene rápidos/cascadas? *ehsteh reeoh tyehneh rahpeedohs/kahskahdahs?*
What does that flag/_____ buoy mean?	¿Qué significa aquella bandera/boya? *keh seegneefeekah ahkehlyah bahndehrah/bohyah?*

Sports

Is there a life guard on duty here?	¿Hay algún vigilante de servicio?
	ay ahlgoon veeheelante deh sehrbeetheeoh?
Are dogs allowed here?	¿Está permitido traer perros?
	ehstah pehrmeeteedoh trahehr pehrrohs?
Is camping on the beach allowed?	¿Está permitido acampar en la playa?
	ehstah pehrmeeteedoh ahkahmpahr ehn lah plahyah?
Are we allowed to build a fire here?	¿Está permitido hacer fuego?
	ehstah pehrmeeteedoh ahthehr fwehgoh?

Peligro	Prohibido pescar	Prohibido bañarse
Danger	No fishing	No swimming
Aguas de pesca	Prohibido hacer	Permiso obligatorio
Fishing water	surfing	Permits only
	No surfing	

🕛 .3 In the snow

Can I take ski lessons here?	¿Dan clases de esquí?
	dahn klahsehs deh eskee?
for beginners/advanced	para principiantes/avanzados
	pahrah preentheepyahntehs/ahbahnthahdohs
How large are the groups?	¿De cuántas personas son los grupos?
	deh kwahntahs pehrsohnahs sohn lohs groopohs?
What language are the classes in?	¿En qué idioma son las clases?
	ehn keh eedyohmah sohn lahs klahsehs?
I'd like a lift pass, please	Quisiera un pase para las telesillas
	keesyehrah oon pahseh pahrah lahs tehlehseelyahs
Must I give you a passport photo?	¿Se necesita foto?
	seh nehthehseetah fohtoh?
Where can I have a passport photo taken?	¿Dónde puedo sacarme fotos?
	dohndeh pwehdoh sahkahrmeh fohtohs?
Where are the beginners' slopes?	¿Dónde están las pistas para principiantes?
	dohndeh ehstahn lahs peestahs pahrah preentheepyahntehs?
Are there any runs for cross-country skiing?	¿Hay pistas de esquí de fondo por aquí?
	ay peestahs deh ehskee deh fohndoh pohr ahkee?
Have the cross-country runs been marked?	¿Las pistas de esquí de fondo están señalizadas?
	lahs peestahs deh ehskee deh fohndoh ehstahn sehnyahleethahdahs?
Are the...in operation?	¿Están abiertos los...?
	ehstahn ahbyehrtohs lohs...?
– the ski lifts	¿Ya funcionan los telesquís?
	yah foonthyohnahn lohs tehlehskees?
– the chair lifts	¿Ya funcionan las telesillas?
	yah foonthyohnahn lahs tehlehseelyahs?
Are the slopes usable?	¿Están abiertas las pistas?
	ehstahn ahbyehrtahs lahs peestahs?

Sports

🕛

Sickness

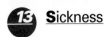

13 Sickness

13.1 Call (fetch) the doctor

Could you call/fetch a_____ doctor quickly, please?
¿Podría llamar/ir a buscar rápido a un médico, por favor?
pohdreeah lyahmahr/eer ah booskahr rahpeedoh ah oon mehdeekoh, pohr fahbohr?

When does the doctor _____ have surgery?
¿Cuándo tiene consulta el médico?
kwahndoh tyehneh kohnsooltah ehl mehdeekoh?

When can the doctor _____ come?
¿Cuándo puede venir el médico?
kwahndoh pwehdeh behneer ehl mehdeekoh?

I'd like to make an_____ appointment to see the doctor
¿Podría pedirme hora con el médico?
pohdreeah pehdeermeh ohrah kohn ehl mehdeekoh?

I've got an appointment ___ to see the doctor at...
Tengo hora con el médico para las...
tehngoh ohrah kohn ehl mehdeekoh pahrah lahs...

Which doctor/chemist _____ has night/weekend duty?
¿Qué médico/farmacia está de guardia esta noche/este fin de semana?
keh mehdeekoh/fahrmahthyah ehstah deh gwahrdyah ehstah nohcheh/ehsteh feen deh sehmahnah?

13.2 Patient's ailments

I don't feel well _____
No me siento bien
noh meh syehntoh byehn

I'm dizzy_____
Tengo mareos
tehngoh mahrehohs

– ill_____
Estoy enfermo
ehstoy ehnfehrmoh

– sick _____
Tengo náuseas
tehngoh nahoosehahs

I've got a cold_____
Estoy acatarrado
ehstoy ahkahtahrrahdoh

It hurts here _____
Me duele aquí
meh dwehleh ahkee

I've been throwing up _____
He devuelto
eh dehbwehltoh

I've got... _____
Tengo molestias de...
tehngoh mohlehstyahs deh...

I'm running a _____ temperature of...degrees
Tengo...grados de fiebre
tehngoh...grahdohs deh fyehbreh

I've been stung by_____ a wasp
Me ha picado una avispa
meh ah peekahdoh oonah ahbeespah

I've been stung by an_____ insect
Me ha picado un insecto
meh ah peekahdoh oon eensehktoh

I've been bitten by _____ a dog
Me ha mordido un perro
meh ah mohrdeedoh oon pehrroh

I've been stung by_____ a jellyfish
Me ha picado una medusa
meh ah peekahdoh oonah mehdoosah

I've been bitten by _____ a snake	Me ha mordido una serpiente *meh ah mohrdeedoh oonah sehrpyehnteh*
I've been bitten by _____ an animal	Me ha picado un insecto *meh ah peekahdoh oon eensehktoh*
I've cut myself _____	Me he cortado *meh eh kohrtahdoh*
I've burned myself _____	Me he quemado *meh eh kehmahdoh*
I've grazed myself _____	Tengo una rozadura *tehngoh oonah rohthahdoorah*
I've had a fall _____	Me he caído *meh eh kaheedoh*
I've sprained my ankle _____	Me he torcido el tobillo *meh eh tohrtheedoh ehl tohbeelyoh*
I've come for the _____ morning-after pill	Vengo a que me dé una píldora del día después *behngoh ah keh meh deh oonah peeldohrah dehl deeah dehspwehs*

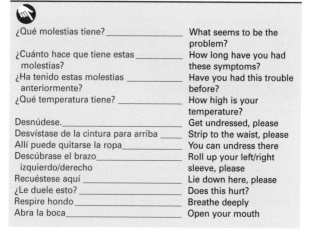

13 .3 The consultation

¿Qué molestias tiene? _____	What seems to be the problem?
¿Cuánto hace que tiene estas _____ molestias?	How long have you had these symptoms?
¿Ha tenido estas molestias _____ anteriormente?	Have you had this trouble before?
¿Qué temperatura tiene? _____	How high is your temperature?
Desnúdese. _____	Get undressed, please
Desvístase de la cintura para arriba _____	Strip to the waist, please
Allí puede quitarse la ropa _____	You can undress there
Descúbrase el brazo _____ izquierdo/derecho	Roll up your left/right sleeve, please
Recuéstese aquí _____	Lie down here, please
¿Le duele esto? _____	Does this hurt?
Respire hondo _____	Breathe deeply
Abra la boca _____	Open your mouth

Patient's medical history

I'm a diabetic _____	Soy diabético *soy deeahbehteekoh*
I have a heart condition _____	Soy enfermo cardíaco *soy ehnfehrmoh kahrdeeahkoh*
I have asthma _____	Soy asmático *soy ahsmahteekoh*
I'm allergic to... _____	Soy alérgico a... *soy ahlehr<u>h</u>eekoh ah...*
I'm...months pregnant _____	Estoy embarazada de...meses *ehstoy ehmbahrahthadah deh...mehsehs*
I'm on a diet _____	Sigo una dieta *seegoh oonah dyehtah*

Sickness

13

I'm on medication/ _____ the pill	Tomo medicamentos/la píldora *tohmoh mehdeekahmehntohs/lah peeldohrah*
I've had a heart attack ____ once before	He tenido un ataque cardíaco anteriormente *eh tehneedoh oon ahtahkeh kahrdeeahkoh ahntehryohrmehnteh*
I've had a(n)...operation ___	Me han operado del/de la... *meh ahn ohpehrahdoh dehl/deh lah...*
I've been ill recently _____	He estado enfermo hace poco *eh ehstahdoh ehnfehrmoh ahtheh pohkoh*
I've got an ulcer_____	Tengo una úlcera *tehngoh oonah oolthehrah*
I've got my period_____	Tengo la regla *tehngoh lah rehglah*

¿Padece alguna alergia?_____	Do you have any allergies?
¿Toma medicamentos?_____	Are you on any medication?
¿Sigue alguna dieta? _____	Are you on a diet?
¿Está embarazada? _____	Are you pregnant?
¿Está vacunado/a contra el tétanos?____	Have you had a tetanus injection?

The diagnosis

No es nada grave _____	It's nothing serious
Se ha fracturado el/la..._____	Your...is broken
Se ha contusionado el/la..._____	You've got a/some bruised...
Se ha desgarrado el/la..._____	You've got (a) torn...
Tiene una inflamación_____	You've got an inflammation
Tiene apendicitis_____	You've got appendicitis
Tiene bronquitis _____	You've got bronchitis
Tiene una enfermedad venérea _____	You've got a venereal disease
Tiene gripe _____	You've got the flu
Ha tenido un ataque al corazón _____	You've had a heart attack
Tiene una infección virósica/_____ bacteriana	You've got an infection (viral..., bacterial...)
Tiene una pulmonía _____	You've got pneumonia
Tiene una úlcera _____	You've got an ulcer
Se ha distendido un músculo _____	You've pulled a muscle
Tiene una infección vaginal_____	You've got a vaginal infection
Tiene una intoxicación alimenticia _____	You've got food poisoning

Sickness

13

Tiene una insolación _____	You've got sunstroke
Es alérgico a... _____	You're allergic to...
Está embarazada _____	You're pregnant
Quisiera hacerle un análisis de sangre/de orina/de materia fecal	I'd like to have your blood/urine/stools tested
Hay que suturar la herida_____	It needs stitching
Lo/la voy a derivar a un especialista/a __ un hospital	I'm referring you to a specialist/sending you to hospital
Tiene que hacerse radiografías _____	You'll need to have some x-rays taken
Vuelva a tomar asiento en la sala de ____ espera	Could you wait in the waiting room, please?
Hay que operarlo/operarla_____	You'll need an operation

Is it contagious?_____	¿Es contagioso?
	ehs kohntah<u>h</u>yohsoh?
How long do I have to _____ stay...?	¿Hasta cuándo tengo que...?
	ahstah kwahndoh tehngoh keh...?
– in bed _____	¿Hasta cuándo tengo que guardar cama?
	ahstah kwahndoh tehngoh keh gwahrdahr kahmah?
– in hospital _____	¿Hasta cuándo tengo que quedarme en el hospital?
	ahstah kwahndoh tehngoh keh kehdahrmeh ehn ehl ohspeetahl?
Do I have to go on _____ a special diet?	¿Tengo que seguir alguna dieta?
	tehngoh keh sehgheer ahlgoonah dyehtah?
Am I allowed to travel? ___	¿Puedo viajar?
	pwehdoh byah<u>h</u>ahr?
Can I make a new _____ appointment?	¿Puedo volver a pedir hora?
	pwehdoh bohlbehr ah pehdeer ohrah?
When do I have to_____ come back?	¿Cuándo tengo que volver?
	kwahndoh tehngoh keh bohlbehr?
I'll come back _____ tomorrow	Vuelvo mañana
	bwehlboh mahnyahnah

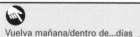

| Vuelva mañana/dentro de...días _____ | Come back tomorrow/in...days' time |

13 .4 Medication and prescriptions

How do I take this _____ medicine?	¿Cómo se toman estos medicamentos?
	kohmoh seh tohmahn ehstohs mehdeekahmehntohs?
How many capsules/ _____ drops/injections/ spoonfuls/tablets each time?	¿Cuántas cápsulas/gotas/inyecciones/ cucharadas/tabletas por vez?
	kwahntahs kahpsoolahs/gohtahs/eenyehkthyohnehs/koo chahrahdahs pohr behth?
How many times a day? ___	¿Cuántas veces al día?

	kwahntahs behthehs ahl deeah?
I've forgotten my_____ medication. At home I take...	Se me ha olvidado traer los medicamentos. En casa tomo...
	seh meh ah olbeedahdoh trahehr lohs mehdeekahmehntohs. ehn kahsah tohmoh...
Could you make out a _____ prescription for me?	¿Podría hacerme una receta?
	pohdreeah ahthehrmeh oonah rehthehtah?
Do you know a good _____	¿Me podría recomendar un buen dentista?

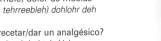

Voy a recetarle unos antibióticos/un_____ jarabe/un calmante/ unos analgésicos	I'm prescribing antibiotics/a mixture/a tranquillizer/pain killers
Tiene que guardar reposo _____	Have lots of rest
No tiene que salir a la calle _____	Stay indoors
Tiene que guardar cama_____	Stay in bed

antes de cada comida	inyecciones	tragar entero
before meals	injections	swallow whole
cápsulas	para uso externo	tabletas
capsules	exclusivamente	tablets
diluir en agua	not for internal use	tomar/ingerir
dissolve in water	ungüento	take
gotas	ointment	estos medicamentos
drops	aplicar/embadurnar	afectan la capacidad
cada...horas	rub on	de conducir
every...hours	cucharadas (soperas/	this medication
seguir la cura hasta	cucharaditas)	impairs your driving
el final	spoonfuls	...vez/veces cada 24
finish the course	(tablespoons/	horas
durante...días	tea-spoons)	...times a day
for...days		

13 .5 At the dentist's

dentist?	*meh pohdreeah rehkohmehndahr oon bwehn dehnteestah?*
Could you make a _____ dentist's appointment for me? It's urgent	¿Me podría pedir hora con el dentista? Es urgente
	meh pohdreeah pehdeer ohrah kohn ehl dehnteestah? ehs oorhehnteh
Can I come in today,_____ please?	¿Me podría atender hoy mismo?
	meh pohdreeah ahtehndehr oy meesmoh?
I have (terrible)_____ toothache	Tengo (un terrible) dolor de muelas
	tehngoh (oon tehrreebleh) dohlohr deh mwehlahs
Could you prescribe/ _____ give me a painkiller?	¿Me podría recetar/dar un analgésico?
	meh pohdreeah rehthehtahr/dahr oon ahnahlhehseekoh?
A piece of my tooth _____	Se me ha caído un pedazo de un diente

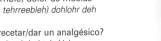
Sickness

13

has broken off	seh meh ah kaheedoh oon pehdahthoh deh oon dyehnteh
My filling's come out _____	Se me ha salido un empaste
	seh meh ah sahleedoh oon ehmpahsteh
I've got a broken crown_____	Se me ha roto la corona
	seh meh ah rohtoh lah kohrohnah
I'd like/I don't want a _____ local anaesthetic	Quisiera que/no quiero que me ponga anestesia local
	keesyehrah keh/noh kyehroh keh meh pohngah ahnehstehsyah lohkahl
Can you do a makeshift_____ repair job?	¿Me podría hacer un arreglo provisional?
	meh pohdreeah ahthehr oon ahrrehgloh prohbeesyohnahl?
I don't want this tooth _____ pulled	No quiero que me extraiga esta muela
	noh kyehroh keh meh ehxtraygah ehstah mwehlah
My dentures are broken. _____ Can you fix them?	Se me ha roto la dentadura postiza ¿Podría arreglármela?
	seh meh ah rohtoh lah dehntahdoorah pohsteethah. pohdreeah arrehglahrmehlah?

¿Qué diente/muela le duele?_____	Which tooth hurts?
Tiene un absceso _____	You've got an abscess
Tengo que tratarle el nervio _____	I'll have to do a root canal
Voy a ponerle anestesia local _____	I'm giving you a local anaesthetic
Tengo que empastarle/extraerle/ _____ pulirle este/esta...	I'll have to fill/pull this tooth/file this...down
Tengo que usar el torno _____	I'll have to drill
Abra la boca_____	Open wide, please
Cierre la boca_____	Close your mouth, please
Enjuáguese_____	Rinse, please
¿Le sigue doliendo?_____	Does it hurt still?

Sickness

13

In trouble

14 In trouble

14 .1 Asking for help

Help!	¡Socorro!
	sohkohrroh!
Fire!	¡Fuego!
	fwehgoh!
Police!	¡Policía!
	pohleetheeah!
Quick!	¡Rápido!
	rahpeedoh!
Danger!	¡Peligro!
	pehleegroh!
Watch out!	¡Cuidado!
	kweedahdoh!
Stop!	¡Alto!
	ahltoh!
Be careful!	¡Cuidado!
	kweedahdoh!
Don't!	¡No, no!
	noh, noh!
Let go!	¡Suelte!
	swehlteh!
Stop that thief!	¡Al ladrón!
	ahl lahdrohn!
Could you help me, please?	¿Podría ayudarme, por favor?
	pohdreeah ahyoodahrmeh, pohr fahbohr?
Where's the police station/emergency exit/fire escape?	¿Dónde está la comisaría/la salida de emergencia/la escalera de incendios?
	dohndeh ehstah lah kohmeesahreeah/lah sahleedah deh ehmehrhehnthyah/lah ehskahlehrah deh eenthehndyohs?
Where's the nearest fire extinguisher?	¿Dónde hay un extintor?
	dohndeh ay oon ehxteentohr?
Call the fire brigade!	¡Llamen a los bomberos!
	lyahmehn ah lohs bohmbehrohs!
Call the police!	¡Llamen a la policía!
	lyahmehn ah lah pohleetheeah!
Call an ambulance!	¡Llamen a una ambulancia!
	lyahmehn ah oonah ahmboolahnthyah!
Where's the nearest phone?	¿Dónde hay un teléfono?
	dohndeh ay oon tehlehfohnoh?
Could I use your phone?	¿Podría llamar por teléfono?
	pohdreeah lyahmahr pohr tehlehfohnoh?
What's the emergency number?	¿Cuál es el número de urgencias?
	kwahl ehs ehl noomehroh deh oorhehnthyahs?
What's the number for the police?	¿Cuál es el número de la policía?
	kwahl ehs ehl noomehroh deh lah pohleetheeah?

I've lost my purse/_____ wallet	Se me ha perdido el monedero/la cartera *seh meh ah pehrdeedoh ehl mohnehdehroh/lah kahrtehrah*
I left my...behind _____ yesterday	Ayer me dejé el/la... *ahyehr meh dehheh ehl/lah...*
I left my...here _____	Me he dejado el/la...aquí *meh eh dehhahdoh ehl/lah...ahkee*
Did you find my...? _____	¿Han encontrado mi...? *ahn ehnkohntrahdoh mee...?*
It was right here_____	Estaba aquí *ehstahbah ahkee*
It's quite valuable _____	Es muy valioso *ehs mwee bahlyohsoh*
Where's the lost_____ property office?	¿Dónde está la oficina de objetos perdidos? *dohndeh ehstah lah ohfeetheenah deh ohbhehtohs pehrdeedohs?*

.3 Accidents

There's been an _____ accident	Ha habido un accidente *ah ahbeedoh oon ahktheedehnteh*
Someone's fallen into ____ the water	Se ha caído alguien al agua *seh ah kaheedoh ahlgyehn ahl ahgwah*
There's a fire_____	Hay un incendio *ay oon eenthehndyoh*
Is anyone hurt? _____	¿Hay algún herido? *ay ahlgoon ehreedoh?*
Some people have _____ been/no one's been injured	(No) hay heridos *(noh) ay ehreedohs*
There's someone in _____ the car/train still	Todavía queda alguien en el coche/tren *tohdahbeeah kehdah ahlgyehn ehn ehl kohcheh/trehn*
It's not too bad. Don't_____ worry	No es grave. No se preocupe *noh ehs grahbeh. noh seh prehohkoopeh*
Leave everything the _____ way it is, please	No toque nada *noh tohkeh nahdah*
I want to talk to the_____ police first	Primero quisiera hablar con la policía *preemehroh keesyehrah ahblahr kohn lah pohleetheeah*
I want to take a _____ photo first	Primero quisiera sacar una foto *preemehroh keesyehrah sahkahr oonah fohtoh*
Here's my name_____ and address	Aquí tiene mi nombre y dirección *ahkee tyehneh mee nohmbreh ee deerehkthyohn*
Could I have your _____ name and address?	¿Me da su nombre y dirección? *meh dah soo nohmbreh ee deerehkthyohn?*
Could I see some_____ identification/your insurance papers?	¿Me permite su carnet de identidad/sus papeles del seguro? *meh pehrmeeteh soo kahrneh deh eedehnteedahdh/soos pahpehlehs dehl sehgooroh?*

In trouble

Will you act as a _____ witness?	¿Le importaría hacer de testigo?
	leh eempohrtahreeah ahtehr deh tehsteegoh?
I need the details for _____ the insurance	Necesito los datos para el seguro
	nehthehseetoh lohs dahtohs pahrah ehl sehgooroh
Are you insured? _____	¿Está asegurado?
	ehstah ahsehgoorahdoh?
Third party or _____ comprehensive?	¿Responsabilidad civil o contra todo riesgo?
	rehspohnsahbeeleedahdh theebeel oh kohntrah tohdoh ryehsgoh?
Could you sign here, _____ please?	Firme aquí, por favor
	feermeh ahkee, pohr fahbohr

🔴 .4 Theft

I've been robbed _____	Me han robado
	meh ahn rohbahdoh
My...has been stolen _____	Me han robado el/la...
	meh ahn rohbahdoh ehl/lah...
My car's been _____ broken into	Me han abierto el coche
	meh ahn ahbyehrtoh ehl kohcheh

🔴 .5 Missing person

I've lost my child/ _____ grandmother	Se ha perdido mi hijo/mi hija/mi abuela
	seh ah pehrdeedoh mee eehoh/mee eehah/mee ahbwehlah
Could you help me _____ find him/her?	¿Podría ayudarme a buscarlo/la?
	pohdreeah ahyoodahrmeh ah booskahrloh/lah?
Have you seen a _____ small child?	¿Ha visto a un niño pequeño/a una niña pequeña?
	ah veestoh ah oon neenyoh pehkehnyoh/ah oonah neenyah pehkehnyah?
He's/she's...years old _____	Tiene...años
	tyehneh...ahnyohs
He's/she's got _____ short/long/blond/red/ brown/black/ grey/curly/ straight/frizzy hair	Tiene el pelo corto/largo/rubio/rojo/castaño/negro/ canoso/rizado/liso/crespo
	tyehneh ehl pehloh kohrtoh/lahrgoh/roobyoh/kahstahnyoh/neh groh/kahnohsoh/reethahdoh/leesoh/krehspoh
with a ponytail _____	con cola de caballo
	kohn kohlah deh kahbahlyoh
with plaits _____	con trenzas
	kohn trehnthahs
in a bun _____	con moño
	kohn mohnyoh
He's/she's got _____ blue/brown/green eyes	Tiene ojos azules/marrones/verdes
	tyehneh ohhohs ahthoolehs/mahrrohnehs/behrdehs

He's wearing swimming trunks/mountaineering boots _____ Lleva bañador/botas de montaña
lyehbah bahnyahdohr/bohtahs deh mohntahnyah

with/without glasses/ _____ a bag con/sin gafas/bolso
kohn/seen gahfahs/bohlsoh

tall/short_____ alto/bajito
ahltoh/bahheetoh

This is a photo of _____ him/her Esta es su foto
ehstah ehs soo fohtoh

He/she must be lost _____ Seguramente se habrá perdido
sehgoorahmehnteh seh ahbrah pehrdeedoh

🖐 14.6 The police

An arrest

Los papeles del coche, por favor_____	Your registration papers, please
Conducía demasiado rápido _____	You were speeding
Tiene mal aparcado el coche_____	You're not allowed to park here
No ha puesto monedas en el parquímetro	You haven't put money in the meter
No le funcionan los faros_____	Your lights aren't working
Le vamos a poner una multa de... _____ pesetas	That's a...pesetas fine
¿Va a pagar la multa en el acto? _____	Do you want to pay on the spot?
Tiene que pagar en el acto_____	You'll have to pay on the spot

I don't speak Spanish_____ No hablo español
noh ahbloh ehspahnyohl

I didn't see the sign _____ No he visto el cartel
noh eh beestoh ehl kahrtehl

I don't understand_____ what it says No entiendo lo que dice
noh ehntyehndoh loh keh deetheh

I was only doing..._____ kilometres an hour Sólo iba a...kilómetros por hora
sohloh eebah ah...keelohmehtrohs pohr ohrah

I'll have my car checked ___ Haré revisar el coche
ahreh rehbeesahr ehl kohcheh

I was blinded by _____ oncoming lights Me cegó un coche que venía de frente
meh thehgoh oon kohcheh keh behneeah deh frehnteh

At the police station

I want to report a_____ collision/missing person/rape Vengo a hacer la denuncia de un choque/un extravío/una violación
behngoh ah ahthehr lah dehnoonthyah deh oon chohkeh/oon ehxtrahbeeoh/oonah beeohlahthyohn

Could you make out _____ a report, please?	¿Podría hacer un atestado? *pohdreeah ahthehr oon ahtehstahdoh?*
Could I have a copy _____ for the insurance?	¿Me podría dar una copia para el seguro? *meh pohdreeah dahr oonah kohpyah pahrah ehl sehgooroh?*
I've lost everything _____	He perdido todo *eh pehrdeedoh tohdoh*

¿Dónde ha sido? _____	Where did it happen?
¿Qué se le ha perdido? _____	What's missing?
¿Qué le han robado? _____	What's been taken?
¿Me permite su documento de_____ identidad?	Could I see some identification?
¿A qué hora ocurrió?_____	What time did it happen?
¿Quiénes estuvieron implicados? _____	Who was involved?
¿Hay testigos? _____	Are there any witnesses?
Rellene este formulario_____	Fill this out, please
Firme aquí, por favor_____	Sign here, please
¿Quiere un intérprete? _____	Do you want an interpreter?

I'd like an interpreter _____	Quisiera un intérprete *keesyehrah oon eentehrprehteh*
I'm innocent _____	Soy inocente *soy eenohthehnteh*
I don't know anything _____ about it	No sé nada *noh seh nahdah*
I want to speak to _____ someone...	Quisiera hablar con alguien de... *keesyehrah ahblahr kohn ahlgyehn deh...*
from the British _____ consulate	Quisiera hablar con alguien del Consulado Británico *keesyehrah ahblahr kohn ahlgyehn dehl kohnsoolahdoh breetahneekoh*
I need to see someone _____ from the British embassy	Quisiera hablar con alguien de la Embajada Británica *keesyehrah ahblahr kohn ahlgyehn deh lah ehmbahhahdah breetahneekah*
I want a lawyer who _____ speaks English	Quisiera un abogado que hable inglés *keesyehrah oon ahbohgahdoh keh ahbleh eenglehs*

In trouble

4

15

Word list

Word list English - Spanish

● **This word list** is meant to supplement the previous chapters.
Nouns are always accompanied by the Spanish definite article in order
to indicate whether it is a masculine (el) or feminine (la) word.
In a number of cases, words not contained in this list can be found
elsewhere in this booklet, namely alongside the diagrams of the car,
the bicycle and the tent. Many food terms can be found in the Spanish-
English list in 4.7.

A

a little	un poco	*oon pohkoh*
above (up)	arriba	*ahrreebah*
abroad	el extranjero	*ehl ehxtrahnhehroh*
accident	el accidente	*ehl ahktheedehnteh*
adder	la víbora	*la veebohrah*
addition	la suma	*lah soomah*
address	la dirección	*lah deerehkthyohn*
admission	la entrada	*lah ehntrahdah*
admission price	el precio de entrada	*ehl prehthyoh deh lah ehntrahdah*
admission ticket	la entrada	*lah ehntrahdah*
advice	el consejo	*ehl kohnseh__h__oh*
after	después de	*dehspwehs deh*
afternoon (in the)	(por) la tarde	*(pohr) lah tahrdeh*
aftershave	la loción para después del afeitado	*lah lohthyohn pahrah dehspwehs dehl ahfeytahdoh*
again	de nuevo	*deh nwehboh*
against	contra	*kohntrah*
age	la edad	*lah ehdahdh*
Aids	el Sida	*ehl seedah*
air conditioning	el aire acondicionado	*ehl ayreh ahkohndeethyohnahdoh*
air mattress	el colchón neumático	*ehl kohlchohn nehoomahteekoh*
air sickness bag	bolsita para el mareo	*bohlseetah pahrah ehl mahrehoh*
aircraft	el avión	*ehl ahbyohn*
airport	el aeropuerto	*ehl ahehrohpwehrtoh*
alarm	la alarma	*lah ahlahrmah*
alarm clock	el despertador	*ehl dehspehrtahdohr*
alcohol	el alcohol	*ehl ahlkohohl*
all the time	cada vez	*kahdah behth*
allergic	alérgico	*ahlehr__h__eekoh*
alone	solo	*sohloh*
always	siempre	*syehmpreh*
ambulance	la ambulancia	*lah ahmboolahnthyah*
amount	el importe	*ehl eempohrteh*
amusement park	el parque de atracciones	*ehl pahrkeh deh ahtrahkthyohnehs*
anaesthetize	anestesiar	*ahnehstehsyahr*
anchovy	la anchoa	*lah ahnchohah*
angry	enfadado	*ehnfahdahdoh*
animal	el animal	*ehl ahneemahl*
ankle	el tobillo	*ehl tohbeelyoh*
answer	la respuesta	*lah rehspwehstah*

ant	la hormiga	*lah ohrmeegah*
antibiotics	los antibióticos	*lohs ahnteebyohteekohs*
antifreeze	el anticongelante	*ehl ahnteekohn̲h̲ehlahnteh*
antique	antiguo	*ahnteegwoh*
antiques	las antigüedades	*lahs ahnteegwehdahdehs*
anus	el ano	*ehl ahnoh*
apartment	el apartamento	*ehl ahpahrtahmehntoh*
aperitif	el aperitivo	*ehl ahpehreeteeboh*
apologies	las disculpas	*lahs deeskoolpahs*
apple	la manzana	*lah mahnthahnah*
apple juice	el zumo de manzana	*ehl thoomoh deh mahnthahnah*
apple pie	la tarta de manzana	*lah tahrtah deh mahnthahnah*
apple sauce	el puré de manzanas	*ehl pooreh deh mahnthahnahs*
appointment	la hora	*lah ohrah*
approximately	más o menos	*mahs oh mehnohs*
April	abril	*ahbreel*
archbishop	el arzobispo	*ehl ahrthohbeespoh*
architecture	la arquitectura	*lah ahrkeetehktoorah*
area	los alrededores	*lohs ahlrehdehdohrehs*
arm	el brazo	*ehl brahthoh*
arrange to meet	quedar	*kehdahr*
arrive	llegar	*lyehgahr*
arrow	la flecha	*lah flehchah*
art	el arte	*ehl ahrteh*
artery	la arteria	*lah ahrtehryah*
artichokes	las alcachofas	*lahs ahlkahchohfahs*
article	el artículo	*ehl ahrteekooloh*
artificial respiration	la respiración artificial	*lah rehspeerahthyohn ahrteefeethyahl*
arts and crafts	la artesanía	*lah ahrtehsahneeah*
ashtray	el cenicero	*ehl thehneethehroh*
ask (a question)	preguntar	*prehgoontahr*
ask for	pedir	*pehdeer*
asparagus	los espárragos	*lohs ehspahrrahgohs*
aspirin	la aspirina	*lah ahspeereenah*
assault	la agresión	*lah ahgrehsyohn*
aubergine	la berenjena	*lah behrehn̲h̲ehnah*
August	agosto	*ahgohstoh*
automatic	automático	*ahootohmahteekoh*
automatic car	el coche con cambio automático	*ehl kohcheh kohn kahmbyoh ahootohmahteekoh*
autumn	el otoño	*ehl ohtohnyoh*
avalanche	el alud	*ehl ahloodh*
awake (adj.)	despierto	*dehspyehrtoh*
awning	el toldo	*ehl tohldoh*

B

English	Spanish	Pronunciation
baby	el bebé	*ehl behbeh*
baby food	la comida para bebés	*lah kohmeedah pahrah behbehs*
babysitter	la niñera	*lah neenyehrah*
back (at the)	atrás	*ahtrahs*
back	la espalda	*lah ehspahldah*
backpack	la mochila	*lah mohcheelah*
bacon	el tocino	*ehl tohtheenoh*
bad	mal, malo	*mahl, mahloh*
bag	la bolsa	*lah bohlsah*
baker	la panadería	*lah pahnahdehreeah*
balcony (theatre)	el palco (alto)	*ehl pahlkoh (ahltoh)*
balcony (to building)	el balcón	*ehl bahlkohn*
ball	la pelota	*lah pehlohtah*
ballet	el ballet	*ehl bahleh*
ballpoint pen	el bolígrafo	*ehl bohleegrahfoh*
banana	el plátano	*ehl plahtahnoh*
bandage	la gasa	*lah gahsah*
bank (river)	la orilla	*lah ohreelyah*
bank	el banco	*ehl bahnkoh*
bank card	la tarjeta del banco	*lah tahrhehtah dehl bahnkoh*
bar (café)	el bar	*ehl bahr*
bar (drinks' cabinet)	la barra	*lah bahrrah*
bar	la barra	*lah bahrrah*
barbecue	la barbacoa	*lah bahrbahkohah*
basketball	el baloncesto	*ehl bahlohnthehstoh*
bath	el baño	*ehl bahnyoh*
bath attendant	el bañista	*ehl bahnyeestah*
bath foam	el gel de baño	*ehl hehl deh bahnyoh*
bath towel	la toalla de baño	*lah tohahlyah deh bahnyoh*
bathing cap	el gorro de baño	*ehl gohrroh deh bahnyoh*
bathing cubicle	la caseta	*lah kahsehtah*
bathing suit	el bañador	*ehl bahnyahdohr*
bathroom	el cuarto de baño	*ehl kwahrtoh deh bahnyoh*
battery (car)	la batería	*lah bahtehreeah*
battery	la pila	*lah peelah*
beach	la playa	*lah plahyah*
beans	las judías blancas	*lahs hoodeeahs blahnkahs*
beautiful	bonito	*bohneetoh*
beauty parlour	el salón de belleza	*ehl sahlohn deh behlyehthah*
bed	la cama	*lah kahmah*
bee	la abeja	*lah ahbehhah*
beef	la carne de vaca	*lah kahrneh deh bahkah*
beer	la cerveza	*lah thehrbehthah*
beetroot	la remolacha	*lah rehmohlahchah*
begin	empezar	*ehmpehthahr*
beginner	el principiante	*ehl preentheepyahnteh*
behind	atrás	*ahtrahs*
Belgian (f)	la belga	*lah behlgah*
Belgian (m)	el belga	*ehl behlgah*

Belgium	Bélgica	*behlheekah*
bellboy	el mozo de cuerda	*ehl mohthoh deh kwehrdah*
belt	el cinturón	*ehl theentoorohn*
berth	la litera	*lah leetehrah*
better	mejor	*mehhohr*
bicarb	el bicarbonato	*ehl beekahrbohnahtoh*
bicycle	la bicicleta	*lah beetheeklehtah*
bicycle pump	el inflador	*ehl eenflahdohr*
bicycle repairman	el mecánico de bicicletas	*ehl mehkahneekoh deh beetheeklehtahs*
bikini	el bikini	*ehl beekeenee*
bill	la cuenta	*lah kwehntah*
billiards, to play	el juego de billar	*ehl hwehgoh deh beelyahr*
birthday (to have a)	cumplir años	*koompleer ahnyohs*
birthday	el cumpleaños	*ehl koomplehahnyohs*
biscuit	la galleta	*lah gahlyehtah*
bite	morder	*mohrdehr*
bitter	amargo	*ahmahrgoh*
black	negro	*nehgroh*
bland	soso	*sohsoh*
blanket	la manta	*lah mahntah*
bleach	teñir de rubio	*tehnyeer deh roobyoh*
blister	la ampolla	*lah ahmpohlyah*
blond	rubio	*roobyoh*
blood	la sangre	*lah sahngreh*
blood pressure	la tensión sanguínea	*lah tehnsyohn sahngheenehah*
blouse	la blusa	*lah bloosah*
blow dry	secar a mano	*sehkahr ah mahnoh*
blue	azul	*ahthool*
boat	el barco	*ehl bahrkoh*
body	el cuerpo	*ehl kwehrpoh*
body milk	la leche corporal	*lah lehcheh kohrpohrahl*
boiled	cocido	*kohtheedoh*
boiled ham	el jamón de York	*ehl hahmohn deh yohrk*
bonbon	el bombón	*ehl bohmbohn*
bone	el hueso	*ehl wehsoh*
bonnet	el capó	*ehl kahpoh*
book (verb)	reservar	*rehsehrbahr*
book	el libro	*ehl leebroh*
booked	reservado	*rehsehrbahdoh*
booking office	la taquilla	*lah tahkeelyah*
bookshop	la librería	*lah leebrehreeah*
border	la frontera	*lah frohntehrah*
bored (be)	aburrirse	*ahboorreerseh*
boring	aburrido	*ahboorreedoh*
born	nacido	*nahtheedoh*
botanical gardens	el jardín botánico	*ehl hahrdeen bohtahneekoh*
both	ambos/ambas	*ahmbohs/ahmbahs*
bottle (baby's)	el biberón	*ehl beebehrohn*
bottle	la botella	*lah bohtehlyah*
bottle-warmer	el calentador de biberones	*ehl kahlehntahdohr de beebehrohnehs*
box (in theatre)	el palco	*ehl pahlkoh*

box	la caja	*kahhah*
boy	el chico	*ehl cheekoh*
bra	el sujetador	*ehl soohehtahdohr*
bracelet	la pulsera	*lah poolsehrah*
braised	estofado	*ehstohfahdoh*
brake	el freno	*ehl frehnoh*
brake fluid	el líquido de frenos	*ehl leekeedoh deh frehnohs*
bread	el pan	*ehl pahn*
bread roll	el panecillo	*ehl pahnehtheelyoh*
breakdown recovery	el auxilio en carretera	*ehl ahooxeelyoh ehn kahrrehtehrah*
break (limb)	fracturarse	*frahktoorahrseh*
breakfast	el desayuno	*ehl dehsahyoonoh*
breast	el pecho	*ehl pehchoh*
bridge	el puente	*ehl pwehnteh*
bring	llevar	*lyehbahr*
brochure	el folleto	*ehl fohlyehtoh*
broken	roto, estropeado	*rohtoh, ehstrohpehahdoh*
broth	el caldo	*ehl kahldoh*
brother	el hermano	*ehl ehrmahnoh*
brown	marrón	*mahrrohn*
bruise (verb)	contusionarse	*kohntoosyohnahrseh*
brush	el cepillo	*ehl thehpeelyoh*
Brussels sprouts	las coles de Bruselas	*lahs kohlehs deh broosehlahs*
bucket	el cubo	*ehl kooboh*
bug	el bicho	*ehl beechoh*
building	el edificio	*ehl ehdeefeethyoh*
bullfight	la corrida de toros	*lah kohrreedah deh tohrohs*
buoy	la boya	*lah boyah*
burglary	el robo en una casa	*ehl rohboh ehn oonah kahsah*
burn (verb)	quemar	*kehmahr*
burn	la quemadura	*lah kehmahdoorah*
burnt	quemado	*kehmahdoh*
bus	el autobús	*ehl ahootohboos*
bus station	la estación de autobuses	*lah ehstahthyohn deh ahootohboos*
bus stop	la parada de autobús	*lah pahrahdah deh ahootohboos*
business class	la clase preferente	*lah klahseh prehfehrehnteh*
business trip	el viaje de negocios	*ehl byahheh deh nehgohthyohs*
busy (crowded)	hay mucha gente	*ay moochah hehnteh*
butane camping gas	el gas butano	*ehl gahs bootahnoh*
butcher's	la carnicería	*lah kahrneethehreeah*
butter	la mantequilla	*lah mahntehkeelyah*
button	el botón	*ehl bohtohn*
buy	comprar	*kohmprahr*
by airmail	el correo aéreo/ vía aérea	*ehl kohrrehoh ahehrehoh/beeah ahehrehah*

C

cabbage	la col, la berza	lah kohl, lah behrthah
cabin	la cabaña	lah kahbahnyah
cake	el pastel	ehl pahstehl
cake shop	la pastelería, la confitería	lah pahstehlehreeah, lah kohnfeetehreeah
call (by phone)	llamar por teléfono	lyahmahr pohr tehlehfohnoh
called, to be	llamarse	lyahmahrseh
camera	la máquina fotográfica	lah mahkeenah fohtohgrahfeekah
camp	acampar	ahkahmpahr
camp shop	la tienda del camping	lah tyehndah dehl kahmpeen
camp site	el camping	ehl kahmpeen
camper van	el autocaravana	ehl ahootohkahrah-bahnah
campfire	la fogata	lah fohgahtah
camping guide	la guía de camping	lah gheeah deh kahmpeen
camping permit	el permiso de acampar	ehl pehrmeesoh deh ahkahmpahr
canal boat	el barco de excursión	ehl bahrkoh deh ehxkoorsyohn
cancel	cancelar	kahnthehlahr
candle	la vela	lah behlah
canoe	la piragua	lah peerahgwah
canoeing	el piragüismo	ehl peerahgweesmoh
cap (hat)	el gorro	ehl gohrroh
car	el coche	ehl kohcheh
car deck	la bodega para coches	lah bohdehgah pahrah kohchehs
car documents	los papeles del coche	lohs pahpehlehs dehl kohcheh
car registration	el permiso de circulación	ehl pehrmeesoh deh theerkoolahthyohn
car trouble	la avería	lah ahbehreeah
carafe	la jarra	lah <u>h</u>ahrrah
caravan	la caravana	lah kahrahbahnah
cardigan	el chaleco	ehl chahlehkoh
careful	con cuidado	kohn kweedahdoh
carrot	la zanahoria	lah thahnahohryah
carton	el cartón	ehl kahrtohn
cartridge	el carrete de cassette	ehl kahrrehteh deh kahseht
cascade	la cascada	lah kahskahdah
cash desk	la caja	lah ka<u>h</u>hah
casino	el casino	ehl kahseenoh
cassette	la cassette	lah kahseht
castle	el castillo	ehl kahsteelyoh
cat	el gato	ehl gahtoh
catalogue	el catálogo	ehl kahtahlohgoh
cathedral	la catedral	lah kahtehdrahl
cauliflower	la coliflor	lah kohleeflohr
cave	la gruta	lah grootah
CD	el compact disc	ehl kohmpahkt deesk

celebrate	celebrar una fiesta	*thehlehbrahr oonah fyehsta*
cellotape	la celo	*lah thehloh*
cemetery	el cementerio	*ehl thehmehntehryoh*
centimetre	centímetro(s)	*thehnteemehtroh(s)*
central heating	la calefacción central	*lah kahlehfakthyohn thehntrahl*
centre (in the)	en el centro/ medio	*ehn ehl thehntroh/ mehdyoh*
centre	el centro	*ehl thehntroh*
chair	la silla	*lah seelyah*
chambermaid	la camarera	*lah kahmahrehrah*
chamois	la gamuza	*lah gahmoothah*
champagne	el champán/el cava	*ehl chahmpahn/ehl kahbah*
change (from paying)	la vuelta	*lah bwehltah*
change (train/plane etc.)	hacer trasbordo	*ahthehr trahsbohrdoh*
change (verb)	cambiar	*kahmbyahr*
change the baby's nappy	cambiar los pañales	*kahmbyahr lohs pahnyahlehs*
change the oil	cambiar el aceite	*kahmbyahr ehl ahtheyteh*
chapel	la capilla	*lah kahpeelyah*
charter flight	el vuelo chárter	*ehl bwehloh chahrtehr*
chat up	ligar	*leegahr*
check (verb)	controlar	*kohntrohlahr*
check in	facturar	*frahktoorahr*
cheers	salud	*sahloodh*
cheese (tasty, mild)	el queso (añejo, blando)	*ehl kehsoh (ahnyeh<u>h</u>oh,blahndoh)*
chef	el jefe	*ehl <u>h</u>ehfeh*
chemist	la droguería	*lah drohguehreeah*
cheque	el cheque	*ehl chehkeh*
cherries	las cerezas	*lahs thehrehthahs*
chess (play)	jugar al ajedrez	*<u>h</u>oogahr ahl a<u>h</u>ehdreth*
chewing gum	el chicle	*ehl cheekleh*
chicken	el pollo	*ehl pohlyoh*
chicory	las endivias	*lahs ehndeebyahs*
child	el hijo, el niño	*ehl ee<u>h</u>oh, ehl neenyoh*
child seat	el asiento para niños	*ehl ahsyehntoh pahrah neenyohs*
child's seat	el sillín para niños	*ehl seelyeen pahrah neenyohs*
chilled	refrigerado	*rehfree<u>h</u>ehrahdoh*
chin	la barbilla	*lah bahrbeelyah*
chips/crisps	las patatas fritas	*lahs pahtahtahs freetahs*
chocolate	el chocolate	*ehl chohkohlahteh*
choose	elegir/escoger	*ehleh<u>h</u>eer/ehskoh<u>h</u>ehr*
chop	la chuleta	*la choolehtah*
christian name	el nombre	*ehl nohmbreh*
church	la iglesia	*lah eeglehsyah*
church service	el servicio religioso	*ehl sehrbeethyoh rehlee<u>h</u>yohsoh*
cigar	el puro	*ehl pooroh*
cigar shop	el estanco	*ehl ehstahnkoh*
cigarette	el cigarrillo	*ehl theegahrreelyoh*

cigarette paper	el papel de fumar	*ehl pahpehl deh foomahr*
cine camera	la filmadora	*lah feelmahdohrah*
circle	el círculo	*ehl theerkooloh*
circus	el circo	*ehl theerkoh*
city map	el plano	*ehl plahnoh*
classic/classical	clásica	*klahseekah*
clean (adj.)	limpio	*leempyoh*
clean (verb)	limpiar	*leempyahr*
clear (adj.)	claro	*klahroh*
clearance	la liquidación	*lah leekeedahthyohn*
closed	cerrado	*thehrrahdoh*
closed off	(la carretera) cerrada	*(lah kahrrehtehrah) thehrrahdah*
clothes	la ropa	*lah rohpah*
clothes hanger	la percha	*lah pehrchah*
clothes peg	la pinza para la ropa	*lah peenthah pahrah lah rohpah*
coat	el abrigo	*ehl ahbreegoh*
cockroach	la cucaracha	*lah kookahrahchah*
cod	el bacalao (fresco)	*ehl bahkahlahoh (frehskoh)*
coffee	el café	*ehl kahfeh*
coffee creamer	la crema para el café	*lah krehmah pahrah ehl kahfeh*
coffee filter	el filtro de café	*ehl feeltroh deh kahfeh*
cognac	el coñac	*ehl kohnyah*
cold	frío	*freeoh*
cold	el constipado	*ehl kohnsteepahdoh*
cold cuts	los fiambres	*lohs fyahmbrehs*
collarbone	la clavícula	*lah klahbeekoolah*
colleague	el/la colega	*ehl/lah kohlehgah*
collision	el choque	*ehl chohkeh*
cologne	el agua de tocador	*ehl ahgwah deh tohkahdohr*
colour	el color	*ehl kohlohr*
colour TV	el televisor color	*ehl tehlehbeesohr kohlohr*
coloured pencils	los lápices de colores	*lohs lahpeethehs deh kohlohrehs*
colouring book	el libro para colorear	*ehl leebroh pahrah kohlohrehahr*
comb	el peine	*ehl peheeneh*
come	venir	*behneer*
compartment	el compartimiento	*ehl kohmpahrteemyehntoh*
complaint (medical)	la molestia	*lah mohlehstyah*
complaint	la queja	*lah keh<u>h</u>ah*
complaints book	el libro de reclamaciones	*ehl leebroh deh rehklahmahthyohnehs*
completely	del todo	*dehl tohdoh*
compliment	el cumplido	*ehl koompleedoh*
compulsory	obligatorio	*ohbleegahtohryoh*
concert	el concierto	*ehl kohnthyehrtoh*
concert hall	la sala de conciertos	*lah sahlah deh kohnthyehrtohs*

Word list

15

concussion	la conmoción cerebral	*lah kohnmohthyohn thehrehbrahl*
condiments	los condimentos	*lohs kohndeemehntohs*
condom	el condón	*ehl kohndohn*
congratulate	felicitar	*fehleetheetahr*
connection	el enlace	*ehl ehnlahtheh*
constipation	el estreñimiento	*ehl ehstrehnyeemyehntoh*
consulate	el consulado	*ehl kohnsoolahdoh*
consultation	la consulta	*lah kohnsooltah*
contact lens	la lentilla	*lah lehnteelyah*
contact lens solution	el líquido para las lentillas	*ehl leekeedoh pahrah lahs lehnteelyahs*
contagious	contagioso	*kohntah<u>h</u>yohsoh*
contest	el concurso	*ehl kohnkoorsoh*
contraceptive	el anticonceptivo	*ehl ahnteekohn-thehpteeboh*
contraceptive pill	la píldora anticonceptiva	*ah peeldohrah lahnteekohnthehpteebah*
convent	el convento	*ehl kohnbehntoh*
cook (verb)	cocinar	*kohtheenahr*
cook	el cocinero	*ehl kohtheenehroh*
copper	el cobre	*ehl kohbreh*
copy	la copia	*lah kohpyah*
corkscrew	el sacacorchos	*ehl sahkahkohrchohs*
corn flour	la maicena	*lah maythehnah*
corner	el rincón	*ehl reenkohn*
correct	correcto	*kohrrehktoh*
correspond	cartearse	*kahrtehahrseh*
corridor	el pasillo	*ehl pahseelyoh*
costume	el traje	*ehl trah<u>h</u>eh*
cot	la cuna	*lah koonah*
cotton	el algodón	*ehl ahlgohdohn*
cotton wool	el algodón	*ehl ahlgohdohn*
cough	la tos	*lah tohs*
cough mixture	el jarabe para la tos	*ehl <u>h</u>ahrahbeh pahrah lah tohs*
counter	el mostrador	*ehl mohstrahdohr*
country	el país	*ehl pahees*
country code	el indicativo del país	*ehl eendeekahteeboh dehl pahees*
country(side)	el campo	*ehl kahmpoh*
courgette	el calabacín	*ehl kahlahbahtheen*
course (of treatment)	la cura	*lah koorah*
cousin (f)	la prima	*lah preemah*
cousin (m)	el primo	*ehl preemoh*
crab	el cangrejo	*ehl kahngre<u>h</u>oh*
cream	la crema, la nata	*lah krehmah, lah nahtah*
credit card	la tarjeta de crédito	*lah tahr<u>h</u>ehtah deh krehdeetoh*
crisps/chips	las patatas fritas	*lahs pahtahtahs freetahs*
croissant	el croissant	*ehl krwahsahn*
cross the road	cruzar la calle	*kroothahr lah kahlyeh*
cross-country run	la pista de esquí de fondo	*lah peestah deh ehskee deh fohndoh*

Word list

cross-country skiing	el esquí de fondo	*ehl ehskee deh fohndoh*
cross-country skis	los esquís de fondo	*lohs ehskees deh fohndoh*
crossing (journey)	la travesía	*lah trahbehseeah*
cry (verb)	llorar	*lyohrahr*
cubic metre(s)	metro(s) cúbico(s)	*mehtroh(s) koobeekoh(s)*
cucumber	el pepino	*ehl pehpeenoh*
cuddly toy	el animal de peluche	*ehl ahneemahl deh pehloocheh*
cuff links	los gemelos	*lohs <u>h</u>ehmehlohs*
culottes	la falda-pantalón	*lah fahldah pahntahlohn*
cup	la taza	*lah tahthah*
curly	rizado	*reethahdoh*
current	la corriente	*lah kohrryehnteh*
cushion	el cojín	*ehl coh<u>h</u>een*
custard	las natillas	*lahs nahteelyahs*
customary	habitual	*ahbeetwahl*
customs	la aduana	*lah ahdwahna*
customs check	el control de aduanas	*ehl kohntrohl deh ahdwahnahs*
cut (verb)	cortar	*kohrtahr*
cutlery	los cubiertos	*lohs koobyehrtohs*
cycling	montar en bicicleta	*mohntahr ehn beetheeklehtah*

D

dairy products	los productos lácteos	*lohs prodooktohs lahktehohs*
damaged	dañado, estropeado	*dahnyahdoh, ehstrohpehahdoh*
dance	bailar	*bahylahr*
dandruff	la caspa	*lah kahspah*
danger	el peligro	*ehl pehleegroh*
dangerous	peligroso	*pehleegrohsoh*
dark	oscuro	*ohskooroh*
date	la cita	*lah theetah*
daughter	la hija	*lah ee<u>h</u>ah*
day	el día, las 24 horas	*ehl deeah, lahs beheenteekwahtroh ohrahs*
day before yesterday	anteayer	*ahntehahyehr*
dead	muerto	*mwehrtoh*
decaffeinated	sin cafeína	*seen kahfeheenah*
December	diciembre	*deethyehmbreh*
deck chair	el sillón de playa	*ehl seelyohn deh plahyah*
declare(customs)	declarar	*dehklahrahr*
deep	hondo	*ohndoh*
deep sea diving	el buceo	*ehl boothehoh*
degrees	los grados	*lohs grahdohs*
delay	el retraso	*ehl rehtrahsoh*
delicious	delicioso	*dehleethyohsoh*
dentist	el dentista	*ehl dehnteestah*
dentures	la dentadura postiza	*lah dehntahdoorah pohsteethah*

Word list

15

deodorant	el desodorante	*ehl dehsohdohrahnteh*
department	la sección	*lah sehkthyohn*
department stores	los grandes almacenes	*lohs grahndehs ahlmahthehnehs*
departure	la partida	*lah pahrteedah*
departure time	la hora de salida	*lah ohrah deh sahleedah*
depilatory cream	la crema depilatoria	*lah krehmah dehpeelahtohryah*
deposit (in)	en consigna	*ehn kohnseegnah*
deposit	la fianza	*lah fyahnzah*
dessert	el postre	*ehl pohstreh*
destination	el destino, el punto final	*ehl dehsteenoh, ehl poontoh feenahl*
develop (photos)	revelar	*rehbehlahr*
diabetic	el diabético	*ehl dyahbehteekoh*
dial (verb)	marcar	*mahrkahr*
diamond	el diamante	*ehl deeahmahnteh*
diarrhoea	la diarrea	*lah deeahrrehah*
dictionary	el diccionario	*ehl deekthyohnahryoh*
diesel	el gasóleo	*ehl gahsohlehoh*
diet	la dieta	*lah dyehtah*
difficulty	la dificultad	*lah deefeekooltahdh*
dining room	el comedor	*ehl kohmehdohr*
dining/buffet car	el coche restaurante	*ehl kohcheh rehstahoorahnteh*
dinner (to have)	cenar	*thehnahr*
dinner	la cena, la comida	*lah thehnah, lah kohmeedah*
dinner jacket	el smoking	*ehl smohkeen*
direction	la dirección	*lah deerehkthyohn*
directly	directo	*deerehktoh*
dirty	sucio	*soothyoh*
disabled person	el minusválido	*ehl meenoosbahleedoh*
disappearance	la desaparición	*lah dehsahpahreethyohn*
disco	la discoteca	*lah deeskohtehkah*
discount	el descuento	*ehl dehskwehntoh*
dish	el plato	*ehl plahtoh*
dish of the day	el plato del día	*ehl plahtoh dehl deeah*
disinfectant	el desinfectante	*ehl dehseenfehktahnteh*
distance	la distancia	*lah deestahnthyah*
distilled water	el agua destilada	*ehl ahgwah dehsteelahdah*
disturb	molestar	*mohlehstahr*
disturbance	el fallo	*ehl fahlyoh*
dive (verb)	bucear	*boothehahr*
diving	el buceo	*ehl boothehoh*
diving board	el trampolín	*ehl trahmpohleen*
diving gear	el equipo de buzo	*ehl ehkeepoh deh boothoh*
divorced	divorciado	*deebohrthyahdoh*
DIY-shop	la tienda de artículos de bricolaje	*lah tyehndah deh ahrteekoolohs deh breekohlaheh*
dizzy	mareado	*mahrehahdoh*

124

do (verb)	hacer	*ahthehr*
doctor	el médico	*ehl mehdeekoh*
dog	el perro	*ehl pehrroh*
doll	la muñeca	*lah moonyehkah*
domestic	nacionales	*nahtheeohnahlehs*
done	hecho	*ehchoh*
door	la puerta	*lah pwehrtah*
double	doble	*dohbleh*
down	abajo	*ahbah<u>h</u>oh*
draught (to be a)	haber corriente	*ahbehr kohrryehnteh*
draughts (play)	jugar a las damas	<u>*hoo*</u>*gahr ah lahs dahmahs*
dream	soñar	*sohnyahr*
dress	el vestido	*ehl behsteedoh*
dressing gown	la bata	*lah bahtah*
drink (verb)	beber	*behbehr*
drinking chocolate	el chocolate	*ehl chohkohlahteh*
drinking water	el agua potable	*ehl ahgwah pohtahbleh*
drive (verb)	ir en coche	*eer ehn kohcheh*
driver	el chófer	*ehl chohfehr*
driving licence	el permiso de conducir	*ehl pehrmeesoh deh kohndootheer*
drought	la sequía	*lah sehkeeah*
dry (verb)	secar	*sehkahr*
dry	seco	*sehkoh*
dry clean	lavar en seco	*lahbahr ehn sehkoh*
dry cleaner's	la tintorería	*lah teentohrehreeah*
dry shampoo	el champú seco	*ehl chahmpoo sehkoh*
dummy	el chupete	*ehl choopehteh*
during	durante	*doorahnteh*
during the day	de día	*deh deeah*

E

ear	la oreja	*lah ohreh<u>h</u>ah*
ear, nose and throat (ENT) specialist	el médico de oídos	*ehl mehdeekoh deh oheedohs*
earache	el dolor de oído	*ehl dohlohr deh oheedoh*
eardrops	las gotas para los oídos	*lahs gohtahs pahrah lohs oheedohs*
early	temprano	*tehmprahnoh*
earrings	los pendientes	*lohs pehndyehntehs*
earth	la tierra	*lah tyehrrah*
earthenware	la cerámica	*lah thehrahmeekah*
east	el este	*ehl ehsteh*
easy	fácil	*fahtheel*
eat	comer	*kohmehr*
eczema	el eczema	*ehl ehkthehmah*
eel	la anguila	*lah ahngeelah*
egg	el huevo	*ehl wehboh*
elastic band	la goma elástica	*lah gohmah ehlahsteekah*
electric	eléctrico	*ehlehktreekoh*
electricity	la corriente	*lah kohrryehnteh*
embassy	la embajada	*lah ehmbah<u>h</u>ahdah*
emergency brake	el freno de emergencia	*ehl frehnoh deh ehmehr<u>h</u>ehnthyah*

emergency exit	la salida de emergencia	lah sahleedah deh ehmehr<u>r</u>hehnthyah
emergency number	el número de urgencias	ehl noomehroh deh oor<u>h</u>ehnthyahs
emergency phone	el teléfono de emergencia	ehl tehlehfohnoh deh ehmehr<u>r</u>hehnthyah
emergency triangle	el triángulo reflectante	ehl treeahngooloh rehflehktahnteh
emery board	la lima (para uñas)	lah leemah (pahrah oonyahs)
empty	vacío	bahtheeoh
engaged (phone)	comunicando	kohmooneekahndoh
engaged	ocupado	ohkoopahdoh
English	inglés	eenglehs
enjoy	disfrutar	deesfrootahr
entertainment guide	la guía de los espectáculos	lah gheeah deh lohs ehspehktahkoolohs
envelope	el sobre	ehl sohbreh
escort	el/la acompañante	ehl/lah ahkohmpahnyahnteh
evening	la tarde	lah tahrdeh
evening wear	el traje de etiqueta	ehl trah<u>h</u>eh deh ehteekehtah
event	el acontecimiento	ehl akohntehthee-myehntoh
event (social)	la función	lah foonthyohn
everything	todo	tohdoh
everywhere	en todas partes	ehn tohdahs pahrtehs
examine	reconocer	rehkohnohthehr
excavation	las excavaciones	lahs ehxkahbahthyohnehs
excellent	excelente, estupendo	ehxthehlehnteh, ehstoopehndoh
exchange (verb)	cambiar	kahmbyahr
exchange office	la oficina de cambio	lah ohfeetheenah deh kahmbyoh
exchange rate	la cotización, el tipo de cambio	lah kohteethahthyohn, ehl teepoh deh kahmbyoh
excursion	la excursión organizada	lah ehxkoorsyohn ohrgahneethahdah
exhibition	la exposición	lah ehxpohseethyohn
exit	la salida	lah sahleedah
expenses	los gastos	lohs gahstohs
expensive	caro	kahroh
explain	explicar	ehxpleekahr
express train	el tren rápido	ehl trehn rahpeedoh
external	tópico, externo	tohpeekoh, ehxtehrnoh
eye	el ojo	ehl oh<u>h</u>oh
eye drops	las gotas para los ojos	lahs gohtahs pahrah lohs oh<u>h</u>ohs
eye shadow	la sombra de ojos	lah sohmbrah deh oh<u>h</u>ohs
eye specialist	el oculista	ehl ohkooleestah
eyeliner	el lápiz de ojos	ehl lahpeeth deh oh<u>h</u>ohs

F

face	la cara	*lah kahrah*
factory	la fábrica	*lah fahbreekah*
fair	la feria	*lah fehryah*
fall	caer(se)	*kahehr(seh)*
family	la familia	*lah fahmeelyah*
famous	famoso	*fahmohsoh*
far away	lejos	*leh<u>h</u>ohs*
farm	la granja	*lah grahn<u>h</u>ah*
farmer	el campesino	*ehl kahmpehseenoh*
farmer's wife	la campesina	*lah kahmpehseenah*
fashion	la moda	*lah mohdah*
fast	rápido	*rahpeedoh*
father	el padre	*ehl pahdreh*
fault (blame)	la culpa	*lah koolpah*
fax (verb)	enviar un fax	*ehnbyahr oon fahx*
February	febrero	*fehbrehroh*
feel (verb)	sentir	*sehnteer*
feel like	apetecer	*ahpehtehthehr*
fence	la verja	*lah behr<u>h</u>ah*
ferry	el transbordador	*ehl trahnsbohrdahdohr*
fever	la fiebre	*lah fyehbreh*
fill (tooth)	empastar	*ehmpahstahr*
fill out	rellenar	*rehlyehnahr*
filling	el empaste	*ehl ehmpahsteh*
film (camera)	el rollo	*ehl rohlyoh*
film	la película	*lah pehleekoolah*
filter	el filtro	*ehl feeltroh*
find (verb)	encontrar	*ehnkohntrahr*
fine	la multa	*lah mooltah*
finger	el dedo	*ehl dehdoh*
fire	el fuego	*ehl fwehgoh*
fire (house etc.)	el incendio	*ehl eenthehndyoh*
fire brigade	los bomberos	*lohs bohmbehrohs*
fire escape	la escalera de incendios	*lah ehskahlehrah deh eenthehndyohs*
fire extinguisher	el extintor	*ehl ehxteentohr*
first	primero	*preemehroh*
first aid	los primeros auxilios	*lohs preemehrohs ahooxeelyohs*
first class	la primera clase	*lah preemehrah klahseh*
fish (verb)	pescar	*pehskahr*
fish	el pescado	*ehl pehskahdoh*
fishing rod	la caña de pescar	*lah kanyah deh pehskahr*
fitness centre	el gimnasio	*ehl <u>h</u>eemnahsyoh*
fitness training	la gimnasia	*lah <u>h</u>eemnahsyah*
fitting room	el probador	*ehl prohbahdohr*
fix puncture	arreglar el pinchazo	*ahrrehglahr ehl peenchahthoh*
flag	la bandera	*lah bahndehrah*
flamenco	el flamenco	*ehl flahmehnkoh*
flash cube	el cuboflash	*ehl koobohflahsh*
flash gun/bulb	el flash	*ehl flahsh*
flat	el piso	*ehl peesoh*

Word list

15

flea market	el mercadillo, el rastro	*ehl mehrkahdeelyoh, ehl rahstroh*
flight	el vuelo	*ehl bwehloh*
flight number	el número de vuelo	*ehl noomehroh deh bwehloh*
flood	la inundación	*lah eenoondathyohn*
floor	el piso	*ehl peesoh*
flour	la harina	*lah ahreenah*
flu	la gripe	*lah greepeh*
fly (insect)	la mosca	*lah mohskah*
fly (verb)	volar	*bohlahr*
fly-over	el viaducto	*ehl beeahdooktoh*
fog	la niebla	*lah nyehblah*
foggy (he)	haber niebla	*ahbehr nyehblah*
folkloristic	folclórico	*fohlklohreekoh*
follow	seguir	*sehgeer*
food	el alimento	*ehl ahleemehntoh*
food poisoning	la intoxicación alimenticia	*lah eentohxeekahthyohn ahleemehnteethyah*
foodstuffs	los víveres	*lohs beebehrehs*
foot	el pie	*ehl pyeh*
for	antes, delante de	*ahntehs, dehlahnteh deh*
for hire	se alquila	*seh ahlkeelah*
forbidden	prohibido	*proheebeedoh*
forehead	la frente	*lah frehnteh*
foreign	extranjero	*ehxtrahnhehroh*
forget	olvidar	*ohlbeedahr*
fork	el tenedor	*ehl tehnehdohr*
form	el formulario	*ehl fohrmoolahryoh*
fort	la fortificación	*lah fohrteefeekahthyohn*
forward (send)	enviar	*ehnbyahr*
fountain	la fuente	*lah fwehnteh*
four-star petrol	súper	*soopehr*
frame	la montura	*lah mohntoorah*
free	libre	*leebreh*
free of charge	gratuito	*grahtweetoh*
free time	el tiempo libre	*ehl tyehmpoh leebreh*
freeze	helar	*ehlahr*
French	francés	*frahnthehs*
French bread	la barra de pan	*lah bahrrah deh pahn*
fresh	fresco	*frehskoh*
Friday	el viernes	*ehl byehrnehs*
fried	frito	*freetoh*
fried egg	el huevo al plato	*ehl wehboh ahl plahtoh*
friend	el amigo	*ehl ahmeegoh*
friendly	cordial, amable	*kohrdyahl, ahmahbleh*
frightened	miedoso	*myehdohsoh*
fringe	el flequillo	*ehl flehkeelyoh*
front (at the)	adelante	*ahdehlahnteh*
frozen goods	los productos congelados	*los prohdooktohs kohnhehlahdohs*
fruit	la fruta	*lah frootah*
fruit juice	el zumo de frutas	*ehl thoomoh deh frootahs*

frying pan	la sartén	lah sahrtehn
full	lleno	lyehnoh
fun	la diversión	lah deebehrsyohn

G

gallery	la galería de arte	lah gahlehreeah deh ahrteh
game	el juego	el hwehgoh
garage (for repairs)	el taller mecánico	ehl tahlyehr mehkahneekoh
garbage bag	la bolsa de basura	lah bohlsah deh bahsoorah
garden	el jardín	ehl hahrdeen
gastroenteritis	la gastroenteritis	lah gahstrohehnteh-reetees
gauze	la gasa esterilizada	lah gahsah ehstehreeleethahdah
gear (bicycle)	el cambio	ehl kahmbyoh
gel	el gel	ehl hehl
German	alemán	ahlehmahn
get married	casarse	kahsahrseh
get off	bajarse	bahhahrse
gift	el regalo	ehl rehgahloh
gilt	dorado	dohrahdoh
ginger	el jengibre	ehl hehnheebreh
girl	la chica	lah cheekah
girlfriend	la amiga	lah ahmeegah
giro card	la tarjeta de la caja postal	lah tahrhehtah deh lah kahhah pohstahl
giro cheque	el cheque postal	ehl chehkeh pohstahl
glacier	el glaciar	ehl glahthyahr
glass (tumbler)	el vaso	ehl bahsoh
glass (wine -)	la copa	lah kohpah
glasses	las gafas	lahs gahfahs
glider	el vuelo sin motor	ehl bwehloh seen mohtohr
glove	el guante	ehl gwahnteh
glue	la cola	lah kohlah
gnat	el mosquito	ehl mohskeetoh
go (verb)	ir	eer
go back, come back	volver	bohlbehr
go backwards	ir para atrás	eer pahrah ahtrahs
go out	salir	sahleer
goat's cheese	el queso de cabra	ehl kehsoh deh kahbrah
gold	el oro	ehl ohroh
golf	el golf	ehl gohlf
golf course	el campo de golf	ehl kahmpoh deh gohlf
gone	perdido	pehrdeedoh
good afternoon	buenas tardes (after 2pm)	bwehnahs tahrdehs
good evening	buenas tardes	bwehnahs tahrdehs
good morning	buenos días (before 2pm)	bwehnohs deeahs
good night	buenas noches	bwehnahs nohchehs
goodbye	la despedida	lah dehspehdeedah
gram	el gramo	ehl grahmoh
grandchild	el nieto	ehl nyehtoh

grandfather	el abuelo	*ehl ahbwehloh*
grandmother	la abuela	*lah ahbwehlah*
grape juice	el zumo de uvas	*ehl thoomoh deh oobahs*
grapefruit	el pomelo	*ehl pohmehloh*
grapes	las uvas	*lahs oobahs*
grave	la tumba	*lah toombah*
grease	la grasa	*lah grahsah*
green	verde	*behrdeh*
green card	la tarjeta verde	*lah tahr<u>h</u>ehtah behrdeh*
greet	saludar	*sahloodahr*
grey (hair)	canoso	*kahnohsoh*
grey	gris	*grees*
grill (verb)	asar a la parrilla	*ahsahr ah lah pahreelyah*
grilled	tostado	*tohstahdoh*
grocer's	la tienda de comestibles	*lah tyehndah deh kohmehsteeblehs*
ground	la tierra	*lah tyehrrah*
group	el grupo	*ehl groopoh*
guest house	la pensión	*lah pehnsyohn*
guide (book)	la guía	*lah gueeah*
guide (person)	el/la guía	*ehl/lah gueeah*
guided tour	la visita guiada	*lah beeseetah gueeahdah*
gynaecologist	el ginecólogo	*ehl <u>h</u>eenehkohlohgoh*

H

hair	el pelo	*ehl pehloh*
hairbrush	el cepillo para el pelo	*ehl thehpeelyoh parah ehl pehloh*
hairdresser (ladies', men's)	la peluquería (de señoras, caballeros)	*lah pehlookehreeah (deh sehnyohrahs, kahbahlyehrohs)*
hairpins	las horquillas	*lahs ohrkeelyahs*
hairspray	la laca para el pelo	*lah lahkah pahrah ehl pehloh*
half	medio, media, la mitad	*mehdyoh, mehdyah, lah meetahdh*
half full	lleno hasta la mitad	*lyehnoh ahstah lah meetahdh*
half kilo	el medio kilo	*ehl mehdyoh keeloh*
hammer	el martillo	*ehl mahrteelyoh*
hand	la mano	*lah mahnoh*
hand brake	el freno de mano	*ehl frehnoh deh mahnoh*
handbag	el bolso de mano	*ehl bohlsoh deh mahnoh*
handbag	el bolso	*ehl bohlsoh*
handkerchief	el pañuelo	*ehl pahnywehloh*
handmade	hecho a mano	*ehchoh ah mahnoh*
happy	contento	*kohntehntoh*
harbour	el puerto	*ehl pwehrtoh*
hard	duro	*dooroh*
haste	la prisa	*lah preesah*
hat	el sombrero	*ehl sohmbrehroh*

hay fever	la fiebre del heno	lah fyehbreh dehl ehnoh
hazelnut	la avellana	lah ahbehlyahnah
head	la cabeza	lah kahbehthah
headache	el dolor de cabeza	ehl dohlohr deh kahbehthah
health	la salud	lah sahloodh
health food shop	la tienda naturista	lah tyehndah nahtooreestah
hear	entender	ehntehndehr
hearing aid	el audífono	ehl ahoodeefohnoh
heart	el corazón	ehl kohrahthohn
heart patient	el enfermo cardíaco	ehl ehnfehrmoh kahrdeeahkoh
heat	calor	kahlohr
heater	la calefacción	lah kahlehfahkthyohn
heavy	pesado	pehsahdoh
heel	el talón	ehl tahlohn
heel (on shoe)	el tacón	ehl tahkohn
hello	hola	ohlah
helmet	el casco	ehl kahskoh
help (verb)	ayudar	ahyoodahr
help	la ayuda	lah ahyoodah
helping/portion	la ración	lah rahthyohn
herbal tea	la infusión	lah eenfoosyohn
here	aquí	ahkee
herring	el arenque	ehl ahrehnkeh
high	alto	ahltoh
high tide	la marea alta	lah mahrehah ahltah
highchair	la silla para niños	lah seelyah pahrah neenyohs
hiking	el excursionismo	ehl ehxkoorsyohneesmoh
hiking trip	la excursión a pie	lah ehxkoorsyohn ah pyeh
hip	la cadera	lah kahdehrah
hire	alquilar	ahlkeelahr
hitchhike	hacer autostop	ahtehhr ahootohstohp
hobby	el hobby	ehl hohbee
hold-up/robbery	el asalto	ehl ahsahltoh
holiday (public)	el día de fiesta	ehl deeah deh fyehstah
holiday house	el chalet	ehl chahleh
holiday park	la urbanización	lah oorbahneethahthyohn
holidays	las vacaciones	lahs bahkahthyohnehs
home (at)	en casa	ehn kahsah
homesickness	la nostalgia	lah nohstahlhyah
honest	sincero	seenthehroh
honey	la miel	lah myehl
horizontal	horizontal	oreethohntahl
horrible	horrible	ohrreebleh
horse	el caballo	ehl kahbahlyoh
hospital	el hospital	ehl ohspeetahl
hospitality	la hospitalidad	lah ohspeetahleedahdh
hot	cálido/caluroso	kahleedoh/ kahloorohsoh
hot (spicy)	picante	peekahnteh

Word list

15

hotel	el hotel	*ehl ohtehl*
hot-water bottle	la bolsa de agua caliente	*lah bohlsah deh ahgwah kahlyehnteh*
hour	la hora	*lah ohrah*
house	la casa	*lah kahsah*
household items	los artículos del hogar	*lohs ahrteekoolohs dehl ohgahr*
houses of parliament	la cámara de diputados	*lah kahmahrah deh deepootahdohs*
housewife	el ama de casa	*ehl ahmah deh kahsah*
how far?	¿a qué distancia?	*ah keh deestahnthyah?*
how long?	¿cuánto tiempo?	*kwahntoh tyehmpoh?*
how much?	¿cuánto?	*kwahntoh?*
how?	¿cómo?	*kohmoh*
hunger	el hambre/el apetito	*ehl ahmbreh/ehl ahpehteetoh*
hurricane	el huracán	*ehl oorahkahn*
hurry	la prisa	*lah preesah*
husband	el marido	*ehl mahreedoh*
hut	el camarote	*ehl kahmahrohteh*
hyperventilation	la hiperventilación	*lah eepehr-behnteelahthyohn*

I

ice cream	el helado	*ehl ehlahdoh*
ice cubes	los cubitos de hielo	*lohs koobeetohs deh yehloh*
ice skating	el patinaje sobre hielo	*ehl pahteenahḥeh sohbreh yehloh*
idea	la idea	*lah eedehah*
identification card	el carnet de identidad	*ehl kahrneh deh eedehnteedahdh*
identify	identificar	*eedehnteefeekahr*
ignition key	la llave de contacto	*lah lyahbeh deh kohntahktoh*
ill	enfermo	*ehnfehrmoh*
illness	la enfermedad	*lah ehnfehrmehdahdh*
imagine	imaginarse	*eemahḥeenahrseh*
immediately	inmediatamente	*eenmehdyahtah-mehnteh*
import duty	los derechos de aduana	*lohs dehrehchohs deh ahdwahnah*
impossible	imposible	*eempohseebleh*
in	en	*ehn*
in the evening	por la tarde	*pohr lah tahrdeh*
in the morning	por la mañana	*pohr lah mahnyahnah*
included	incluido	*eenklooeedoh*
indicate	señalar	*sehnyahlahr*
indicator	el intermitente	*ehl eentehrmeetehnteh*
inexpensive	barato	*bahrahtoh*
infection (viral -, bacterial -)	la infección (vírica, bacteriana)	*lah eenfehkthyohn (beereekah, bahktehryahnah)*
inflammation	la inflamación	*lah eenflahmahthyohn*
information	la información	*lah eenfohrmahthyohn*
information office	la oficina de información	*lah ohfeetheenah deh eenfohrmahthyohn*

injection	la inyección	*lah eenyehkthyohn*
injured	herido	*erhreedoh*
inner ear	el oído	*ehl oheedoh*
inner tube	la cámara	*lah kahmahrah*
innocent	inocente	*eenohthehnteh*
insect	el insecto	*ehl eensehktoh*
insect bite	la picadura de insecto	*lah peekahdoorah deh eensehktoh*
insect repellant	el aceite para los mosquitos	*ehl ahthehyteh pahrah lohs mohskeetohs*
inside	adentro	*ahdehntroh*
insole	la plantilla	*lah plahnteelyah*
instructions	las instrucciones	*lahs eenstrookthyohnehs*
insurance	el seguro	*ehl sehgooroh*
intermission	la pausa	*lah pahoosah*
international	internacional	*eentehrnahthyohnahl*
interpreter	el intérprete	*ehl eentehrprehteh*
intersection/crossing	el cruce	*ehl krootheh*
introduce oneself	presentarse	*prehsehntahrseh*
invite (verb)	invitar	*eenbeetahr*
iodine	el yodo	*ehl yohdoh*
iron (metal)	el hierro	*ehl yehrroh*
iron (verb)	planchar	*plahnchahr*
iron	la plancha	*lah plahnchah*
ironing board	la tabla de planchar	*lah tahblah deh plahnchahr*
island	la isla	*lah eeslah*
it's a pleasure	de nada	*deh nahdah*
Italian	italiano	*eetahlyahnoh*
itch	la picazón	*lah peekahthohn*

J

jack	el gato	*ehl gahtoh*
jacket	la chaqueta	*lah chahkehtah*
jam	la mermelada	*lah mehrmehlahdah*
January	enero	*ehnehroh*
jaw	la mandíbula	*lah mahndeeboolah*
jellyfish	la medusa	*lah mehdoosah*
jeweller	la joyería	*lah hoyehreeah*
jewels	las alhajas	*lahs ahlahhahs*
jog (verb)	hacer footing	*ahthehr footeen*
joke	la broma	*lah brohmah*
journey	el viaje	*ehl byahheh*
juice	el zumo/el jugo	*ehl thoomoh/ehl hoogoh*
July	julio	*hoolyoh*
jump leads	el cable de arranque	*ehl kahbleh deh ahrrahnkeh*
jumper	el jersey	*ehl hehrsehee*
June	junio	*hoonyoh*

K

key	la llave	*lah lyahbeh*
kilo	el kilo	*ehl keeloh*
kilometre	kilómetro(s)	*keelohmehtroh(s)*
king	el rey	*ehl rehee*

kiss (verb)	besar	*behsahr*
kiss	el beso	*ehl behsoh*
kitchen	la cocina	*lah kohtheenah*
knee	la rodilla	*lah rohdeelyah*
knee socks	las medias cortas	*lahs mehdyahs kohrtahs*
knife	el cuchillo	*ehl koocheelyoh*
know	saber	*sahbehr*

L

lace	el encaje	*ehl ehnkahheh*
ladies'	el servicio para señoras	*ehl sehrbeethyoh pahrah sehnyohrahs*
lake	el lago	*ehl lahgoh*
lamp	la lámpara	*lah lahmpahrah*
land (verb)	aterrizar	*ahtehrreethahr*
lane	el carril	*ehl kahrreel*
language	el idioma	*ehl eedyohmah*
large	grande	*grahndeh*
last	pasado, último	*pahsahdoh, oolteemoh*
last night	anoche	*ahnohcheh*
late	tarde	*tahrdeh*
later	luego	*lwehgoh*
latest (at the)	a más tardar	*ah mahs tahrdahr*
laugh	reír	*reheer*
launderette	la lavandería (automática)	*lah lahbahndehreeah (ahootohmahteekah)*
law	el derecho	*ehl dehrehchoh*
laxative	el laxante	*ehl lahxahnteh*
leak	pinchado	*peenchahdoh*
leather	la piel, el cuero	*lah pyehl, ehl kwehroh*
leather goods	los artículos de piel	*lohs ahrteekoolohs deh pyehl*
leave (verb)	partir, salir	*pahrteer, sahleer*
leek	el puerro	*ehl pwehrroh*
left (on the)	a la izquierda	*ah lah eethkyehrdah*
left	izquierda	*eethkyehrdah*
left luggage	el depósito de equipajes	*ehl dehpohseetoh deh ehkeepahhehs*
leg	la pierna	*lah pyehrnah*
lemon	el limón	*ehl leemohn*
lemonade	la limonada	*lah leemohnahdah*
lend	prestar	*prehstahr*
lens	el objetivo	*ehl ohbhehteeboh*
lentils	las lentejas	*lahs lehntehhahs*
less	menos	*mehnohs*
lesson	la clase	*lah klahseh*
letter	la carta	*lah kahrtah*
lettuce	la lechuga	*lah lehchoogah*
level crossing	el paso a nivel	*ehl pahsoh ah neebehl*
library	la biblioteca	*lah beeblyohtehkah*
lie	mentir	*mehnteer*
lie down	estar tumbado	*ehstahr toombahdoh*
lift (hitchhike)	el viaje (en autostop)	*ehl byahheh (ehn ahootohstohp)*
lift (in building)	el ascensor	*ehl ahsthehnsohr*

lift (ski)	el telesquí, el telesilla	*ehl tehlehskee,ehl tehlehseelyah*
light (for cigarette)	el fuego	*ehl fwehgoh*
light (not dark)	claro	*klahroh*
light (not heavy)	ligero	*leehehroh*
lighter	el mechero	*ehl mehchehroh*
lighthouse	el faro	*ehl fahroh*
lightning	el rayo	*ehl rahyoh*
like	gustar	*goostahr*
line	la línea	*lah leenehah*
linen	el hilo	*ehl eeloh*
lipstick	la barra de labios	*lah bahrrah deh lahbyohs*
liqueur	la copa	*lah kohpah*
liquorice	el regaliz	*ehl rehgahleeth*
listen	escuchar	*ehskoochahr*
literature	la literatura	*lah leetehrahtoorah*
litre	el litro	*ehl leetroh*
little	poco	*pohkoh*
live (verb)	vivir	*beebeer*
live together	vivir con otra persona	*beebeer kohn ohtrah pehrsohnah*
lobster	la langosta	*lah lahngohstah*
local	local	*lohkahl*
lock	la cerradura	*lah thehrrahdoorah*
long	largo	*lahrgoh*
look (verb)	mirar	*meerahr*
look for	buscar	*booskahr*
look up (person)	buscar	*booskahr*
lorry	el camión	*ehl kahmyohn*
lose	perder	*pehrdehr*
loss	la pérdida	*lah pehrdeedah*
lost (to get)	perderse, extraviarse	*pehrdehrseh, ehxtrahbyahrseh*
lost	extraviado, perdido	*ehxtrahbyahdoh, pehrdeedoh*
lost item	extravío	*ehxtrahbeeoh*
lost property office	los objetos perdidos	*lohs ohbhehtohs pehrdeedohs*
lotion	la loción	*lah lohthyohn*
loud	alto	*ahltoh*
love (be in - with)	estar enamorado de	*ehstahr ehnahmohrahdoh deh*
love (verb)	querer	*kehrehr*
love	el amor	*ehl ahmohr*
low	bajo	*bahhoh*
low tide	la marea baja	*lah mahrehah bahhah*
luck	la suerte	*lah swehrteh*
luggage	el equipaje	*ehl ehkeepahheh*
luggage locker	la consigna automática	*lah kohnseegnah ahootohmahteekah*
lunch	el almuerzo, la comida	*ehl ahlmwehrthoh, lah kohmeedah*
lungs	los pulmones	*lohs poolmohnehs*

M

macaroni	los macarrones	*lohs mahkahrrohnehs*
madam/Mrs	señora	*sehnyohrah*
magazine	la revista	*lah rehbeestah*
magnificent	magnífico	*mahgneefeekoh*
mail	el correo	*ehl kohrrehoh*
main post office	la oficina central de Correos	*ah ohfeetheenah thehntrahl deh kohrrehohs*
main road	la carretera principal	*lah kahrrehtehrah preentheepahl*
make an appointment	pedir hora	*pehdeer ohrah*
make love	acostarse/hacer el amor	*ahkohstahrseh/ahtehr ehl ahmohr*
makeshift	provisional(mente)	*prohbeesyohnahl (mehnteh)*
man	el hombre	*ehl ohmbreh*
manager	el encargado	*ehl ehnkahrgahdoh*
mandarin	la mandarina	*lah mahndahreenah*
manicure	la manicura	*lah mahneekoorah*
map	el mapa	*ehl mahpah*
marble	el mármol	*ehl mahrmohl*
March	marzo	*mahrthoh*
margarine	la margarina	*lah mahrgahreenah*
marina	el puerto deportivo	*ehl pwehrtoh dehpohrteeboh*
market	el mercado	*ehl mehrkahdoh*
marriage	el matrimonio	*ehl mahtreemohnyoh*
married	casado	*kahsahdoh*
mass	la misa	*lah meesah*
massage	el masaje	*ehl mahsah<u>h</u>eh*
mat	mate	*mahteh*
matches	las cerillas	*lahs thehreelyahs*
May	mayo	*mahyoh*
maybe	quizá	*keethah*
mayonnaise	la mayonesa	*lah mahyohnehsah*
mayor	el alcalde	*ehl ahlkahldeh*
meal	la comida	*lah kohmeedah*
mean (verb)	significar	*seegneefeekahr*
meat	la carne	*lah kahrneh*
medical insurance	el seguro de enfermedad	*ehl sehgooroh deh ehnfehrmehdahdh*
medication	el medicamento	*ehl mehdeekahmehntoh*
medicine	el medicamento, la medicina	*ehl mehdeekahmehntoh, lah mehdeetheenah*
meet	conocer	*kohnohthehr*
melon	el melón	*ehl mehlohn*
membership	el ser socio	*ehl sehr sohthyoh*
menstruate	tener la regla	*tehnehr lah rehglah*
menstruation	la menstruación	*lah mehnstrooahthyohn*
menu	el menú, la carta	*ehl mehnoo, lah kahrtah*
menu of the day	el menú del día	*ehl mehnoo dehl deeah*
message	el recado/mensaje	*ehl rehkahdoh/ mehnsah<u>h</u>eh*

metal	el metal	*ehl mehtahl*
meter (taxi)	el taxímetro	*ehl tahxeemehtroh*
metre	metro(s)	*mehtroh(s)*
migraine	la jaqueca	*lah hahkehkah*
mild (tobacco)	rubio	*roobyoh*
milk	la leche	*lah lehcheh*
millimetre(s)	milímetro(s)	*meeleemehtroh(s)*
milometer	el cuentakilómetros	*ehl kwehntah-keelohmehtrohs*
mince	la carne picada	*lah kahrneh peekahdah*
mineral water	el agua mineral	*ehl ahgwah meenehrahl*
minute	el minuto	*ehl meenootoh*
mirror	el espejo	*ehl ehspehoh*
miss (person)	echar de menos	*ehchahr deh mehnohs*
missing (be)	faltar	*fahltahr*
mistake	el error, la equivocación	*ehl ehrrohr, lah ehkeebohkahthyohn*
mistaken (be)	equivocarse	*ehkeebohkahrseh*
misunderstanding	el malentendido	*ehl mahlehntehndeedoh*
mixture	el jarabe, la poción	*ehl hahrahbeh, lah pohthyohn*
mocha	el moca	*ehl mohkah*
modern art	el arte moderno	*ehl ahrteh mohdehrnoh*
molar	la muela	*lah mwehlah*
moment	el momento	*ehl mohmehntoh*
Monday	el lunes	*ehl loonehs*
money	el dinero	*ehl deenehroh*
month	el mes	*ehl mehs*
moped	el ciclomotor	*ehl theeklohmohtohr*
morning-after pill	la píldora para el día después	*lah peeldohrah pahrah ehl deeah dehspwehs*
mosque	la mezquita	*lah methkeetah*
motel	el motel	*ehl mohtehl*
mother	la madre	*lah mahdreh*
motor cross	el motocrós	*ehl mohtohkrohs*
motorbike	la moto	*lah mohtoh*
motorboat	la lancha motora	*lah lahnchah mohtohrah*
motorway	la autovía, la autopista	*lah ahootohbeeah, lah ahootohpeestah*
mountain	la montaña	*lah mohntahnyah*
mountain hut	el refugio	*ehl rehfoohyoh*
mountaineering	el montañismo	*ehl mohntahnyeesmoh*
mountaineering shoes	las botas de alpinismo	*lahs bohtahs deh ahlpeeneesmoh*
mouse	el ratón	*ehl rahtohn*
mouth	la boca	*lah bohkah*
much/many	mucho	*moochoh*
multi-storey car park	el estacionamiento	*ehl ehstahthyohnah-myehntoh*
muscle	el músculo	*ehl mooskooloh*
muscle spasms	los calambres (en los músculos)	*lohs kahlahmbrehs (ehn lohs mooskoolohs)*
museum	el museo	*ehl moosehoh*
mushrooms	las setas	*lahs sehtahs*
music	la música	*lah mooseekah*

Word list

15

musical show	la comedia musical	*lah kohmehdyah mooseekahl*
mussels	los mejillones	*lohs meheelyohnehs*
mustard	la mostaza	*lah mohstahthah*

N

nail (on hand)	la uña	*lah oonyah*
nail	el clavo	*ehl klahboh*
nail polish	el esmalte (para uñas)	*ehl ehsmahlteh(pahrah oonyahs)*
nail polish remover	el quitaesmalte	*ehl keetahehsmahlteh*
nail scissors	las tijeras de uñas	*lahs tee<u>h</u>ehrahs pahrah oonyahs*
naked	desnudo	*dehsnoodoh*
nappy	el pañal	*ehl pahnyahl*
nationality	la nacionalidad	*lah nahthyohnahlee-dahdh*
nature	la naturaleza	*lah nahtoorahlehthah*
naturism	el naturismo	*ehl nahtooreesmoh*
nauseous	con náuseas	*kohn nahoosehahs*
near	junto a	*<u>h</u>oontoh ah*
nearby	cerca	*thehrkah*
necessary	necesario	*nehthehsahryoh*
neck	la nuca	*lah nookah*
necklace	la cadena	*lah kahdehnah*
needle	la aguja	*lah ahoo<u>h</u>ah*
negative	el negativo	*ehl nehgahteeboh*
neighbours	los vecinos	*lohs behtheenohs*
nephew	el sobrino	*ehl sohbreenoh*
Netherlands	los Países Bajos	*lohs paheesehs bah<u>h</u>ohs*
never	jamás/nunca	*<u>h</u>ahmahs/noonkah*
new	nuevo	*nwehboh*
news	las noticias	*lahs nohteethyahs*
news stand	el quiosco	*ehl kyohskoh*
newspaper	el periódico	*ehl pehryohdeekoh*
next	próximo, que viene	*prohxeemoh, keh byehneh*
next to	al lado de	*ahl lahdoh deh*
nice (friendly)	amable	*ahmahbleh*
nice (to look at)	bonito, mono	*bohneetoh, mohnoh*
nice	bien, agradable	*byehn, ahgrahdahbleh*
niece	la sobrina	*lah sohbreenah*
night (at)	por la noche	*pohr lah nohcheh*
night	la noche	*lah nohcheh*
night duty	la guardia nocturna	*lah gwahrdyah nohktoornah*
nightclub	el cabaré	*ehl kahbahreh*
nightlife	la vida nocturna	*lah beedah nohktoornah*
nipple	la tetina	*lah tehteenah*
no	no	*noh*
no overtaking	la prohibición de adelantar	*lah proheebeethyohn deh ahdehlahntahr*
noise	el ruido	*ehl rooeedoh*
nonstop	sin escalas	*seen ehskahlahs*
no-one	nadie	*nahdyeh*

normal	normal, corriente	*nohrmahl, kohrryehnteh*
north	el norte	*ehl nohrteh*
nose	la nariz	*lah nahreeth*
nose bleed	la hemorragia nasal	*lah ehmohrrahhyah nahsahl*
nose drops	las gotas para la nariz	*lahs gohtahs pahrah lah nahreeth*
notepaper	el papel de escribir	*ehl pahpehl deh ehskreebeer*
nothing	nada	*nahdah*
November	noviembre	*nohbyehmbreh*
nowhere	en ninguna parte	*ehn neengoonah pahrteh*
nudist beach	la playa nudista	*lah plahyah noodeestah*
number	el número	*ehl noomehroh*
number plate	la matrícula	*lah mahtreekoolah*
nurse	la enfermera	*lah ehnfehrmehrah*
nutmeg	la nuez moscada	*lah nwehth mohskahdah*
nuts	los frutos secos	*lohs frootohs sehkohs*

O

October	octubre	*ohktoobreh*
of course	claro	*klahroh*
off	podrido	*pohdreedoh*
offer	ofrecer	*ohfrehthehr*
office	la oficina	*lah ohfeetheenah*
off-licence	la bodega, la tienda de vinos y licores	*lah bohdehgah, lah tyehndah deh beenohs ee leekohrehs*
oil	el aceite	*ehl ahtheyteh*
oil level	el nivel del aceite	*ehl neebehl deh ahtheyteh*
ointment	la pomada, el ungüento	*lah pohmahdah, ehl oongwehntoh*
ointment for burns	la pomada contra las quemaduras	*lah pohmahdah kohntrah lahs kehmahdoorahs*
okay	vale, de acuerdo	*bahleh, deh ahkwehrdoh*
old	viejo	*byehhoh*
old part of town	el casco antiguo	*ehl kahskoh ahnteegwoh*
olive oil	el aceite de oliva	*ehl ahtheyteh deh ohleebah*
olives	las aceitunas	*lahs ahtheytoonahs*
omelette	la tortilla	*lah tohrteelyah*
on	sobre	*sohbreh*
on board	a bordo	*ah bohrdoh*
oncoming car	el vehículo que viene	*ehl beheekooloh keh byehneh*
one hundred grams	los cien gramos	*lohs thyehn grahmohs*
one-way traffic	la dirección única	*lah deerehkthyohn ooneekah*
onion	la cebolla	*lah thehbohlyah*
open (adj.)	abierto	*ahbyehrtoh*
open (verb)	abrir	*ahbreer*

opera	la ópera	*lah ohpehrah*
operate	operar	*ohpehrahr*
operator (telephone)	la operadora	*lah ohpehrahdohrah*
operetta	la opereta, la zarzuela	*lah ohpehrehtah, lah thahrthwehlah*
opposite	al frente, enfrente de	*ahl frehnteh, ehnfrehnteh deh*
optician	la óptica	*lah ohpteekah*
orange	la naranja	*lah nah<u>rah</u>n<u>h</u>ah*
orange (adj.)	naranja	*nah<u>rah</u>n<u>h</u>ah*
orange juice	el zumo de naranja	*ehl thoomoh deh nah<u>rah</u>n<u>h</u>ah*
order (in -,) tidy	en orden, ordenado	*ehn ohrdehn, ohrdehnahdo*
order (verb)	pedir	*pehdeer*
order	el pedido	*ehl pehdeedoh*
other	otro	*ohtroh*
other side	el otro lado	*ehl ohtroh lahdoh*
outside	afuera	*ahfwehrah*
overtake	adelantar	*ahdehlahntahr*
oysters	las ostras	*lahs ohstrahs*

P

packed lunch	el paquete con bocadillos	*ehl pahkehteh kohn bohkahdeelyohs*
page	la página	*lah pah<u>h</u>eenah*
pain	el dolor	*ehl dohlohr*
painkiller	el analgésico	*ehl ahnahl<u>h</u>ehseekoh*
paint (verb)	pintar	*peentahr*
paint	la pintura	*lah peentoorah*
painting (art)	el cuadro	*ehl kwahdroh*
painting (object)	la pintura	*lah peentoorah*
palace	el palacio	*ehl pahlahthyoh*
pancake	la crepe	*lah krehp*
pane	el cristal	*ehl kreestahl*
pants (briefs)	las bragas	*lahs brahgahs*
panty liner	el protegeslip	*ehl prohteh<u>h</u>ehsleep*
paper	el papel	*ehl pahpehl*
paraffin oil	el querosén	*ehl kehrohsehn*
parasol	el quitasol	*ehl keetahsohl*
parcel	el paquete	*ehl pahkehteh*
pardon	perdone	*pehrdohneh*
parents	los padres	*lohs pahdrehs*
park	el parque	*ehl pahrkeh*
park (verb)	aparcar	*ahpahrkahr*
parking space	el sitio para aparcar	*ehl seetyoh pahrah ahpahrkahr*
parsley	el perejil	*ehl pehreh<u>h</u>eel*
partition	la secreción	*lah sehkrehthyohn*
partner	la pareja	*lah pahreh<u>h</u>ah*
party	la fiesta	*lah fyehstah*
passable	practicable	*prahkteekahbleh*
passenger	el pasajero	*ehl pahsah<u>h</u>ehroh*
passport	el pasaporte	*ehl pahsahpohrteh*
passport photo	la foto de carnet	*lah fohtoh deh kahrneh*
patient	el paciente	*ehl pahthyehnteh*
pavement	la acera	*lah ahthehrah*

pay (verb)	pagar	*pahgahr*
pay the bill	pagar la cuenta	*pahgahr lah kwehntah*
peach	el melocotón	*ehl mehlohkohtohn*
peanuts	los cacahuetes	*lohs kahkahwehtehs*
pear	la pera	*lah pehrah*
peas	los guisantes	*lohs gueesahntehs*
pedal	el pedal	*ehl pehdahl*
pedestrian crossing	el paso de peatones	*ehl pahsoh deh pehahtohnehs*
pedicure	la pedicura	*lah pehdeekoorah*
pen	la pluma	*lah ploomah*
pencil (hard/soft)	el lápiz (duro/blando)	*ehl lahpeeth (dooroh /blahndoh)*
penis	el pene	*ehl pehneh*
pepper (capsicum)	el pimiento	*ehl peemyehntoh*
pepper (condiment)	la pimienta	*lah peemyehntah*
performance	la función de teatro /música	*lah foonthyohn deh tehahtroh/mooseekah*
perfume	el perfume	*ehl pehrfoomeh*
perm (verb)	hacer una permanente	*ahthehr oonah pehrmahnehnteh*
perm	la permanente	*lah pehrmahnehnteh*
permit	el permiso	*ehl pehrmeesoh*
person	la persona	*lah pehrsohnah*
personal	personal	*pehrsohnahl*
petrol	la gasolina	*lah gahsohleenah*
petrol station	la gasolinera	*lah gahsohleenehrah*
pets	los animales domésticos	*lohs ahneemahles dohmehsteekohs*
pharmacy	la farmacia	*lah fahrmahthyah*
phone (by)	por teléfono	*pohr tehlehfohnoh*
phone (tele-)	el teléfono	*ehl tehlehfohnoh*
phone (verb)	llamar por teléfono	*lyahmahr pohr tehlehfohnoh*
phone box	la cabina telefónica	*lah kahbeenah tehlehfohneekah*
phone directory	la guía de teléfonos	*lah gheeah deh tehlehfohnohs*
phone number	el número de teléfono	*ehl noomehroh deh tehlehfohnoh*
photo	la foto	*lah fohtoh*
photocopier	la fotocopiadora	*lah fohtohkohpyahdohrah*
photocopy (verb)	fotocopiar	*fohtohkohpyahr*
photocopy	la fotocopia	*lah fohtohkohpyah*
pick up (fetch person)	(ir a) buscar, pasar a buscar	*(eer ah) booskahr, pahsahr ah booskahr*
picnic	el picnic	*ehl peekneek*
piece of clothing	la prenda	*lah prehndah*
pier	el muelle	*ehl mwehlyeh*
pigeon	la paloma	*lah pahlohmah*
pill (contraceptive)	la píldora (anticonceptiva)	*lah peeldohrah (ahnteekohnthehp-teebah)*
pillow	la almohada	*lah ahlmohahdah*
pillowcase	la funda de almohada	*lah foondah deh ahlmohahdah*

pin	el alfiler	*ehl ahlfeelehr*
pineapple	la piña	*lah peenyah*
pipe	la pipa	*lah peepah*
pipe tobacco	el tabaco de pipa	*ehl tahbahkoh deh peepah*
pity	lástima	*lahsteemah*
place of entertainment	el sitio para salir	*ehl seetyoh pahrah sahleer*
place of interest	el punto de interés	*ehl poontoh deh eentehrehs*
plan/map	el plano	*ehl plahnoh*
plant	la planta	*lah plahntah*
plasters	las tiritas, los esparadrapos	*lahs teereetahs, lohs ehspahrahdrahpohs*
plastic	el plástico	*ehl plahsteekoh*
plastic bag	la bolsita	*lah bohlseetah*
plate	el plato	*ehl plahtoh*
platform	la vía, el andén	*lah beeah, ehl ahndehn*
play (theatre)	la obra de teatro	*lah ohbrah deh tehahtroh*
play (verb)	jugar	*hoogahr*
playground	el parque infantil	*ehl pahrkeh eenfahnteel*
playing cards	los naipes	*lohs naypehs*
pleasant	agradable	*ahgrahdahbleh*
please	por favor	*pohr fahbohr*
pleasure	el placer	*ehl plahthehr*
plum	la ciruela	*lah theerwehlah*
pocketknife	la navaja	*lah nahbahhah*
point (verb)	indicar	*eendeekahr*
poison	el veneno	*ehl behnehnoh*
police	la policía	*lah pohleetheeah*
police station	la comisaría	*la kohmeesahreeah*
policeman	el guardia	*ehl gwahrdyah*
pond	el estanque	*ehl ehstahnkeh*
pony	el poney	*ehl pohnehy*
pop concert	el concierto pop	*ehl kohnthyehrtoh pohp*
population	la población	*lah pohblahthyohn*
pork	la carne de cerdo	*lah kahrneh deh thehrdoh*
port wine	el oporto	*ehl ohpohrtoh*
porter	el portero	*ehl pohrtehroh*
post code	el código postal	*ehl cohdeegoh pohstahl*
post office	la oficina de Correos	*lah ohfeetheenah deh cohrrehohs*
postage	el franqueo	*ehl frahnkehoh*
postbox	el buzón	*ehl boothohn*
postcard	la (tarjeta) postal	*lah (tahrhehtah) pohstahl*
postman	el cartero	*ehl kahrtehroh*
potato	la patata	*lah pahtahtah*
poultry	las aves	*lahs ahbehs*
powdered milk	la leche en polvo	*lah lehcheh ehn pohlboh*

power point	la toma de corriente	*lah tohmah deh kohrryehnteh*
pram	el cochecito	*ehl kohchehtheetoh*
prawns	las gambas	*lahs gahmbahs*
precious	querido	*kehreedoh*
prefer	preferir	*prehfehreer*
preference	la preferencia	*lah prehfehrehnthyah*
pregnant	embarazada	*ehmbahrahthahdah*
present	presente	*prehsehnteh*
present (gift)	el regalo	*ehl rehgahloh*
press (verb)	apretar	*ahprehtahr*
pressure	la tensión	*lah tehnsyohn*
price	el precio	*ehl prehthyoh*
price list	la lista de precios	*lah leestah deh prehthyohs*
print (verb)	copiar	*kohpyahr*
print	la copia	*lah kohpyah*
probably	probablemente	*prohbahblehmehnteh*
problem	el problema	*ehl prohblehmah*
profession	la profesión	*lah prohfehsyohn*
programme	el programa	*ehl prohgrahmah*
pronounce	pronunciar	*prohnoonthyahr*
propane camping gas	el gas propano	*ehl gahs prohpahnoh*
pull	sacar	*sahkahr*
pull a muscle	distender un músculo	*deestehndehr oon mooskooloh*
pure	puro	*pooroh*
purple	violeta	*beeohlehta*
purse	el monedero	*ehl mohnehdehroh*
push	empujar	*ehmpoohahr*
puzzle	el rompecabezas	*ehl rohmpehkahbehthahs*
pyjamas	el pijama	*ehl peehahmah*

Q

quarter	la cuarta parte	*lah kwahrtah pahrteh*
quarter of an hour	el cuarto de hora	*ehl kwahrtoh deh ohrah*
queen	la reina	*lah reheenah*
question	la pregunta	*lah prehgoontah*
quick	rápido	*rahpeedoh*
quiet	tranquilo	*trahnkeeloh*

R

radio	la radio	*lah rahdyoh*
railways	los ferrocarriles	*lohs fehrrohkahrreelehs*
rain (verb)	llover	*lyohbehr*
rain	la lluvia	*lah lyoobyah*
raincoat	el impermeable	*ehl eempehrmehahbleh*
raisins	las uvas pasas	*lahs oobahs pahsahs*
rape	la violación	*lah beeohlahthyohn*
rapids	el rápido	*ehl rahpeedoh*
rash (skin)	la erupción cutánea	*lah ehroopthyohn kootahnehah*
raspberries	las frambuesas	*lahs frahmbwehsahs*
raw	crudo	*kroodoh*
raw ham	el jamón (serrano)	*ehl hahmohn sehrrahnoh*

Word list

15

raw vegetables	las verduras crudas	*lahs behrdoorahs kroodahs*
razor blades	las hojas de afeitar	*lahs ohahs deh ahfeheetahr*
read (verb)	leer	*lehehr*
ready	listo	*leestoh*
really	en realidad	*ehn rehahleedahdh*
receipt	el recibo	*ehl rehtheeboh*
recipe	la receta	*lah rehthehtah*
reclining chair	la tumbona	*lah toombohnah*
recommend	recomendar	*rehkohmehndahr*
rectangle	el rectángulo	*ehl rehktahngooloh*
red	rojo	*rohhoh*
red wine	el vino tinto	*ehl beenoh teentoh*
refrigerator	el refrigerador	*ehl rehfreehehrahdohr*
regards	recuerdos	*rehkwehrdohs*
region	la región	*lah rehhyohn*
registered	certificado	*thehrteefeekahdoh*
relatives	los parientes	*lohs pahryehntehs*
reliable	fiable/seguro	*fyahbleh/sehgooroh*
religion	la religión	*lah rehleehyohn*
rent out	alquilar	*ahlkeelahr*
repair (verb)	arreglar	*ahrrehglahr*
repairs	el arreglo	*ehl ahrrehgloh*
repeat	repetir	*rehpehteer*
report	el atestado	*ehl ahtehstahdoh*
resent	tomar a mal	*tohmahr ah mahl*
responsible	responsable	*rehspohnsahbleh*
rest (verb)	descansar	*dehskahnsahr*
restaurant	el restaurante	*ehl rehstahoorahnteh*
retired	jubilado	*hoobeeladoh*
retirement	la jubilación	*lah hoobeelahthyohn*
return (ticket)	el billete de ida y vuelta	*ehl beelyehteh deh eedah ee bwehltah*
reverse (vehicle)	dar marcha atrás	*dahr mahrchah ahtrahs*
rheumatism	el reuma	*ehl rehoomah*
rice	el arroz	*ehl ahrrohht*
ridiculous	tontería(s)	*tohntehreeah(s)*
riding (horseback)	montar a caballo	*mohntahr ah kahbahlyoh*
riding school	el picadero	*ehl peekahdehroh*
right	derecha	*dehrehchah*
right (on the)	a la derecha	*ah lah dehrehchah*
right of way	la preferencia	*lah prehfehrehnthyah*
ripe	maduro	*mahdooroh*
risk	el riesgo	*ehl ryehsgoh*
river	el río	*ehl reeoh*
road	el camino	*ehl kahmeenoh*
roadway	la calzada	*lah kahlthahdah*
roasted	asado	*ahsahdoh*
rock	la roca	*lah rohkah*
rolling tobacco	el tabaco para liar	*ehl tahbahkoh pahrah leeahr*
roof rack	la baca	*lah bahkah*
room	la habitación	*lah ahbeetahthyohn*
room number	el número de la habitación	*ehl noomehroh deh lah ahbeetahthyohn*

room service	el servicio en la	_ehl sehrbeethyoh ehn_
	habitación	_lah ahbeetahthyohn_
rope	la cuerda	_lah kwehrdah_
rosé	el vino rosado	_ehl beenoh rohsahdoh_
roundabout	la rotonda	_lah rohtohndah_
route	la ruta	_lah rootah_
rowing boat	el bote de remos	_ehl bohteh deh_
		rehmohs
rubber	la goma	_lah gohmah_
rubbish	tontería(s)	_tohntehreeah(s)_
rucksack	la mochila	_lah mohcheelah_
rude	descortés/	_dehskohrtehs/_
	maleducado	_mahlehdookahdoh_
ruins	las ruinas	_lahs rweenahs_
run into	encontrar	_ehnkohntrahr_

S

sad	triste	_treesteh_
safari	el safari	_ehl sahfahree_
safe	la caja fuerte	_lah ka<u>h</u>ah fwehrteh_
safe/secure	seguro	_sehgooroh_
safety pin	el imperdible	_ehl eempehrdeebleh_
sail	la vela	_lah behlah_
sailing boat	el velero	_ehl behlehroh_
salad	la ensalada	_lah ehnsahlahdah_
salad oil	el aceite	_ehl ahthehyteh_
salami	el salami	_ehl sahlahmee_
sale	las rebajas, la	_lahs rehbah<u>h</u>ahs,_
	liquidación	_lah leekeedahthyohn_
salt	la sal	_lah sahl_
same	mismo	_meesmoh_
same	lo mismo	_loh meesmoh_
sandwich	el bocadillo	_ehl bohkahdeelyoh_
sandy beach	la playa de arena	_lah plahyah deh_
		ahrehnah
sanitary towel	la compresa	_lah kohmprehsah_
sardines	las sardinas	_lahs sahrdeenahs_
satisfied	contento	_kohntehntoh_
Saturday	el sábado	_ehl sahbahdoh_
sauce	la salsa	_lah sahlsah_
saucepan	la cacerola	_lah kahthehrohlah_
sauna	la sauna	_lah sahoonah_
sausage	el embutido	_ehl ehmbooteedoh_
savoury	salado	_sahlahdoh_
say (verb)	decir	_dehtheer_
scarf	la bufanda (woollen)	_lah boofahndah_
scarf	el pañuelo	_ehl pahnywehloh_
scenic walk	la visita a la ciudad	_lah beeseetah ah_
	(a pie)	_lah thyoodahdh_
		(ah pyeh)
school	la escuela	_lah ehskwehlah_
scissors	las tijeras	_lahs teehehrahs_
scooter	la vespa	_lah behspah_
scorpion	el escorpión	_ehl ehskohrpyohn_
scrambled eggs	los huevos revueltos	_lohs wehbohs_
		rehbwehltohs
screw	el tornillo	_ehl tohrneelyoh_

screwdriver	el destornillador	_ehl dehstohrneelyahdohr_
sculpture	la escultura	_lah ehskooltoorah_
sea	el mar	_ehl mahr_
seasick	mareado	_mahrehahdoh_
seat	el asiento	_ehl ahsyehntoh_
seat	el asiento, la butaca	_ehl ahsyehntoh, lah bootahkah_
second (adj.)	segundo	_sehgoondoh_
second	el segundo	_ehl sehgoondoh_
second-hand	de segunda mano	_deh sehgoondah mahnoh_
sedative	el calmante	_ehl kahlmahnteh_
see (person)	visitar	_beeseetahr_
see	mirar	_meerahr_
self-timer	el disparador automático	_ehl deespahrahdohr ahootohmahteekoh_
semi-skimmed	semidesnatado	_sehmeedehsnahtahdoh_
send	enviar	_ehnbyahr_
sentence	la frase	_lah frahseh_
September	septiembre	_sehptyehmbreh_
serious	grave	_grahbeh_
service	el servicio	_ehl sehrbeethyoh_
serviette	la servilleta	_lah sehrbeelyehtah_
set (verb)	marcar	_mahrkahr_
sewing thread	el hilo de coser	_ehl eeloh deh kohsehr_
shade	la sombra	_lah sohmbrah_
shallow	poco profundo	_pohkoh prohfoondoh_
shampoo	el champú	_ehl chahmpoo_
shark	el tiburón	_ehl teeboorohn_
shave (verb)	afeitar	_ahfeheetahr_
shaver	la afeitadora eléctrica	_lah ahfehytahdohrah ehlehktreekah_
shaving brush	la brocha de afeitar	_lah brohchah deh ahfeheetahr_
shaving cream	la crema de afeitar	_lah krehmah deh ahfeheetahr_
shaving soap	el jabón de afeitar	_ehl <u>h</u>ahbohn deh ahfeheetahr_
sheet	la sábana	_lah sahbahnah_
sherry	el jerez	_ehl <u>h</u>ehrehht_
shirt	la camisa	_lah kahmeesah_
shoe	el zapato	_ehl thahpahtoh_
shoe polish	la crema de zapatos	_lah krehmah deh thahpahtohs_
shoe shop	la zapatería	_lah thahpahtehreeah_
shoelaces	los cordones	_lohs kohrdohnehs_
shoemaker	el zapatero	_ehl thahpahtehroh_
shop (verb)	hacer la compra	_ahthehr lah kohmprah_
shop	la tienda	_lah tyehndah_
shop assistant	la vendedora	_lah behndehdohrah_
shop window	el escaparate	_ehl ehskahpahrahteh_
shopping centre	el centro comercial	_ehl thehntroh kohmehrthyahl_
short	corto	_kohrtoh_
short circuit	el cortocircuito	_ehl kohrtohtheer-kweetoh_

shoulder	el hombro	*ehl ohmbroh*
show	el espectáculo	*ehl ehspehktahkooloh*
shower	la ducha	*lah doochah*
shutter	el obturador	*ehl ohbtoorahdohr*
sieve	el tamiz	*ehl tahmeeth*
sign (verb)	firmar	*feermahr*
sign	el cartel	*ehl kahrtehl*
signature	la firma	*lah feermah*
signposted walk	la excursión	*lah ehxkooresyohn*
	señalizada	*sehnyahleethahdah*
silence	el silencio	*ehl seelehnthyoh*
silver	la plata	*lah plahtah*
silver-plated	plateado	*plahtehahdoh*
simple	sencillo	*sehntheelyoh*
single (unmarried)	soltero	*sohltehroh*
single	individual	*eendeebeedwahl*
single ticket	el billete de ida	*ehl beelyehteh deh*
		eedah
sir	señor	*sehnyohr*
sister	la hermana	*lah ehrmahnah*
sit	estar sentado	*ehstahr sehntahdoh*
size (shoes)	el número	*ehl noomehroh*
size	la talla	*lah tahlyah*
ski boots	las botas de esquí	*lahs bohtahs deh*
		ehskee
ski goggles	las gafas de esquí	*lahs gahfahs deh*
		ehskee
ski instructor	el profesor de esquí	*ehl prohfehsohr deh*
		ehskee
ski lessons/class	la clase de esquiar	*lah klahseh deh*
		ehskeeahr
ski lift	el telesquí	*ehl tehlehskee*
ski pants	los pantalones de	*lohs pahntahlohnehs*
	esquiar	*deh ehskeeahr*
ski pass	el bono (de remontes/	*ehl bohnoh (deh*
	esquí)	*rehmohntehs/ehskee)*
ski slope	la pista de esquí	*lah peestah deh*
	(alpino)	*ehskee (ahlpeenoh)*
ski stick	el bastón de esquí	*ehl bahstohn deh*
		ehskee
ski suit	el traje de esquiar	*ehl tra<u>h</u>heh deh*
		ehskeeahr
ski wax	la cera para esquí	*lah thehrah pahrah*
		ehskee
ski/skiing	esquiar, el esquí	*ehskeeahr, ehl ehskee*
skin	la piel	*lah pyehl*
skirt	la falda	*lah fahldah*
skis	los esquís	*lohs ehskees*
sleep (verb)	dormir	*dohrmeer*
sleep well!	que descanse	*keh dehskahnseh*
sleeping car	el coche cama	*ehl kohcheh kahmah*
sleeping pills	los somníferos	*lohs sohmneefehrohs*
slide	la diapositiva	*lah deeahpohseeteebah*
slip (women's)	la combinación	*lah kohmbeenahthyohn*
slip road	la entrada	*lah ehntrahdah*
slow	despacio	*dehspahthyoh*
slow train	el tren ómnibus	*ehl trehn ohmneeboos*

small	pequeño	*pehkehnyoh*
small change	el cambio, el dinero suelto	*ehl kahmbyoh, ehl deenehroh swehltoh*
smell unpleasant (verb)	oler mal	*ohlehr mahl*
smoke	el humo	*ehl oomoh*
smoke (verb)	fumar	*foomahr*
smoked	ahumado	*ahoomahdoh*
smoking compartment	el departamento de fumadores	*ehl dehpahrtahmehntoh deh foomahdohrehs*
snake	la serpiente	*lah sehrpyehnteh*
snorkel	el esnórquel	*ehl ehsnohrkehl*
snow (verb)	nevar	*nehbahr*
snow	la nieve	*lah nyehbeh*
snow chains	la cadena antideslizante	*lah kahdehnah ahnteedehsleethahnte*
soap	el jabón	*ehl ḥahbohn*
soap box	la jabonera	*lah ḥahbohnehrah*
soap powder	el jabón en polvo	*ehl ḥahbohn ehn pohlboh*
soccer	el fútbol	*ehl footbohl*
soccer match	el partido de fútbol	*ehl pahrteedoh deh footbohl*
socket	el enchufe	*ehl ehnchoofeh*
socks	los calcetines	*lohs kahlthehteenehs*
soft drink	el refresco	*ehl rehfrehskoh*
sole (fish)	el lenguado	*ehl lehngwahdoh*
sole	la suela	*lah swehlah*
solicitor	el abogado	*ehl ahbohgahdoh*
someone	alguien	*ahlgyehn*
sometimes	a veces	*ah behthehs*
somewhere	en alguna parte	*ehn ahlgoonah pahrteh*
son	el hijo	*ehl eeḥoh*
soon	pronto	*prohntoh*
sorbet	el sorbete	*ehl sohrbehteh*
sore	la úlcera	*lah oolthehrah*
sore throat	el dolor de garganta	*ehl dohlohr deh gahrgahntah*
sorry	perdón	*pehrdohn*
sort/type	la clase	*lah klahseh*
soup	la sopa	*lah sohpah*
sour	agrio	*ahgreeoh*
sour cream	la nata ácida	*lah nahtah ahteedah*
source	la fuente	*lah fwehnteh*
south	el sur	*ehl soor*
souvenir	el recuerdo de viaje	*ehl rehkwehrdoh deh byahḥeh*
spaghetti	los espaguetis	*lohs ehspahgehtees*
Spanish	español	*ehspahnyohl*
spanner (openended)	la llave (de boca)	*lah lyahbeh(deh bohkah)*
spanner	la llave de tuercas	*lah lyahbeh deh twehrkahs*
spare	la reserva	*lah rehsehrbah*
spare part	la pieza de recambio	*lah pyehthah deh rehkahmbyoh*
spare tyre	el neumático de reserva	*ehl nehoomahteekoh deh rehsehrbah*

spare wheel	la rueda de recambio	*lah rwehdah deh rehkahmbyoh*
speak	hablar	*ahblahr*
special	especial	*ehspehthyahl*
specialist	el especialista	*ehl ehspethyahleestah*
specialty	la especialidad	*lah ehspehthyahleedah*
speed limit	la velocidad máxima	*lah behlohtheedahdh mahxeemah*
spell (verb)	deletrear	*dehlehtrehahr*
spicy	picante	*peekahnteh*
splinter	la astilla	*lah ahsteelyah*
spoon	la cuchara	*lah koocharah*
spoonful	la cucharada	*lah koochahrahdah*
sport (play)	hacer deporte	*ahthehr dehpohrteh*
sport	el deporte	*ehl dehpohrteh*
sports centre	la sala de deportes	*lah sahlah deh dehpohrtehs*
spot/place	el sitio	*ehl seetyoh*
sprain (verb)	torcerse	*tohrthehrseh*
spring	la primavera	*lah preemahbehrah*
square	el cuadrado	*ehl kwahdrahdoh*
square (town)	la plaza	*lah plahthah*
square metre(s)	metro(s) cuadrado(s)	*mehtroh(s) kwahdrahdoh(s)*
squash	el squash	*ehl skwahsh*
stadium	el estadio	*ehl ehstahdyoh*
stain	la mancha	*lah mahnchah*
stain remover	el quitamanchas	*ehl keetahmahnchahs*
stairs	las escaleras	*lahs ehskahlehrahs*
stalls (theatre)	la platea	*lah plahtehah*
stamp	el sello	*ehl sehlyoh*
start (car)	arrancar	*ahrrahnkahr*
station	la estación	*lah ehstahthyohn*
statue	la estatua	*lah ehstahtooah*
stay (lodge)	alojarse	*ahloh<u>h</u>ahrseh*
stay (verb)	quedarse	*kehdahrseh*
stay	la estancia	*lah ehstahnthyah*
steal (verb)	robar	*rohbahr*
steel, stainless	el acero, inoxidable	*ehl ahthehroh, eenohxeedahbleh*
stench	el mal olor	*ehl mahl ohlohr*
sting (verb)	picar	*peekahr*
stitch (med.)	el punto	*ehl poontoh*
stitch (verb)	suturar	*sootoorahr*
stock	el caldo	*ehl kahldoh*
stockings	las medias	*lahs mehdyahs*
stomach	el estómago, el vientre	*ehl ehstohmahgoh, ehl byehntreh*
stomach ache	el dolor de vientre/ estómago	*ehl dohlohr deh byehntreh/ ehstohmahgoh*
stomach cramps	los retortijones	*lohs rehtohrtee<u>h</u>ohnehs*
stools	las heces	*lahs ehtehs*
stop (verb)	parar	*pahrahr*
stop	la parada	*lah pahrahdah*
stopover	la escala	*lah ehskahlah*
storm	la tormenta	*lah tohrmehntah*

15

straight	liso	*leesoh*
straight ahead	todo recto	*tohdoh rehktoh*
straw	la pajita	*lah pah̲heetah*
strawberries	las fresas	*lahs frehsahs*
street	la calle	*lah kahlyeh*
street side	el lado de la calle	*ehl lahdoh deh lah kahlyeh*
strike	la huelga	*lah wehlgah*
strong (tobacco)	negro	*nehgroh*
study (verb)	estudiar	*ehstoodyahr*
stuffing	el relleno	*ehl rehlyehnoh*
subscriber's number	el número de abonado	*ehl noomehroh deh ahbohnahdoh*
subtitled	subtitulada	*soobteetoolahdah*
succeed	salir bien	*sahleer byehn*
sugar	el azúcar	*ehl ahthookahr*
sugar lumps	los terrones de azúcar	*lohs tehrrohnehs deh ahthookahr*
suit	el traje	*ehl trah̲heh*
suitcase	la maleta	*lah mahlehtah*
summer	el verano	*ehl behrahnoh*
summertime	la hora de verano	*lah ohrah deh behrahnoh*
sun	el sol	*ehl sohl*
sun hat	el sombrero de playa	*ehl sohmbrehroh deh plahyah*
sunbathe	tomar el sol	*tohmahr ehl sohl*
Sunday	el domingo	*ehl dohmeengoh*
sunglasses	las gafas de sol	*lahs gahfahs deh sohl*
sunrise	la salida del sol	*lah sahleedah dehl sohl*
sunset	la puesta del sol	*lah pwehstah dehl sohl*
sunstroke	la insolación	*lah eensohlahthyohn*
suntan lotion	la crema solar	*lah krehmah sohlahr*
suntan oil	el aceite bronceador	*ehl ahthehyteh brohnthehahdohr*
supermarket	el supermercado	*ehl soopehrmehrkahdoh*
surcharge	el suplemento	*ehl sooplehmehntoh*
surf	el surf	*ehl soorf*
surf board	la tabla de surf	*lah tahblah deh soorf*
surgery	la consulta	*lah kohnsooltah*
surname	el apellido	*ehl ahpehlyeedoh*
surprise	la sorpresa	*lah sohrprehsah*
swallow (verb)	tragar	*trahgahr*
swamp	el terreno pantanoso	*ehl tehrrehnoh pahntahnohsoh*
sweat	el sudor	*ehl soodohr*
sweet	el caramelo	*ehl kahrahmehloh*
sweet	dulce	*doolteh*
sweetcorn	el maíz	*ehl maheeth*
sweetener	la sacarina	*lah sahkahreenah*
sweets	las golosinas	*lahs gohlohseenahs*
swim (verb)	nadar	*nahdahr*
swimming pool	la piscina	*lah peestheenah*
swimming trunks	el bañador	*ehl bahnyahdohr*
swindle	la estafa	*lah ehstahfah*
switch	el interruptor	*ehl eentehrrooptohr*

synagogue	la sinagoga	*lah seenahgohgah*

T

table	la mesa	*lah mehsah*
table tennis	el pingpong	*ehl peenpohn*
tablet	la tableta	*lah tahblehtah*
take (photograph)	sacar	*sahkahr*
take (time)	durar, tardar	*doorahr, tahrdahr*
take (verb)	emplear, usar, tomar	*ehmplehahr, oosahr, tohmahr*
take pictures	fotografiar, sacar fotos	*fohtohgrahfyahr, sahkahr fohtohs*
taken	ocupado	*ohkoopahdoh*
talcum powder	el talco	*ehl tahlkoh*
talk (verb)	hablar	*ahblahr*
tampons	los tampones	*lohs tahmpohnehs*
tap	el grifo	*ehl greefoh*
tap water	el agua del grifo	*ehl ahgwah dehl greefoh*
tart	la tarta	*lah tahrtah*
taste (verb)	probar	*prohbahr*
tax free shop	la tienda libre de impuestos	*lah tyehndah leebreh deh eempwehstohs*
taxi	el taxi	*ehl tahxee*
taxi stand	la parada de taxis	*lah pahrahdah deh tahxees*
tea	el té	*ehl teh*
teapot	la tetera	*lah tehtehrah*
teaspoon	la cuchara de té	*lah koochahrah deh teh*
telegram	el telegrama	*ehl tehlehgrahmah*
telephoto lens	el teleobjetivo	*ehl tehlehohbhehteeboh*
television	la televisión	*lah tehlehbeesyohn*
telex	el télex	*ehl tehlehx*
temperature	la temperatura	*lah tehmpehrahtoorah*
temporary filling	el empaste provisional	*ehl ehmpahsteh prohbeesyohnahl*
tender	tierno	*tyehrnoh*
tennis	el tenis	*ehl tehnees*
tennis ball	la pelota de tenis	*lah pehlohtah deh tehnees*
tennis court	la pista de tenis	*lah peestah deh tehnees*
tennis racket	la raqueta de tenis	*lah rahkehtah deh tehnees*
tennis shoes	los zapatos de tenis	*lohs thahpahtohs deh tehnees*
tenpin bowling	los bolos	*lohs bohlohs*
tent	la tienda	*lah tyehndah*
tent peg	la estaca	*lah ehstahkah*
terrace	la terraza	*lah tehrrahthah*
terrible	terrible	*tehrreebleh*
thank (verb)	agradecer	*ahgrahdehthehr*
thank you	gracias	*grahthyahs*
thaw	deshelar	*dehsehlahr*
the day after tomorrow	pasado mañana	*pahsahdoh mahnyahnah*

Word list

15

theatre	el teatro	*ehl tehahtroh*
theft	el robo	*ehl rohboh*
there	allí	*ahlyee*
thermal bath	el baño termal	*ehl bahnyoh tehrmahl*
thermometer	el termómetro	*ehl tehrmohmehtroh*
thick	grueso/gordo	*grwehsoh/gohrdoh*
thief	el ladrón	*ehl lahdrohn*
thigh	el muslo	*ehl moosloh*
thin	fino, flaco	*feenoh, flahkoh*
things	las cosas	*lahs kohsahs*
think	pensar	*pehnsahr*
third	la tercera parte	*lah tehrthehrah pahrteh*
thirsty, to be	la sed	*lah sehd*
this afternoon	esta tarde	*ehstah tahrdeh*
this evening	esta noche	*ehstah nohcheh*
this morning	esta mañana	*ehstah mahnyahnah*
thread	el hilo	*ehl eeloh*
throat	la garganta	*lah gahrgahntah*
throat lozenges	las pastillas para la garganta	*lahs pahsteelyahs pahrah lah gahrgahntah*
throw up	vomitar	*bohmeetahr*
thunderstorm	la tormenta eléctrica	*lah tohrmehntah ehlehktreekah*
Thursday	el jueves	*ehl <u>h</u>wehbehs*
ticket (admission)	la entrada	*lah ehntrahdah*
ticket (travel)	el billete	*ehl beelyehteh*
tickets	los billetes	*lohs beelyehtehs*
tidy (verb)	recoger	*rehko<u>h</u>ehr*
tie	la corbata	*lah kohrbahtah*
tights	el leotardo, el panty	*ehl lehohtahrdoh, ehl pahntee*
time (occasion)	la vez	*lah behth*
time	el tiempo	*ehl tyehmpoh*
timetable	el horario	*ehl ohrahryoh*
tin	la lata	*lah lahtah*
tip (money)	la propina	*lah prohpeenah*
tissues	los pañuelitos de papel	*lohs pahnywehleetohs de pahpehl*
toast	el pan tostado, las tostadas	*ehl pahn tohstahdoh, lahs tohstahdahs*
tobacco	el tabaco	*ehl tahbahkoh*
toboggan	el trineo	*ehl treenehoh*
today	hoy	*oy*
toe	el dedo del pie	*ehl dehdoh dehl pyeh*
together	juntos	*<u>h</u>oontohs*
toilet	el water/los servicios/ el lavabo	*ehl bahtehr/lohs sehrbeethyohs, ehl lahbahboh*
toilet paper	el papel higiénico	*ehl pahpehl ee<u>h</u>yehneekoh*
toiletries	los artículos de tocador	*lohs ahrteekoolohs deh tohkahdohr*
tomato	el tomate	*ehl tohmahteh*
tomato purée	el tomate triturado	*ehl tohmahteh treetoorahdoh*
tomato sauce	el ketchup	*ehl kehchoop*
tomorrow	mañana	*mahnyahnah*

tongue	la lengua	*lah lehngwah*
tonic water	el agua tónica	*ehl agwah tohneekah*
tonight	esta noche	*ehstah nohcheh*
too much	demasiado	*dehmahsyahdoh*
tools	las herramientas	*lahs ehrrahmyehntahs*
tooth	el diente	*ehl dyehnteh*
toothache	el dolor de muelas	*ehl dohlohr deh mwehlahs*
toothbrush	el cepillo de dientes	*ehl thehpeelyoh deh dyehntehs*
toothpaste	el dentífrico	*ehl dehnteefreekoh*
toothpick	el palillo	*ehl pahleelyoh*
top up	rellenar	*rehlyehnahr*
total	el total	*ehl tohtahl*
tough	duro	*dooroh*
tour	la excursión, el paseo	*lah ehxkoorsyohn, ehl pahsehoh*
tour guide	el guía	*ehl gheeah*
tourist card	la tarjeta de turista	*lah tahrhehtah deh tooreestah*
tourist class	la clase turista	*lah klahseh tooreestah*
Tourist Information office	la oficina de (información y) turismo	*lah ohfeetheenah deh (eenfohrmahthyohn ee) tooreesmoh*
tourist menu	el menú turístico	*ehl mehnoo tooreesteekoh*
tow	remolcar	*rehmohlkahr*
tow cable	el cable de remolque	*ehl kahbleh deh rehmohlkeh*
towel	la toalla	*lah tohahlyah*
tower	la torre	*lah tohrreh*
town hall	el ayuntamiento	*ehl ahyoontahmyehntoh*
town/city	la ciudad	*lah thyoodahdh*
toys	los juguetes	*lohs hoogehtehs*
traffic	el tráfico	*ehl trahfeekoh*
traffic light	el semáforo	*ehl sehmahfohroh*
trailer tent	el remolque tienda	*ehl rehmohlkeh tyehndah*
train	el tren	*ehl trehn*
train ticket	el billete de tren	*ehl beelyehteh deh trehn*
train timetable	la guía de trenes	*lah gueeah deh trehnehs*
translate	traducir	*trahdootheer*
travel (verb)	viajar	*byahhahr*
travel agent	la agencia de viajes	*lah ahhehnthyah deh byahhehs*
travel guide	la guía	*lah gheeah*
traveller	el pasajero	*ehl pahsahhehroh*
traveller's cheque	el cheque de viajero	*ehl chehkeh deh byahhehroh*
treacle/syrup	la melaza	*lah mehlahthah*
treatment	el tratamiento	*ehl trahtahmyehntoh*
triangle	el triángulo	*ehl treeahngooloh*
trim	cortar las puntas	*kohrtahr lahs poontahs*

trip	el paseo, la excursión	*ehl pahsehoh,lah ehxkoorsyohn*
trouble	la molestia	*lah mohlehstyah*
trousers (long, short)	los pantalones (cortos, largos)	*lohs pahntahlohnehs (kohrtohs,lahrgohs)*
trout	la trucha	*lah troochah*
trunk call	interurbano	*eentehroorbahnoh*
trunk code	el prefijo	*ehl prehfeehoh*
trustworthy	digno de confianza	*deegnoh deh kohnfyahnthah*
try on (clothes)	probarse	*prohbahrseh*
T-shirt	la camiseta	*lah kahmeesehtah*
tube	el tubo	*ehl tooboh*
Tuesday	el martes	*ehl mahrtehs*
tumble drier	la secadora	*lah sehkahdohrah*
tuna	el atún	*ehl ahtoon*
tunnel	el túnel	*ehl toonehl*
turn	la vez	*lah behth*
TV	la televisión	*lah tehlehbeesyohn*
tv and radio guide	la guía de radio y televisión	*lah gheeah deh rahdyoh ee tehlehbeesyohn*
tweezers	los alicates	*lohs ahleekahtehs*
tyre (bicycle)	la cubierta	*lah koobyehrtah*
tyre lever	el desmontador de neumáticos	*ehl dehsmohntahdohr deh nehoomahteekohs*
tyre pressure	la presión de los neumáticos	*lah prehsyohn deh lohs nehoomahteekohs*

U

ugly	feo	*fehoh*
umbrella	el paraguas	*ehl pahrahgwahs*
under	abajo, debajo de	*ahbahhoh, dehbahhoh deh*
underground railway	el metro	*ehl mehtroh*
underground railway system	la red de metro	*lah rehdh deh mehtroh*
underground station	la estación de metro	*lah ehstahthyohn deh mehtroh*
underpants	los calzoncillos	*lohs kahlthohntheelyohs*
understand	entender	*ehntehndehr*
underwear	la ropa interior	*lah rohpah eentehryohr*
undress (verb)	desvestirse	*dehsbehsteerseh*
unemployed	en paro	*ehn pahroh*
uneven	desigual	*dehseegwahl*
university	la universidad	*lah ooneebehrseedah*
unleaded	sin plomo	*seen plohmoh*
urgent	urgente	*oorhehnteh*
urine	la orina	*lah ohreenah*
usually	por lo general	*pohr loh hehnehrahl*

V

vacate	desalojar	*dehsahlohhahr*
vaccinate	vacunarse	*bahkoonahrseh*
vagina	la vagina	*lah bahheenah*
vaginal infection	la infección vaginal	*lah eenfehkthyohn bahheenal*

valid	válido	*bahleedoh*
valley	el valle	*ehl bahlyeh*
valuable	costoso	*kohstohsoh*
van	la furgoneta	*lah foorgohnehtah*
vanilla	la vainilla	*lah baheeneelyah*
vase	el florero	*ehl flohrehroh*
vaseline	la vaselina	*lah bahsehleenah*
veal	la carne de ternera	*lah kahrneh deh tehrnehrah*
vegetable soup	la sopa de verduras	*lah sohpah deh behrdoorahs*
vegetables	la verdura	*lah behrdoorah*
vegetarian	vegetariano	*behhehtahryahnoh*
vein	la vena	*lah vehnah*
vending machine	la máquina automática	*lah mahkeenah ahootohmahteekah*
venereal disease	la enfermedad venérea	*lah ehnfehrmehdahdh behnehrehah*
via	pasando por	*pahsahndoh pohr*
video recorder	el video	*ehl beedehoh*
video tape	la cinta de vídeo	*lah theentah deh beedehoh*
view	la vista	*lah beestah*
village	el pueblo	*ehl pwehbloh*
visa	el visado	*ehl beesahdoh*
visit (verb)	visitar	*beeseetahr*
visit	la visita	*lah beeseetah*
vitamin tablets	las tabletas de vitaminas	*lahs tahblehtahs deh beetahmeenahs*
vitamins	la vitamina	*lah beetahmeenah*
volcano	el volcán	*ehl bohlkahn*
volleyball (play)	jugar al vóleibol	*hoogahr ahl bohleheebohl*
vomit (verb)	vomitar	*bohmeetahr*

W

wait (verb)	esperar	*ehspehrahr*
waiter	el camarero	*ehl kahmahrehroh*
waiting room	la sala de espera	*lah sahlah deh ehspehrah*
waitress	la camarera	*lah kahmahrehrah*
wake up (verb)	despertar	*dehspehrtahr*
walk	el paseo	*ehl pahsehoh*
walk (take a)	salir a caminar	*sahleer ah kahmeenahr*
walk (verb)	ir (andando)	*eer(ahndahndoh)*
wallet	la cartera	*lah kahrtehrah*
wardrobe	el guardarropa	*ehl gwahrdahrrohpah*
warm	caliente	*kahlyehnteh*
warn	avisar, llamar	*ahbeesahr,lyahmahr*
warning	el aviso	*ehl ahbeesoh*
wash (verb)	lavar	*lahbahr*
washing (dirty)	la ropa sucia	*lah rohpah soothyah*
washing line	la cuerda de colgar la ropa	*lah kwehrdah deh kohlgahr lah rohpah*
washing machine	la lavadora	*lah lahbahdohrah*
washing-powder	el detergente	*ehl dehtehrhehnteh*
wasp	la avispa	*lah ahbeespah*

watch	el reloj	*ehl rehlohh*
water	el agua	*ehl ahgwah*
water ski	el esquí acuático	*ehl ehskee ahkwahteekoh*
waterproof	impermeable	*eempehrmehahbleh*
wave-pool	la piscina con oleaje	*lah peestheenah kohn ohlehahheh*
way (means)	el remedio	*ehl rehmehdyoh*
way (on the)	en el camino	*ehn ehl kahmeenoh*
way	el lado	*ehl lahdoh*
we	nosotros	*nohsohtrohs*
weak	débil	*dehbeel*
weather	el tiempo	*ehl tyehmpoh*
weather forecast	el pronóstico del tiempo	*ehl prohnohsteekoh dehl tyehmpoh*
wedding	la boda	*lah bohdah*
Wednesday	el miércoles	*ehl myehrkohlehs*
week	la semana	*lah sehmahnah*
weekend	el fin de semana	*ehl feen deh sehmahnah*
weekend duty	la guardia de fin de semana	*lah gwahrdyah deh feen deh sehmahnah*
weekly ticket	el abono semanal	*ehl ahbohnoh sehmahnahl*
welcome	bienvenido	*byehnbehneedoh*
well	bien, bueno	*byehn, bwehnoh*
west	el oeste	*ehl ohehsteh*
wet	mojado	*mohahdoh*
wet (weather)	lluvioso	*lyoobyohsoh*
wetsuit	el traje de surf	*ehl trahheh deh soorf*
what?	¿qué?	*keh?*
wheel	la rueda	*lah rwehdah*
wheelchair	la silla de ruedas	*lah seelyah deh rwehdahs*
when?	¿cuándo?	*kwahndoh?*
where?	¿dónde?	*dohndeh?*
which?	¿cuál?	*kwahl?*
whipped cream	el chantilly	*ehl chahnteelyee*
whipping cream	la nata para batir	*lah nahtah pahrah bahteer*
white	blanco	*blahnkoh*
who?	¿quién?	*kyehn?*
wholemeal	integral	*eentehgrahl*
wholemeal bread	el pan integral	*ehl pahn eentehgrahl*
why?	¿por qué?	*pohr keh?*
wide-angle lens	el objetivo gran angular	*ehl obhehteeboh grahn ahngoolahr*
widow	la viuda	*lah byoodah*
widower	el viudo	*ehl byoodoh*
wife	la mujer	*lah moohehr*
wind	el viento	*ehl byehntoh*
windbreak	la protección contra el viento	*lah prohtehkthyohn kohntrah ehl byehntoh*
windmill	el molino	*ehl mohleenoh*
window	la ventanilla, la ventana	*lah behntahneelyah, lah behntahnah*

15 Word list

windscreen wiper	el limpiaparabrisas	*ehl leempyahpahrah-breesahs*
wine	el vino	*ehl beenoh*
wine list	la carta de vinos	*lah kahrtah deh beenohs*
winter	el invierno	*ehl eenbyehrnoh*
witness	el testigo	*ehl tehsteegoh*
woman	la mujer	*lah moohehr*
wood	la madera	*lah mahdehrah*
wool	la lana	*lah lahnah*
word	la palabra	*lah pahlahbrah*
work	el trabajo	*ehl trahbahhoh*
working day	el día laborable	*ehl deeah lahbohrahbleh*
worn/used	gastado	*gahstahdoh*
worried	inquieto	*eenkyehtoh*
wound	la herida	*lah ehreedah*
wrap (verb)	envolver	*ehnbohlbehr*
wrist	la muñeca	*lah moonyehkah*
write	escribir	*ehskreebeer*
write down	apuntar	*ahpoontahr*
writing pad	el bloc (cuadriculado, a rayas)	*ehl blohk(kwahdreekoo-lahdoh, ah rahyahs)*
writing paper	el papel de escribir	*ehl pahpehl deh ehskreebeer*
written	por carta	*pohr kahrtah*
wrong	mal, equivocado	*mahl, ehkeebohkahdoh*

Y

yacht	el yate	*ehl yahteh*
year	el año	*ehl anyoh*
yellow	amarillo	*ahmahreelyoh*
yes	sí	*see*
yes, please	con (mucho) gusto	*kohn (moochoh) goostoh*
yesterday	ayer	*ahyehr*
yoghurt	el yogur	*ehl yohgoor*
you (formal)	usted	*oostehd*
you too	igualmente	*eegwahlmehnteh*
youth hostel	el albergue juvenil	*ehl ahlbehrgeh hoobehneel*

Z

zip	la cremallera	*lah krehmahlyehrah*
zoo	el parque zoológico	*ehl pahrkeh thohohlohheekoh*

Word list

15

Basic grammar

1 The article

Spanish nouns and adjectives are divided into 2 categories: masculine and feminine. The definite article (the) is **el** or **la**. Most masculine words end in **o** and most feminine words end in **a**.

el is used before masculine nouns, as in **el tren** (the train)
la is used before feminine nouns, as in **la playa** (the beach)
el is also used before feminine nouns beginning with a vowel, as in **el agua** (water).

Other examples are:

el techo	the roof	**la casa**	the house
el hambre	hunger	**el alma**	the soul

The plural of **el** is **los**; the plural of **la** is **las**.

In the case of the indefinite article (**a, an**):

un is used before masculine nouns, as in **un libro** (a book).

una is used before feminine nouns, as in **una mesa** (a table).

The plural is constructed by adding s, as in **unos camiones** (some lorries), **unas tazas** (some cups).

Other examples are:

un padre	a father	**una madre**	a mother
un hombre	a man	**una mujer**	a woman
unos hombres	men	**unas mujeres**	women

2 The plural

The plural of Spanish nouns and adjectives ends in **s**. Examples are:

singular	plural
el avión (the plane)	**los aviones**
la manzana (the apple)	**las manzanas**

3 Personal pronouns

I	**yo**
You	**tú/Usted**
He/she/it	**él/ella**
We	**nosotros/nosotras**
You	**vosotros/vosotras/Ustedes**
They	**ellos/ellas**

When speaking to a person one does not know well, **Usted** is used with the third person of the verb:

e.g. **Usted sabe/Ustedes saben**   you know